Community Structures and Processes on Lives of Refugee Children

Edited by

Sofia Leitão
Rinova Ltd

Yvonne Vissing
Salem State University

Series in Sociology

VERNON PRESS

In the Americas:	*In the rest of the world:*
Vernon Press	Vernon Press
1000 N West Street, Suite 1200,	C/Sancti Espiritu 17,
Wilmington, Delaware 19801	Malaga, 29006
United States	Spain

Series in Sociology

Library of Congress Control Number: 2023932573

ISBN: 978-1-64889-892-1

Also available: 978-1-64889-648-4 [Hardback]; 978-1-64889-748-1 [PDF, E-Book]

Cover design by Vernon Press.
Cover image by Gordon Johnson from Pixabay.

Contents

George Weagba
United Methodist University, Liberia

Joe Buttner
Salem State University

David Mercer
Salem State University

Sofia Leitão
Rinova Ltd

Amanda Francis
Rinova Ltd

Sami Atif
Rinova Ltd

Richard Thickpenny
University of West of England; Aston University; The New Penny Ltd

Yvonne Vissing
Salem State University

Sofia Leitão
Rinova Ltd

List of Tables and Figures

Tables

Figures

Authors' Biographies

Editors

Sofia Leitão, PhD, is a Sociologist, Senior Development Manager at Rinova Ltd (UK), and Senior Advisory Board Member at 'Hope For Children' CRC Policy Center (Cyprus). Sofia's work reflects her interest in children's agency in matters related to their spheres of action. She is particularly interested in raising awareness on the Rights of the Child; developing learning programmes promoting child-friendly practices, children's entrepreneurship, social inclusion and participation; non-formal education with an emphasis on storytelling and the use of media and arts as means to enhance self-expression and learning. Sofia has directed the development and implementation of numerous programmes in the field of the Rights of the Child, including the transnational programme *INTEGRA: Multidisciplinary Mentorship program to support the entrepreneurship of children in care and young care-leavers; BASE: Migrant and Refugee Child-friendly Support Services in cases of sexual and gender-based violence; HIT: Hate Interrupter Teams* (funded by the Rights, equality & Citizenship programme of the European commission); *FATIMAII: Preventing Honour Related Violence against women through Social Impact Projects and Peer Learning led by Young men.* She is the author of a book on media discourses and childhood constructions, *Desenhos Animados – Discursos sobre ser criança* (Edições 70) and co-editor of *The Rights of Unaccompanied Minors: Perspectives and Case Studies on Migrant Children* (Springer).

Yvonne Vissing, PhD is a sociologist and Professor of Healthcare Studies at Salem State University in Salem, Massachusetts. Yvonne has worked in the area of child and youth advocacy for her entire career, collaborating with different child rights groups in the USA. Her work is driven by the pursuit of human rights, community-building, resiliency, peace and justice. Yvonne has worked as a teacher, researcher, consultant, therapist, award-winning filmmaker, mediator, guardian-ad-litem, and helps organizations to decrease child abuse and improve child well-being. She is a former fellow at the National Institute of Mental Health, University of Connecticut Center for Democracy, and Whiting Foundation. Author/co-author of 19 books and hundreds of chapters, professional journal articles and other publications, including *Children's Human Rights in the USA*: Challenges and Opportunities (Springer), The Rights of Unaccompanied Minors: Perspectives and Case Studies on Migrant Children (Springer), Children's *Human Rights as a Buffer to Extremism* (Springer); *Changing the Paradigm* *of Homelessness* (Routledge) and *Out of Sight, Out of Mind: Homeless Children in Small Town America* (Lexington).

Authors

Allan Shwedel is Professor Emeritus and Adjunct Professor in the Secondary and Higher Education Department at Salem State University. He was a Fulbright Specialist at Petro Mohyla Black Sea State University in Mykolaiv, Ukraine, in 2015-16 and the Associate Director of the Office of Research, Assessment and Evaluation for the Boston Public Schools from 1987 to 2001. His current research interests include classroom assessment, program assessment and youth resiliency. He has conducted longitudinal research on the impact of early childhood education among children with special needs, with gifts and talents, and from low-income families.

Amanda Francis is the Director and CEO of Rinova Ltd, with 37 year's experience in the field of social regeneration, economic, cultural and educational inclusion, with a particular focus on vocational education, employment and training. Amanda is Governor, Trustee and Director on a number of boards, but her passion is always focused on representation, diversity and equity, particularly in relation to under-represented or disadvantaged groups, including women and children. Over the past 35 years, Amanda has devised, authored and delivered multiple programmes aimed at raising the aspirations and achievement of those facing multiple barriers. During her 12 years as Director and CEO of Rinova Ltd, she has devised, directed and implemented numerous programmes, including national and transnational programmes such as: £108 million National Lottery funded Talent Match aimed at supporting vulnerable and disadvantaged young people; Head2Work, which focuses on young people with complex needs or characteristics of disadvantage and BASE; aimed at training cross-agency professionals to provide refugee child-friendly support services.

Blaž Lenarčič is a senior research associate and assistant professor at the Science and research centre Koper. As a sociologist, he is primarily interested in research topics related to the impact of ICT on society in general, social capital, and migration studies. Recently, he has focused on the study of ICT in the context of migration processes.

Cristobal Pérez is an Educational Psychologist who obtained his Bachelor's degree in Denver, Colorado and his Master's degree in Santiago, Chile. He currently works as the Deputy Director of Programs and Data for the Coalition for Independent Living Options, Inc. (CILO), a non-profit agency in West Palm Beach, Florida, that works with children and adults with disabilities. As Deputy Director, he analyzes agency-wide programmatic data and provides oversight and management of the Information & Referral, Food Pantry, Social Security

Advocacy, and Treasure Coast Services staff. In addition to his role in CILO, Cristobal is also a consultant, working on subjects related to vulnerable populations like unaccompanied refugee minors and victims of sex and labour trafficking. A published author and academic guest lecturer, Cristobal has received local and nationwide recognition for his work on human trafficking.

David Mercer, MD, has retired from Family Practice in Florida after thirteen years. In his "chapter two", he taught human biology courses at Salem State University for an additional fifteen years with an interest in human pathology. For the past four years, he has served as the Chair of the Biology Department.

Dialechti Chatzoudi, Licensed School Psychologist in Cyprus, as well as a PhD Candidate in Psychology at the University of Cyprus. Her doctoral dissertation focuses on early assessment and differential diagnosis of specific learning disability, attention difficulties and behavioural problems. She has worked for five years at the Humanitarian Division of the International Organization "Hope For Children" CRC Policy Center, first as a School Psychologist at the shelters for unaccompanied minors and later as the Coordinator of the Psychology Department, focusing on the quality provision of psychological services to various groups of children and youth.

Dora Cabete, Assistant Guest Professor at the University of the Azores and Assistant Guest Professor at the University of Santiago - Cape Verde.

George Weagba is the Vice President for Research and Planning of the United Methodist University of Liberia. He is an ordained minister and a Counselling Elder at the Liberia Annual Conference of the United Methodist Church. He is a passionate leader of leaders and an author. One of his most recent works is "Conflict and Resolution: Suggested Strategies for Resolving Intragroup Church Conflict from a Leadership Perspective". His research interests are leadership development, conflict resolution, biblical preaching, qualitative research, and youth resiliency. He is the 2022 Recipient of the Life Time Achievement Award for Innovative Research from the Universal Chaplain Corps & Rescue Mission.

Graça Santos holds a PhD in Educational Sciences from the University of Coimbra. She is an Assistant Professor at the Escola Superior de Educação of the Polytechnic Institute of Bragança (Portugal). She is an integrated member of the Research Center on Adult Education and Community Intervention (CEAD) and a member of the Portuguese Society of Educational Sciences. She is Chair of the 'Hope For Children' CRC Policy Center (Cyprus). She has scientific production in the area of Educational Sciences.

Greg Carroll is a Professor of Peace and Conflict Studies at Salem State University. His research interests include youth nation-building in divided societies, having worked extensively in Liberia and Timor-Leste. His most recent works are Human Rights and Globalization, viewpoints from the Global South. In Zajda, J., Vissing, Y. & Majhanovich, S. Discourses of globalisation, ideology and social justice. Dordrecht: Springer; and Fragmentation and Integration: Education in the Context of Globalization. In Maniam, V., (Ed.), Interrogating Common Sense: Teaching for Social Justice, 4th Edition. Melbourne, Vic., Australia, Pearson.

Isolde Quandranti is the documentalist head of the European Documentation Centre at the Department of Law - the University of Verona as well as the contact person for the networks Scholars at Risk, Manifesto on an Inclusive University (UNHCR) and the action University Corridors for Refugees in the same University. Her main areas of research and interest cover international and European protection of Human Rights, Migration law, freedom of expression and communication policy. She was the coordinator of the EDC Italian Network from 2004 until 2017. For the EDC, she is charged with didactic laboratories and seminars within courses and events at the academic and high school level. She is also committed to several projects regarding EU Migration Law, EU Human rights Law, Education and Migrants.

Joe Buttner has four decades of experience using aquatic science and aquaculture as a means to achieve food security and enhance the quality of life for diverse audiences. Dr Joe is currently a Professor Emeritus and Visiting Lecturer in the Department of Biology. He has worked with K-12 youth, undergraduate and graduate students, aspiring and practising aquaculturists, regulators and elected officials, friendly and less than embracive audiences, disenfranchised fishermen, minorities, inner-city youth, and Indigenous Peoples globally (First Nation People in North America, Polynesian youth in Hawaii, youth and adults in Liberia).

José Noronha Rodrigues is the Chair of the 'Hope For Children', CRC Policy Center, a researcher at CEEAplA, CEIS20, IUS GENTIUM COIMBRIGAE and collaborating member of CEDIS, IDILP, CINETS, CEDUE, IDCLB. He is the Vice-President of the Faculty of Economics and Management and Assistant Professor at the University of the Azores. He is the Scientific Coordinator of the Masters in Business and Labor Law. He received his Law Degree at the University of Santiago, Cape Verde.

Raúl Fernández-Calienes is a professor of ethics at several universities and colleges in South Florida and a researcher, writer, and editor. At St. Thomas University, he is Adjunct Professor of Ethics in the Gus Machado School of Business and was formerly a Visiting Associate Professor in the School of Law and a staff member with the Human Rights Institute. Widely published himself, he also has served as Deputy Editor of the American Bar Association Section of International Law, The Year in Review; co-editor of the three-volume series

Women Moving Forward; and co-editor of a book on ethics (Routledge, 2019). Currently, he is the Managing Editor of the peer-reviewed Journal of Multidisciplinary Research. He has been involved in Human Trafficking education and awareness and has been part of the South Florida Human Trafficking Task Force for many years.

Regina Bernadin is the Senior Technical Advisor for Protection and Anti-trafficking Program at the International Rescue Committee (IRC), where she supports the organizations' protection efforts in the United States and Europe. She is a consultant for the Department of Justice Office for Victims of Crime Training and Technical Assistance Center and the National Human Trafficking Training and Technical Assistance Center on human rights issues. She holds a B.A. in International Studies and Criminology from the University of Miami and an M.A. in International Administration, and a Certificate in Non-profit Management from that same institution. She received her PhD in Conflict Analysis and Resolution at Nova Southeastern University. Her dissertation focused on refugee self-sufficiency. Regina is a published author and blogger and an active member of various advisory boards and committees, including the Board of Directors of the Florida Council Against Sexual Violence and Freedom Network's USA Steering Committee. Regina is the recipient of the Sarlo Distinguished Humanitarian Award and the Janita Lee Award for Victim Advocate Professional of the Year.

Richard Thickepenny, FRSA, CQP, MCQI MIEP. He is a visiting Fellow in the Faculty of Health and Applied Sciences, University of West of England. Engaged Scholar at the Centre for Research in Enthic Minority Entrepreneurship, Aston University. Director of Research and Innovation at The New Penny Ltd. He has developed strong research practitioner partnerships with renowned academic research groups (CREME at Aston University, Everyday Integration and Bristol Digital Futures at the University of Bristol), positioning himself as a Lived Experience Elder, Ally and Accomplice specialising in the field of refugee integration. As an engaged scholar at Aston University, he brings significant experience in linking practice research with academic research and, through combining these into action research, has been able to secure significant funding and opened up new areas of study in entrepreneurship.

Sami Atif is a project officer at Rinova Ltd (UK) and has worked as a researcher across a number of projects addressing GBV, refugee/migrant integration and entrepreneurial development. One of his focuses as a project officer has been curriculum and learning resource development for digital learning platforms. He has a bachelor's degree in Film and Television studies from Brunel University London, with main research interests in the representation of class, race and gender in popular media.

Sofia Bergano holds a PhD in Educational Sciences from the University of Coimbra. She is an Assistant Professor at the Escola Superior de Educação of the Polytechnic Institute of Bragança (Portugal). She is an integrated member of the Research Center on Adult Education and Community Intervention (CEAD), a member of the Portuguese Society of Educational Sciences and a member of APEM [Portuguese Association of Women Studies]. She coordinates the IPB team in the Voices of Immigrant Women project consortium (Erasmus+ project, with reference 2020-1-ES01-KA203-082364). Her research interests are gender studies, adult education, migration and social pedagogy.

Tanya Herring PhD's academic pursuits are motivated by her desire to be a 'voice-for-the-voiceless' unaccompanied refugee and asylum-seeking child. Her work includes research in the prevention and protection measures and mechanisms against the multiple forms of exploitation of children, legal empowerment, and self-determination focus on the stateless child, refugee, and non-refugee. Her socio-legal approach in supporting Children's Rights and the Law has globally engaged international government officials, legal and academic practitioners, and a host of child advocates in North America, Southeast Asia, the Oceania Region, Russia, and Europe. Her research and body of work include *Prevention and Protection Interventions for Stateless Non-Refugee and Force Displaced Children* (*New England Journal of Public Policy* and *The Palermo Protocols as a Conduit to Legal Empowerment and Peaceful Self-Determination* (Ateliers Doctoraus).

Zorana Medarić, sociologist and researcher at the Science and Research Centre. Her research interests include migration, integration, migrant children, and child-centredness. She was the principal investigator for the Horizon 2020 - MiCREATE: Migrant Children and Communities in a Transforming Europe (2019-2021), led by the Science and Research Centre Koper. She is co-editor of the book Children's voices: studies of interethnic conflict and violence in European schools, published by Routledge in 2014.

Introduction:
Why Community Structures and Processes Matter in the Lives of Refugee Children

Sofia Leitão

Rinova Ltd

Yvonne Vissing

Salem State University

Abstract

This chapter provides an overview of the chapters in this book that describe the importance of how social structures and institutional processes impact the lives of refugee and asylum-seeking children. A child is defined as anyone under the age of 18, according to the United Nations Convention on the Rights of the Child. Social structures that work as a unified system create more streamlined services for children compared with institutions that operate as silos. Processes that utilize a trauma-informed approach are more conducive to creating positive outcomes for the children as they transition into their new communities. Social institutions around the world tend to experience similar types of challenges in their serving this population. These challenges are examined in this book as recommendations for actions are provided. A human rights approach frames this book.

Keywords: Human Rights, UNCRC, ACEs, refugee/asylum-seeking children, community

***

Introduction

Children's development and wellbeing are always contingent upon how social systems interact with them and provide for them (Viner *et al.*, 2015). When a child is a refugee, they are undergoing massive physical, emotional, social, cultural, and geographic shifts. How they will fare in their new country and situation is largely dependent upon how adequately these changes and challenges are met. While some children will be more resourceful and resilient than others, the wellbeing of all of them will be impacted by what community structures provide. The lives of refugee and asylum-seeking children will be influenced by the social processes that are instituted to interact with them. This chapter will examine the importance of the ways in which community structures and processes impact the lives of children who are refugees. How their communities and institutions have designed programmes, services, policies and practices will influence how they adapt to their new environment and both their short-term and long-term chances of living happy, healthy and successful lives (Hodes, 1998).

Overview of Refugee Children

The number of refugee children has increased substantially in recent years (UNICEF, 2020). While children constitute less than a third of the world's population, they were half (50%) of the world's refugees in 2018, and that number has increased since then. The United Nations Refugee Agency (UNHRC, 2020) reports that in 2020 over 80 million people were forcibly displaced that year alone, with 26.3 million people being refugees and 4.2 million more seeking asylum. How many were under the age of 18 is not clear, but estimates indicate that that number is high. The UNICEF (2020) report found that in 2018 one in three children living outside the countries of their birth are child refugees, but for adults, that figure is less than 5%. There are over 33 million children who migrated in 2018, including 13 million child refugees, one million asylum-seeking children, and 17 million children displaced in their own country due to violence or conflict. These numbers do not include the millions of children who have been displaced due to natural and human-made disasters. UNICEF reports that the number of child refugees increased by 119% between 2010 and 2018.

Who are these refugee children? Some are refugees travelling with their parents, siblings or families. Others may be travelling with friends or acquaintances. Some parents have paid smugglers or others to escort their children to new locales. Others may have been trafficked. Increasingly, refugee children may be unaccompanied and travelling alone, without any guardian or anyone to watch over them or protect them. They may be teenagers, toddlers, or even new-borns (Russell, 1999; Vissing and Leitao, 2021).

What are the causes for children to become refugees? Refugee children did not cause and can't control the conditions underscoring their mobility, which are largely due to disasters, violence and conflicts found in their locales. Common causes include war, and violence between groups in their communities, whether by military, coups, gangs, or those pressing ideological and power directives. Escaping poverty is a big cause for fleeing in search of better futures. The lack of services, education, and opportunity is real for millions of people. Corruption, oppression, discrimination, torture, kidnappings, targeting of certain groups, and lack of protection are big causes for people to seek other homes. Natural disasters, including floods, fires, earthquakes, and tsunamis have displaced millions more than are counted. When home countries fail to serve and protect citizens, it is understandable that they may flee to places where they hope life will be better. Parents may take huge risks to protect their children, knowing that where they are could be a potential death-sentence unless they escape. While their journeys to new destinations may be dangerous and challenging, where they were before, may be even worse.

UNICEF reports that violence and displacement in home countries set the stage for refugees that seek help from other nations. Demographically, in 2018 two countries, South Sudan and Syria, accounted for about half of all child refugees in the world. Most child refugees (84%) found asylum in their home countries or neighbouring nations. Nine of the ten major host countries for refugees globally are located in Asia and Africa, with Turkey hosting the most. Germany is the only exception in the top-ten host countries.

The numbers available are low estimates of the likely reality experienced, and it appears that breakdowns of numbers by age are not regularly counted. But one thing seems sure - children bear the physical, emotional, and social burdens of problems that are caused by adults.

Trauma in Refugee Children

Trauma, including post-traumatic stress disorder, are common in young refugees (Barnett and Hambien, 2017). Child refugees, because of their unique situation, are at risk of suffering from a variety of physical ailments, cognitive and developmental challenges, behavioural issues and psychopathologies (Rutter, 1999). The traumas that they experience may be preventable in the first instance. When they do occur, their traumas could be lessened by the use of processes, interactions, policies, practices, and laws that are embedded in a variety of institutions and community social structures.

Fazel and Stein (2002) have identified three major stress points for refugee children. These occur: (1) while in their country of origin; (2) during the flight to safety; and (3) when having to settle in a country of refuge. At each point, there are things that community structures and providers could do to lessen the trauma, especially from a mental health perspective.

While in their home country, before they become refugees, children may have experienced considerable trauma. These including being forced to flee their homes and communities, perhaps because of war, death or injury of family members, or as a result of environmental disasters. Children's lives may have been chronically unstable, where they witnessed any number of losses in the form of violence, poverty, and suffering. They may have been recipients of abuse or have witnessed the torture of others. Sources of normal stability, such as schools, friends, neighbours, and community groups, may suddenly be gone due to situational crises, with no replacements for them.

When children are forced to abandon whatever stability they had, their journey to a new place may be fraught with challenges and new forms of trauma. Many children travel long distances through dangerous environments, confront people who threaten their safety, and be subjected to physical violence, hunger, harsh weather, difficult terrain, and physical, sexual, emotional and verbal abuse (Hjern, Angel, and Hojer, 1991). Children may be separated from loved ones, perhaps by accident or by intention, as a way to get them to safety and a better life than their futures hold in their home countries. Smugglers and strangers may be their paid companions on difficult journeys through lands that are unfamiliar to them. The smugglers may be far from caring and compassionate to them. The exposure to life chaos and disruption, including violence and deprivation, results in post-traumatic stress disorders that include depression, anxiety, paranoia, sleeping, and eating impacts (Kinzie *et al.*, 1986, 1990; Yule and Williams, 1997).

Once refugee children arrive at their destination, new challenges and potential traumas await them. Their transition across the border can be frightening as their lives are held in the hands of people who speak a different language and whose customs are unfamiliar to them. Sometimes military members or people who may hold weapons over them, or the children may find themselves separated from everyone they know and be alone, not knowing where they are or what will happen to them next. Loved-ones could have died. Beloved possessions are likely gone, either by being left behind, lost, destroyed, or stolen. Studies have found that refugee children may arrive hungry, tired and sick (Vissing and Leitao, 2021). Common physical conditions found in refugee children include communicable diseases, parasitic infestations, anaemia, dental problems, hepatitis B, and tuberculous (Fazel and Stein, 2002). Once settled they may experience traumas trying to integrate into the new society in a phenomenon referred to as secondary trauma. Trying to adjust to a new home, family members, peers, schools, and community may be very challenging.

Because children are at significant risk for trauma and psychological disturbance before, during and after their travel as refugees, the number of adverse child experiences (ACEs) may be high. Research has found that the more exposure to trauma, the greater the negative long-term impacts of physical and mental illnesses, as well as social and behavioural disruptions (Anda, Felitti and Bemner, 2006; Cronholm *et al.*, 2015; Finkelhor *et al.*, 2015; Hunt, Slack and Berger, 2017). Realizing that refugee children will arrive carrying a variety of traumas, how they are managed when they arrive in their new country is of utmost importance to creating stability and the chances of positive transitions and successful lives.

Importance of Social Structures

How a refugee child will fare in the future depends much upon how the new country provides support to the child during their initial transition (Williams and Westermeyer, 1986). A systems approach to helping refugee children is essential. Addressing the treatment needs of refugee children may seem overwhelming because they arrive at their new destination having experienced many challenges and traumatic exposures (Fazel and Stein, 2002). Refugee children will need care and assistance from governments, the legal community, immigration officials, translators, schools, healthcare professionals, mental health, social services, child protective services, housing, food, clothing, and recreational communities, to name a few. Some geographic locales will have more developed helping systems than others. When these helping organizations work together as a coordinated care system, this benefits the children much more than when the organizations exist as isolated silos. Developing a case-management approach where different organizations coordinate their services in a team-like manner to ensure that the children are receiving the care they need and do not fall through the cracks is important to their success.

Development of community systems, collaborations and partnerships are essential for the creation of good outcomes in service delivery. Many social systems are not well developed and efficient in streamlining effective services to vulnerable populations such as refugee children. How social systems operate may vary and is directly related to their outcomes in service delivery (Porter and Córdoba, 2009; Walker, 2019). Viewing social institutions as a part of a complex system in which chaos is a natural component requires that organizations and social systems take a more developed, sophisticated and enlightened approach to service development (Hudson, 2000; 2010). The use of a clinical, sociological approach that integrates both structural or macro-level components as well as micro-level processes and procedures can also result in more positive results not just for individuals but for organizations (Fritz, 2008).

Schools are likely the institution that most children access on a daily basis, and they are fundamentally important in supporting refugee children (Thomas, 2016). Schools play a critical role in helping refugee children find a sense of stability, safety and predictability while helping them maximize their learning potential and opportunities for success (Crosnoe, 2013). Even very young refugee children have likely experienced a variety of traumas. Early childhood education and care (ECEC) programmes are an important vehicle that can mitigate many of the risks these children face (Park *et al.*, 2018).

Education programmes boost not just children's education and career trajectories but also support longer-term integration success. Schools provide not just educational content but also help students to: develop peer relationships; learn norms, folkways and mores; gain emotional and social support; and obtain career guidance and training. Nurses may provide healthcare, students may get lunch and food given to them, and some schools may have social workers who help the student obtain needed community resources. It is within the school environment that children's self-esteem, identity, social adaptation, and resilience are influenced (Fazel and Stein, 2002).

Refugee children find that schools provide much more than academic learning, as valuable as language, history, math, science, and other subjects may be. They provide socio-emotional grounding and support that help them to make successful transitions into their new communities and to become active participants in them. Schools, the communities in which they exist, can create climates that are welcoming, and have a wide array of resources and places to go for refugee families to find what they need to make a positive contribution to student adjustment (Hess, 2017).

Over half of the world's refugee children do not have access to education that will help them to become self-sustaining, productive adults (UN News, 2019). UNESCO (2020) reports that refugee children are five times more likely to be out of school. Millions lack adequate healthcare, especially during the time of COVID-19, putting refugee children at dire risk (Browne *et al.*, 2021; Hawke, 2021). Even very young children may be alone, unaccompanied by siblings, parents or caregivers, putting them at extreme vulnerability to a wide array of life-threatening problems (Vissing and Leitao, 2021).

Social structures like schools and humanitarian organizations work to organize and interact with refugee children by teaching them norms about what to expect in their new countries. A rights-respecting approach can be present in the way institutions are designed, the services they provide, and the way they process and interact with children. Their structures and processes directly impact what children learn about human rights and social inclusion. A successful human rights approach requires involvement from the entire social system, including government, school administration, teachers, social workers, students, parents, and the community, to partner together to create an environment for active learning and socialization for productive citizenry (Thomas, 2016). Research by Devonald *et al.* (2021) found that human rights education should be a core pillar of humanitarian responses for refugee children. When human rights education is provided in humanitarian settings, it creates opportunities for adolescent refugees to understand and exercise their human rights, respect the rights of others, and gain active citizenship skills. Studying the extent to which education about, through and for human rights are embedded in refugee humanitarian programmes, researchers found stark differences in how programmes are structured. They found in Jordan, the Makani programme integrates human rights across subjects and teacher pedagogy and fosters skills for active citizenship, while in Cox's Bazar, Bangladesh, a lack of basic rights hinders the delivery of meaningful human rights education for Rohingya adolescents. A human rights framework can make refugee youth aware of their rights, open dialogue between students and teachers, and encourage youth to become social change agents in their communities. The lack of a rights approach disempowers youth to develop the skills necessary for active global citizenship.

Challenges Facing Social Structures Serving Refugee Children

An international analysis of challenges facing education and care programmes that serve refugee children notes common problems (Park, Katsiaficas and McHugh, 2018; Refugee Processing Centre, 2017). While it is well-documented that refugee children have experienced traumas, programmes recognize the importance of providing trauma-informed care – yet the resources and training to provide quality trauma-informed care are lacking almost everywhere. Young children appear to be a lower priority for refugee resettlement and integration programmes, despite their developmental needs. Waiting lists may exist in many places for services, housing or support. This is counter-productive to addressing their immediate needs and setting them up for longer-term stability and success. No matter what country studied, there is a shortage of qualified multilingual staff with extensive knowledge of the cultures and languages of the refugee children they serve. Many programmes do not have stable long-term funding, which complicates how many refugees they can serve and what kinds of resources they can provide them.

Programmes find that refugee and asylum-seeking families may continue to move from place to place even after being settled into a new country. When they move, this makes it difficult to provide continuity in services. Bureaucratic and logistical processes may become uncomplicated and result in refugees falling through the cracks in service delivery systems. A general lack of coordination among disparate government departments, NGOs, and other key stakeholders exists. This means that programmes often act in isolation from one another, with limited access to critical information and a heightened risk that scarce resources are used inefficiently (Park, Katsiaficas and McHugh, 2018).

A systems approach integrates the role of social work, physical and mental health, education, and social wellbeing. The Centre for Immigration and Child Welfare (2015) has created a very comprehensive manual of child welfare practices with immigrant and refugee families. It contains detailed guidelines for how to integrate child welfare practices with trauma-informed care. The manual also describes how to build child welfare agency capacity to be more supportive of creating cultural competencies that support refugee children. These capacity strategies include organizational policies and protocols, administrative support, staff and volunteer training, and the creation of collaborations and partnerships. It also describes the interface of the elements of good child welfare practices and their implications for immigrant families who are exposed to traumatic stress.

Resilience of Refugee Children

Studies of refugee children indicate that while they have experienced significant traumas, many demonstrate resilience (Masten, Best and Garmzey, 1990; Werner and Smith, 1982). Providing them with resources that will enhance protection and well-being are essential influences of their success (Fazel and Stein, 2002). These protective factors include the child's personality or disposition, having a supportive family or family environment, external social agencies that help children cope, and agencies that provide them with meaningful services and resources they can use. Providing comprehensive services to children will help increase their resilience. Not providing services to even the most resilient children will disempower their ability to move forward successfully. Resilience and resource are intertwined concepts.

The Centre for Immigration and Child Welfare (2015) reminds us that in order to survive the multiplicity of chaos and traumas, children may cope by engaging in some behaviours that may, on the surface, seem maladaptive or pathological. As children adjust to their new homes, cultures and locations, they may have a transition period where the coping strategies they used in order to survive are no longer necessary but still used. Therefore, resilience may be present but not always perceived as such by people in their new countries. Helping young people to find constructive coping mechanisms and to fit into their new environments and peer groups will be important for their success.

Program Directions

Social structures and processes that embed a children's human rights framework have been found to produce better quality outcomes for refugee children, families and their integration into being active and productive members of their communities. The UN Convention on the Rights of the Child outlines standards necessary for the wellbeing of children. These include provision, protection and participation. Provisions include food, housing, services, education, healthcare, and socio-emotional support. Protections from violence, abuse, torture, and trauma are essential; when such things do occur, finding ways to help the child recover successfully from them is part of the treaty. Helping young people to have a sense of agency and how to use that agency to participate in decisions that pertain to their own life is an essential part of the treaty. So is having the opportunity to participate meaningfully in their homes, schools, and communities. Adhering to the basic guidelines of the universal child rights treaty by refugee organizations would be in the best interests of the child.

Welcome Centres can be the first point of introduction to a new country, and staff can meet and interview refugee individuals and families to help link them to the services and support they need. Refugees will arrive likely frightened, weary, hungry, tired, without extensive paperwork, and may not know the language. Their needs may be extensive, to having staff who can meet them, welcome them, and assist them is crucial (Sevazzi, 2016).

Governments and institutions that serve refugees need better coordination and greater capacities to ensure comprehensive service delivery and longitudinal sustainability. A holistic set of services for an extended period of time could greatly assist refugee children. This would necessitate a good data collection and monitoring system so that children can be followed-up over time to ensure that they receive the services they need. Prioritization of young refugees would benefit them substantially in programmes. Employing staff or volunteers who are multilingual and have a keen understanding of the culture and conflicts that the refugee children have experienced would be very valuable. Having available and accessible written documents and resource guides so that refugees can learn where to go to obtain services and how to apply for them is very important. They cannot be expected to use services that they don't even know exist. Having transportation systems that enable them to get to locations to access help is critically important.

When children are part of a family system, there can be a symbiotic assistance system that develops where parents can learn from children just as children may learn from parents. Working with parents and entire family units is therefore essential to the stability and success of the family collective.

Sometimes newcomers like refugee children are resented by people in the new countries. This may be because they require substantial assistance that taxpayers may subsidize. Newcomers who don't know the rules and norms of the new community may violate them, which may result in crime, misbehaviour, and resentment. If people do not have the language, training, education, and skill-sets to make contributions to the community, they may be regarded as loafers who want to take from and not give to the community. But it is important to realize that all of these factors can be eliminated or reduced when new refugees are provided the array of supports they need to in order to make a successful adjustment to their new homes. Instead of viewing them as detrimental to the wellbeing of a community, history documents that supporting immigrants and newcomers to a country can result in substantial benefits to both the individuals and the community (OECD/ILO (2018)). Investing in the resources to support refugee children who come in distress could result in emotional and social loyalty to the new community. The community could benefit substantially from their work, employment, volunteerism, and civic contributions. This assumption guides the purpose of our book – to make life better for children, families, and for their new host communities.

Chapter Relevance

The contributions in this book present different perspectives on processes, interactions, policies, practices, and laws embedded in a variety of institutions and community social interactions.

Noronha and Cabete address the transnational character of transnational migrant families and communities and the uses of new information and communication technologies in the process of family reorganisation, arguing the need for states to acknowledge and support this potential. Lenarčič and Medarić analyse the role of information-communication technologies (ICT) in the lives of children on the move at different stages of their migration process (preparation, sociability, integration). The authors draw on qualitative research with unaccompanied migrant children in Slovenia deriving from the project *Migrant Children and Communities in a Transforming Europe* (MiCREATE) funded by the EU Horizon 2020 Research and Innovation Programme of the EC.

Herring's chapter examines whether states ensure that a child seeking refugee status receives appropriate protection and humanitarian assistance looking at protection gaps in international community structures for the accompanied and unaccompanied asylum-seeking refugee child. Quadranti looks at the social inclusion programmes for legal residents and the security approach focused on opposing illegal immigration, analysing the provisions of the EU Pact on Migration and Asylum and Action Plan on Integration and Inclusion for both accompanied and unaccompanied minors. The author places an emphasis on European mechanisms concerning the detention of minors, reception conditions and so-called 'Dublin transfers' to then provide an analysis of the Italian integration plan and the failure to recognize the principle of social inclusion.

Chatzoudi presents an account of the vulnerability of unaccompanied children in southern Europe, presenting the shelters 'Homes for Hope' in Cyprus and the holistic model developed to provide multidisciplinary services on rehabilitation, integration, and durable solutions strategies. The chapter focuses on the psychological support services provided to unaccompanied minors; the challenges faced, good practices, and recommendations. Santos and Bergano look at immigration and the integration of refugees in Portugal and at the social inclusion of children and adults through community processes that facilitate access to education, health, housing and employment, analysing data provided by national and international organisations. Carrol et al. present a study of student resilience in Liberia, a country with a recent history of civil wars and pandemics. The authors make use of the concepts of ACEs and HOPEs (Adverse Childhood Experiences and Healthy Outcomes from Positive Experiences), proposing general guidelines for practice in educational contexts and for the Government of Liberia. Bernardine et al. examine community approaches to the integration process in the U.S. federally funded programmes that combine education, social services, and social integration aiming at the integration of unaccompanied refugee children and survivors of Human Trafficking, introduce the programming and explain why they are necessary for assisting unaccompanied refugee, asylee, and trafficked youth. Francis et al. looks at lifelong learning as a catalyst for the sustained promotion of safe communities in the context of migration through a case study based on the implementation of a capacity-building programme to equip migrant women with competences to raise awareness on, and counteract, female genital mutilation (FGM). Thickpenny explores the specificities of refugee communities looking beyond the general perspective of policy makers to focus on understanding individual refugee needs and their family's future wellbeing towards service to refugees that work for the individual.

References

Anda, R. F., Felitti, V. J., Bemner, J. D. 2006. 'The enduring effects of abuse and related adverse experiences in childhood'. *European Archives of Psychiatry ClinicalNeuroscience, 256,* 174-186.

Barnett, E. R. and Hambien, J. 2017. 'Trauma, PTSD, and Attachment in Infants and Young Children'. *National Centre for PTSD.* Viewed 2.22.22. www.ptsd.va. gov/professional/treatment/children/trauma_ptsd_attachment.asp

Browne, D.T. *et al.* 2021. 'Refugee Children and Families During the COVID-19 Crisis: A Resilience Framework for Mental Health', *Journal of Refugee Studies,* feaa113, https://doi.org/10.1093/jrs/feaa113

Centre for Immigration and Child Welfare. 2015. 'A social worker's tool kit for working with immigrant families'. Viewed 3.2.22. https://bettercarenetwork. org/sites/default/files/A%20Social%20Worker%27s%20Toolkit%20for%20W orking%20with%20Immigrant%20Families.pdf

Cronholm, P. F. *et al.* 2015. 'Adverse childhood experiences: Expanding the concept of adversity'. *American Journal of Prevention Medicine, 49,* 354- 361.

Crosnoe, R. 2013. 'Preparing the Children of Immigrants for Early Academic Success'. *Washington, DC: Migration Policy Institute.* Viewed 4.2.22 www.migration policy.org/research/preparing-children-immigrants-early-academic-success

Devonald, M. *et al.* 2021. 'Human rights education in humanitarian settings: opportunities and challenges'. *Human Rights Education Review.* Volume 4, no 1. Viewed 2.27.22. https://journals.oslomet.no/index.php/human/article/view/39 86/3736

Fazel M. and Stein A. 2002. 'The mental health of refugee children'. *Archives of Disease in Childhood.* 87:366-370. Viewed 1.17.22. https://adc.bmj.com/content/87/5/366

Finkelhor, D. *et al.* 2015. 'A revised inventory of adverse childhood experiences'. *Child Abuse and Neglect, 48,* 13-21.

Fritz, J. M. 2008. *International Clinical Sociology.* Springer.

Hawke, A. 2021. 'Safeguarding health for refugee and migrant children during the COVID-19 pandemic'. *UNICEF.* Viewed 5.27.22. https://www.unicef.org/eca/stories/safeguarding-health-refugee-and-migrant-children-during-COVID-19-pandemic

Hess, R. 2017. 'Social and emotional support for refugee families'. *Color in Colorado.* Viewed 6.12.22. https://www.colorincolorado.org/article/social-and-emotional-support-refugee-families-school-psychology-perspective

Hjern, A., B. Angel, and B. Hojer 1991. Persecution and Behavior: A Report of Refugee Children from Chile. Child Abuse and Neglect 15: 239-48.

Hodes, M. 1998. *Refugee children.* BMJ 1998;316:793–4.

Hudson, C. 2000. 'At the Edge of Chaos', *Journal of Social Work Education,* 36:2, 215-230, DOI: 10.1080/10437797.2000.10779003

Hudson, C. 2010. *Complex Systems and Social Behavior.* New York: Oxford University Press.

Hunt, T. K. A., Slack, K. S., and Berger, L M. 2017. 'Adverse childhood experiences and behavioral problems in middle childhood'. *Child Abuse and Neglect, 67,* 391-402.

Internal Displacement Monitoring Centre. 2019. Global Internal Displacement Database (GIDD), IDMC.

Kinzie, J.D. et al. 1986. 'The psychiatric effects of massive trauma on Cambodian children'. *J Am Acad Child Adolesc Psychiatry.* 25:370–6.

Kinzie J.D. *et al.* 1990. 'The prevalence of posttraumatic stress disorder and its clinical significance among Southeast Asian refugees'. *Am J Psychiatry.* 147:913–17.

Masten, A., Best, K. and Garmezy, N. 1990. 'Resilience and development: contributions from the study of children who overcome adversity'. *Dev Psychopathol.* 2:425–44.

OECD and International Labour Organization. 2018. 'How Immigrants Contribute to Developing Countries' Economies', *OECD Publishing,* Paris. http://dx.doi.org/10.1787/9789264288737-en/

Park, M., Katsiaficas, C. and McHugh, M. 2018. *Responding to the ECEC needs of children of refugees and asylum seekers in Europe and North America.* Viewed 7.1.21. https://www.migrationpolicy.org/sites/default/files/publications/ECECforRefugeeChildren_FINALWEB.pdf

Porter, T., and Córdoba, J. 2009. 'Three views of systems theories and their implications for sustainability education'. *Journal of Management Education,* *33*(3), 323–347. https://doi.org/10.1177/1052562908323192

Refugee Processing Centre. 2017. Refugee Admissions Report. Viewed 1.4.22. www.wrapsnet.org/s/Refugee-Admissions-Report-2017_11_30.xls

Russell, S. 1999. *Most vulnerable of all: the treatment of unaccompanied refugee children in the UK.* UK: Amnesty International.

Rutter, M.L. 1999. 'Psychosocial adversity and child psychopathology'. *Br J Psychiatry.* 174:480–93.

Sevazzi, H. 2016. 'Supporting the Settlement Needs of Young Refugee Children'. *The Early Child Educator.* Spring: 7–12. Viewed 7.2.22. www.ecebc.ca/resources/ journal/2016_Spring/Savazzi.pdf

Thomas, R.L. 2016. 'The Right to Quality Education for Refugee Children Through Social Inclusion'. *J. Hum. Rights Soc. Work* 1, 193–201. https://doi.org/10.1007/ s41134-016-0022-z

UNESCO. 2020. 'Refugee children are five times more likely to be out of school'. Viewed 6.22.22. https://en.unesco.org/news/refugee-children-are-five-times-more-likely-be-out-school-others

UNICEF. 2020. Displaced children. Viewed 3.3.22. https://data.unicef.org/topic/ child-migration-and-displacement/displacement/

United Nations, Department of Economic and Social Affairs, Population Division. 2019. World Population Prospects: The 2019 Revision, United Nations, New York.

United Nations, Department of Economic and Social Affairs, Population Division, 2017. Trends in International Migrant Stock: The 2019 Revision, United Nations, New York.

United Nations, Department of Economic and Social Affairs, Population Division. 2019. Trends in International Migrant Stock: Migrants by Destination and Origin. United Nations, New York.

United Nations High Commissioner for Refugees. 2019. Global Trends: Forced Displacement in 2018. UNHCR, Geneva.

United Nations High Commissioner for Refugees. 2019. Global Trends: Forced Displacement in 2018. UNHCR, Geneva.

United Nations News. 2019. 'More than half of world's refugee children to not have access to education'. *UN News.* Viewed 8.2.22. https://news.un.org/en/ story/2019/08/1045281

United Nations Refugee Agency (UNHCR). 2020. Refugee Statistics. Viewed 2.9.22. https://www.unhcr.org/refugee-statistics/

Viner, R. *et al.* 2015. 'Life course epidemiology: Recognising the importance of adolescence'. *Journal of Epidemiology and Community Health,* 69(8), 719-720. https://doi.org/10.1136/jech-2014-205300

Vissing, Y. and Leitao, S. 2021. *The Rights of Unaccompanied Minors: Perspectives and Case Studies of Migrant Children.* Springer.

Walker, S. 2019. *Systems Theory and Social Work.* Sage. Viewed 8.1.22. https:// www.researchgate.net/publication/335228435_Systems_Theory_and_Social _Work

Werner, E.E and Smith, R.S. 1982. *Vulnerable but invincible: a longitudinal study of resilient children and youth.* New York: McGraw Hill.

Williams, C. and Westermeyer, J. 1986. *Refugee mental health in resettlement countries.* Washington, DC: Hemisphere Publishing Corporation.

Yule, W. and Willams, C. 1997. *Post-traumatic stress reactions in children. J Trauma Stress.*3:279–95.

Chapter 1

Transnational Families
- A Vulnerability of Migration

José Noronha Rodrigues

Universidade dos Açores, Portugal

Dora Cabete

Universidade dos Açores, Portugal

Abstract

There is no unanimous definition of family. However, it is established that the family is the fundamental foundation of support and of the integral development of man, and its members need to be in permanent connection. Thus, it is essential to address the topic of transnational families and/or transnational communities since they are the by-products of migration in all its fullness as a global phenomenon. Dealing with homesickness, family reorganization, and hope for better days are part of the challenges for thousands of migrants, but until they are fully realized, the use of new information and communication technologies by transmigrants is a device that host states must foster and support.

Keywords: Transnational families, information and communication technology, migration, refugees

***

Introduction

This article focuses on two themes that we have been working hard on in recent times, namely, the issue of migrants in its entirety and the issue of the family. It is worth mentioning a priori that the overwhelming majority of people migrate internationally for reasons related to work, family and study - which involves migration processes that occur largely without fundamentally challenging the migrants or the countries they enter. On the other hand, other people leave their homes and countries for a range of compelling and sometimes tragic reasons, such as conflict, persecution and disasters. While people who have been displaced, such as refugees and internally displaced persons, represent a relatively small percentage of all migrants, overall, they are the most in need of assistance and support (World Migration Report, 2020, p. 23).

That said, we will focus the analysis specifically on transnational families and/or transnational communities, which, in practice, reflect the socio-legal-economic and cultural implications of migration, displaced persons, stateless persons and, in particular, refugee migrants and/or asylum seekers.

However, before addressing the issue of migrants and transnational families, it is important to define the concept of family because there is not a single definition of family, as Borsa and Feil show.

> [According to] the classical conceptualization proposed by Lévi-Strauss (1972), the term family is used to define a social group originating in marriage, consisting of a husband, a wife and the children resulting from their union, as members duly united by legal ties, economic, religious and other rights and obligations with a variety of psychological feelings, such as love, affection, respect and fear. For Lévi-Strauss, the family is configured on the basis of three types of relations: alliance between the couple (marriage or marital legalization), filiation and consanguinity. These relations give the idea that the concept of family is directly related to the concept of kinship (...). The author of various studies on family, Osório (2002), opts for an operative concept, where the family represents a group unit in which three types of personal relations are developed, as proposed by Lévi-Strauss - alliance (home), filiation (parents/children) and consanguinity (siblings) and which, from the generic objectives of preserving the species, nurturing and protecting the offspring and providing them with conditions for acquiring their personal identities, has developed through time diversified functions of transmitting ethical, aesthetic, religious and cultural values. (Borsa and Feil, 2008, p. 2).

The family is designated by a group of people who have a degree of kinship or affective ties and live in the same house, forming a home. A traditional family is usually formed by the father and mother, united by marriage, and one or more children, making up a nuclear or elementary family. However, we must never forget that the family is not only the result of marriage; there are several other forms of organisation based on affective relationships and cohabitation. Regardless of this, the family is considered an institution responsible for promoting the education and care of children, as well as the one responsible for influencing their behaviour in the social environment. The role of the family is related to socialization. In this process, moral and social values are transmitted, as well as traditions, customs and knowledge perpetuated through generations. By law, the family environment is expected to be a place of affection, care, safety, comfort and well-being, providing respect for the dignity of each of its members.

Thus, as we can see, the concept of family per se is a broad and comprehensive concept where all affective and consanguineous relationships may intersect. Thus, it is fundamental to address this topic of transnational families since migration in all its fullness has become a global phenomenon and has provided a new family model. As a matter of fact, as Vasconcelos stated

> [The] processes of transnational displacement end up bringing to the surface a series of ethno-cultural and identity phenomena that impact the transformations in the world of work and in the lives of men and women who experience this reality. The material and symbolic exchange between social subjects of different cultures influences the changes in values and the (re) formulation of the new way of seeing and perceiving the 'we/others', including reinforcing or redefining notions of paternity and maternity (...). In this sense, the transnational family is understood not only by the fact that the family members reside in different countries and establish contacts and affective bonds, but also because it consists of members of different nationalities and that physically and symbolically move between different territories and cultures. (Vasconcelos, 2010, pp.3-4)

In this context, Vasconcelos argues that in the field of social sciences, the term 'family' has several meanings. In the context of cross-border reality, it is no different. Thus, the notion of family is linked not only to consanguineous aspects, national identity and a network of support and collaboration but also symbolic ones.

> 'We Brazilians here (Las Claritas) have no help from anyone, neither from the government, nor from the national guard, so one paisano helps the other paisano in case of need. We are one big family!'. This demonstrates the reconfigurations of the dominant concept of family, linked to marriage, descent, kinship and cohabitation, which starts to give centrality to a context of diverse relationships, marked by a collective identity and solidarity networks (...).(*Idem*, p.5)

In this same line of thought, Vasconcelos also states that

> [The] transnational family assumes a multiplicity of senses and meanings, which reflect in the characterization of its social organization and in the choice and elaboration of family survival mechanisms and strategies. The nationality in conjunction constituted and experienced in the everyday life of the place, provides a 'field of possibilities', in which

family members can play and articulate various identities. The exercise of fathers and mothers and their relationship of caring for their sons and daughters are exercised and conceived in different ways, between men and women, mediated by mobility and cross-border social dynamics that give new meaning to affective ties and family belonging. (*Ibidem*, p.12)

For her part, Risson understands that

migrant families are those whose members manage to stay together or meet again in a new place other than the one where they were constituted as a family. It is common to find in immigrant communities those families which, after much effort and, in most cases, after a certain period of time, manage to reunite in the new country. The family, which was inserted in a social, cultural context and with a support network already formed in its country of origin, finds itself in a completely different scenario (language, culture, religion, food), which may reject it, either because it is an immigrant, because of religion or culture. (Risson, 2019)

In this sense, also Bryceson and Vuorela define transnational families as

families whose members live some or most of the time apart from each other, but nevertheless remain united and create something that can be seen as a sense of collective well-being and unity, that is, 'familiarity', even across national borders'. Through the e/immigration experience these families, as 'real and imagined communities' (...) bring new and delicate questions to migration studies, demanding approaches that privilege a 'transnational perspective of migration' (Bryceson and Vuorela, 2002, p.3).

Shiller, Basch and Blanc also maintain that

[transmigrantes] are immigrants whose daily lives depend on multiple and constant interconnections across international borders and whose public identities are configured in relation-ship to more than one nation-state. (...) They are not sojourners because they settle and become incorporated in the economy and political institutions, localities, and patterns of daily life of the country in which they reside. However, at the very same time, they are engaged elsewhere in the sense that they maintain connections, build institutions, conduct transactions, and influence local and national events in the countries from which they emigrated. Transnational migration is the process by which immigrants forge and sustain simultaneous multi-stranded social relations that link together their societies of origin and settlement (Schiller, Basch and Blanc, 1995, p.48).

Finally, Grassi and Vivet define transnational families as those 'families where there is a geographical separation between parents and children, and a social and family unit based on the organisation of parenthood at a distance' (Grassi and Vivet, 2015, p87; Bryceson and Vuorela, 2002, p.3). In general terms, we can state that transnational families and/or 'transnational communities' result from migrations, or rather, they are fruits or side effects of migrations, and in particular, they produce devastating effects on migrants when for any reason, they cannot be connected internationally.

However, as Machado *et al.* argue, in some specific cases, "transnationalizing the family can also become a strategic move made to fulfil specific projects aimed at generally improving the family's well-being or status in the face of new circumstances" (Machado *et al.* 2008, p. 91).

Moreover, the new forms of family, in fact, force us to rethink contemporary European society, which has an increasingly important presence of migrants from other countries and their families (Grassi and Vivet, 2015, pp. 86-88). However, for refugees and asylum seekers, the transnationalisation of the family is often not an option but an obligation imposed by the spatial circumstances resulting from socio-political-economic and/or military constraints which violate the most basic human rights for them. The consequences are devastating and minimised by information and communication technologies where possible.

An immigrant leaves his country of origin by choice and has the possibility to plan his going abroad, namely by choosing the means, the destination and the family group accompanying him. In the case of refugees, they leave their country or move internally within their country, by necessity or by external imposition, alien to their will and, consequently, often do not even have the opportunity to take with them the necessary technological means to make up for missing their family. They do not choose the final destination but prefer any destination regardless of cultural affinity or not with this destination, provided that it safeguards and protects them in their most basic human rights. Finally, many times they do not even have the possibility to be safely accompanied by their small family because they are persecuted and have to separate in order to protect themselves. Because they are persecuted, they cannot freely access the technological means of communication to minimise their homesickness. Those refugees who fortunately have the good fortune to be provided with these technological means of information and communication are undoubtedly the privileged ones who manage to minimise family homesickness and integrate better into the host society.

Globalisation and the Importance of Information and Communication Technologies for Transmigrants and/or Transnational Families

The socio-political-economic, cultural and technological globalisation has changed the experience of migrants in relation to their country of origin. In fact, the geophysical distances between countries have been shortened with the rise of information technologies. In this sense, as Bacigalupe and Parker have rightly argued,

> for both the immigrant and the family who have stayed behind, emerging technologies change the meaning of immigration, albeit in different ways. For some, such technology helps family members justify their decision to live apart. For others, they help immigrants adjust to their new land, providing them with an emotional and familial connection as they strive to create a new social network (...). For most immigrant families, emerging technologies provide a means to hear and see with some frequency aspects of their country of origin that would otherwise be forgotten, thus partially alleviating some painful experiences of loss and loneliness. Even though these technologies have been largely anticipated by socioeconomic areas, they are now more accessible than ever, even to immigrants with limited resources. (Bacigalupe and Parker, 2016, p.16).

In this direction, Machado *et al.* also argue that

> globalization changes the dynamics between space and time, due to technological advances in means of transport and communications. This affected the experience of migration, because many migrants, far from being incorporated into the chosen receiving society, created extensive ties not only with some instances of the society to which they migrated but also with the society of origin, making us think, therefore, in 'transmigrants' and non-migrants: 'transmigrants are migrants whose daily lives depend on multiple and constant interconnections that cross international borders and whose public identities are configured in relationship with more than one nation-state', i.e. they create cultural, social, political and even economic ties with both the receiving nation and the nation of origin (Machado *et al.* , 2008, pp. 85-86).

Bacigalupe and Parker also point out that

> information and communication technologies shape human development and identity. Immigrant children and young people are no exceptions (...) emerging technologies shape and influence intergenerational relationships within and between families (...) emerging technologies, known as information and communication technologies (ICTs), constitute an

integral and everyday aspect of family members' lives, easing the pain of transition, but also complicating it in some ways. With the rapid evolution of emerging technologies, the experience of young immigrants in the United States has been significantly transformed. By participating in this new media ecology, this 'millennium' youth, born at the turn of the century, relates to their country of origin in a qualitatively different way than generations before the advent of these technologies. (Bacigalupe and Parker, 2016, pp.94-95)

In fact, these authors portray well the importance of information technology for transnational families

[in] the Bay Area in California, two teenagers are glued to a mobile phone talking to their 4-year-old sister and their parents in Guatemala, the joy is palpable - not even poor connection spoils their enthusiasm. Holding a prepaid phone card, the youngster's speech quickens when a voice message informs them that only one minute of credit remains. The call ends before he has a chance to say goodbye. Some time later, at her 14th birthday party, her parents appear on the webcam and watch their daughter blow out the candles. They stay on the webcam throughout the party, watching with joy, but not participating fully in it. Their virtual presence is significant, but perhaps not enough, as we can deduce from a closer look at the birthday girl's face (...) Immigrants use mobile phones, text messages, e-mails, online instant messaging and videoconferencing programmes, such as Skype, to communicate with family and friends back home and talk about a variety of topics, from more prosaic information, for example, about the weather, to more serious matters such as births, deaths and crossing the border. (...)Some of the emerging technologies allow family members separated by time and space to be virtually present for an extended period of time, thus providing the opportunity for physically distant relatives to 'participate' in family events. Emerging technologies enable an intimacy between friends and relatives that did not exist before; a separated mother and daughter can shop together online, a distant father can monitor his son's progress on schoolwork, relatives in the home country can watch migrants choosing items for home decoration, or even participate virtually in family gatherings. The list of possibilities for using emerging technologies is endless, although depending on the type of activity, certain types of technology are more appropriate. Moreover, several technologies combined, a 'polymedia', create different, context-specific communication environments. For many transnational users of emerging technology, the content of the communication is not as important as its social and, most often, its emotional function. (...) The sense of another person's

presence that technology enables is, in and of itself, significant for the family and for children's development. (Bacigalupe and Parker, 2016, pp.94-95)

On the other hand, but in the same line of thought, Cogo refers

[from] reports obtained in interviews, migrants of different nationalities highlighted the daily and weekly routines of family meetings and monitoring of the children's schoolwork through the use of communication software such as Skype or social networking sites; or, still, the effort of family members to introduce themselves in the world of the internet in cities in the interior where access is restricted in order to establish connections with the migrated family member. Some young interviewees, especially women, also expressed concerns about the excessive control exercised by family members from the imposition of daily connection and communication routines via internet. There were also migrant women who, as a strategy to strengthen ties with the places to which they migrated, showed a commitment to reducing the time spent using the internet in order to prioritize experiences of a daily life less mediated by family relationships in the country of origin. (Cogo, 2017, p. 185)

As a matter of fact, as reiterated by Francisco

[research] on recent international migration flows have shown that contemporary e/immigrants do not completely assimilate to the culture of their countries of destination, nor do they break the ties with their countries of origin. The global social context, marked by the presence of all kinds of flows (including that of workers) and by technological modernisation, has allowed that through e/immigratory networks in the form of families, communities or social organisations, the e/immigrants continue participating in the economic, social and even political life of their countries of origin, even when they are physically and temporally distant from them. These are experiences of ordinary people living between two or more 'different worlds', but which are connected through family, economic, affective, caring, political and religious ties. (Francisco, 2017, p.1)

In these families, maternal, paternal and conjugal relationships, among others, are carried out at a distance, and therefore, access to technology has decisive importance. For all this, it should be noted that the challenges imposed by migration are not only in social, economic and governmental structures. Migrations, especially international ones, impose new dynamics on families, whether those in which all its members migrate to a new country or those in which part of it remains, and the other migrates. Dealing with homesickness, family reorganization and hoping for better days are part of the challenges for thousands of families that are crossed by migration (Risson, 2019).

In short, with globalization, the use of new information technologies by transmigrants and/or transnational families makes it possible to realize 'for example, the changing nature of the family as a unit of socioeconomic strategy and how family ties are reconfigured across time and space.' (Levitt and Glick-Shiller, 2004, p.196)

In fact, the border is simultaneously a plural and singular space. Singular because it has its own logic, distinguishing itself geopolitically and culturally from the other social spaces of the Nation-State of which it is part. Plural, for converging in its core cultures and identities of the most diverse possible, which are affirmed or merged at the same time. The border dynamics are marked by mobility through continuous displacements of the social subjects that transit in this space. The social space shared in the cross-border allows its social actors a life of interaction with differences, which undergoes changes as the definitions of public space and private space modify the symbolic content that the host society attributes to them. Culture is re-signified since it is constituted as a web of meanings elaborated and interpreted by the subjects in the process of social interaction (Vasconcelos, 2010, pp.12-13).

For all these reasons, information and communication technologies and/or emerging technologies are fundamental instruments to kill homesickness, annihilate the distance between continents and, above all, they are technological instruments of success for migrants because, by means of these same instruments, transnational families flourish and proliferate in the migratory global world. It is easy to kill the homesickness of the family when one has basic information and communication technologies.

The Role of Women in Transnational Families

Contemporary migratory movements have been intensifying since the last decade of the twentieth century. In fact, as referred by Bógus and Silva, '[with] globalization, international migrations have reached new origins, destinations and routes, enhanced by the reduction of transport costs and the ease in obtaining information, creating, at first, the idea that distances had been reduced and space would be free for all' (Bógus and Silva, 2017, p.35).

However, in most discussions about migration, in general, the starting point is numbers. Understanding the shifting scales, emerging trends, and variable demographics related to global social and economic transformations, such as migration, helps us understand the dynamic world we live in and plan for the future. The current global estimate is that there were about 272 million

international migrants in the world in 2019, equivalent to 3.5% of the global
population (World Migration Report, 2020, p. 23). However, the growth of
international migration has supposedly slowed by 27% due to the COVID-19
pandemic. Effectively, in 2020, the pandemic interrupted all forms of human
mobility because of social confinement and the closing of borders. In addition,
travel has been suspended, but despite all this, the number of current migrants
has reached 281 million (United Nations, 2021).

The quantitative record of the growth of international migration in these last
decades is, however, only one dimension of a phenomenon for which different
factors of qualitative order concur and which contribute to attribute complexity to
contemporary migration movements (Cogo, 2017, p. 178). Indeed,

> [it] is important to understand migration and displacement, and how
> they are changing globally, given their relevance to states, local
> communities and individuals. Human migration may be an ancient
> phenomenon dating back to the earliest periods of history, but its
> manifestations and impacts have changed over time as the world has
> become more globalised. Now, more than at any other time in history,
> we have more information about migration and displacement globally
> at our disposal. And yet the very nature of migration in an interconnected
> world means that its dynamism can be difficult to capture in statistical
> terms. Migration involves 'events' that can be rapid and complex, [so it
> is virtually impossible to identify with complete accuracy the exact
> number of migrants in the world]. (World Migration Report, 2020, p. 55)

However, as Grassi and Vivet point out

> [despite] increasingly restrictive migration policies, migration flows
> from Africa to Europe remain significant. Many families unable to move
> together live increasingly separated from their children, using local and
> transnational networks adapted to the care of their 'children'. Thus, we
> are witnessing the emergence of transnational migrant families derived
> from the migration of their members. (Grassi and Vivet, 2015, p.86)

It is in this socio-historical and cultural framework that women play a crucial
role in solidifying transnational families. Currently, increasingly valued as an
alternative for women, migration is seen as a solution for those experiencing
high levels of poverty and unmet basic needs. In this context, most migrant
women are single, abandoned or separated mothers who act as heads of family
and, as such, are the breadwinners for their children. Faced with difficulties,
they leave in search of a better life for themselves and their children (Schuler
and Dias, 2016, p.1021).

In fact, in Europe, as in the rest of the world, the number of migrant women has increased in the last decades, and this trend is based on a growing demand for autonomy on the part of women. If in the past women migrated mainly to reunite their families, today they often do so alone and for reasons that have nothing to do with the family universe. A significant number of women migrate today in search of better living conditions, trying to blur social minority statuses and escape discrimination, prejudice and oppression to which they are exposed in their countries of origin (Neves *et al.*, 2016, pp.723-724).

The role of women in the twenty-first century is completely different from that of women in the nineteenth and twentieth century. Nowadays, the number of women is slightly higher than the number of men, women tend to marry and start a family later, and many aspire to a different quality of life, security and respect for their most basic human rights. This is because women generally have a higher level of education and training than their counterparts in the last century, so they aspire to enter the labour market in the same way as men and try to reconcile their personal and professional lives. Women are the pillars of the migratory process. They are the shelter for their children. They are the leverage of many men since they are more resourceful and determined and, at the same time, they are the handicap in the whole migratory process since they are victims of domestic violence and all kinds of attacks on the most basic human rights during the migratory journey.

Moreover, with maternal migration, single-parent families also become the families currently called 'transnational families'. These are those families whose relatives are divided between two or more countries. The element of transnationalism, therefore, challenges the notion of shared residence in families that are geographically separate but maintain social, cultural, reproductive and income links across borders.

> (...) Here are some examples of transnational families: parents who leave their families (children, wife) to go work abroad; a child who is sent to live with relatives; women who live and work abroad and leave their children behind. (...) [Transnational families] constitute a common aspect of migration, and are linked to the increase in migration worldwide (Schuler and Dias, 2016, p.1021).

However, it should be noted that '[t]he experiences of a migrant woman and a migrant man are very different, mainly due to the different accumulated experiences, both in terms of what they learned in the country of origin and what is expected from them in the host country' (Vasconcelos, 2010, p.5).

In this context, Valderrama also mentions that among the diversity of experiences that make up the migration scenario nowadays, it is possible to notice an expansion of the countries involved in the migratory networks; a greater diversity of ethnic and cultural groups that make up these networks; a significant number of women who migrate independently or as heads of the family; an increase in the number of people living and working abroad without legal regularization, as well as refugees and asylum seekers; a growth of migrations resulting from environmental disasters; and the intensification of temporary migratory movements and circulation (Valderrama, 2006, pp. 11-30).

On the other hand, it should be noted that

> [through] increased female migration, grandmothers have often been called upon to take full responsibility for their grandchildren. (...) [Grandmothers], but especially grandfathers, assume a role as carers of their grandchildren until they are reunited with their parents or even permanently. (...) [It is] important to note that migration can have a psychological impact not only on children, but also on older people and other family members who remain in the country of origin. (...) [Older] people are often forgotten, but take on important roles as caregivers in transnational families (Schuler and Dias, 2016, p.1022).

Therefore, and because we consider the family as a central unit of analysis in understanding the relationships of individuals in transnational contexts, it becomes crucial to take into account that these relationships are developed in different countries, each of which has a specific social and family organisation from a historical, cultural and political point of view, and which condition the representations and self-perception of the roles played by individuals (Grassi and Vivet, 2015, p. 87). In fact, the changes that have occurred in family configurations due to the dynamism of society show us how the family has become fragmented and pluralistic (Schuler and Dias, 2016, p. 1020). However, it should be stressed that transnational families are fundamental in the migration process to the extent that they create a network that allows other relatives to migrate.

The Exceptionality of Refugees and 'Friendly Law' on Migration in Portugal

Portuguese migration law is an inclusive law, or rather, it can be considered a law that values the family in comparison with other European countries. Moreover, article 15, paragraph 1 of the Constitution of the Portuguese Republic states the following: '[foreigners and stateless persons who are or live in Portugal shall enjoy the rights and be subject to the duties of Portuguese citizens' (Constitution of the Portuguese Republic, 1976).

In fact, paragraphs 1 and 2 of article 99, under the heading (family members) of Law no. 23/2007, of 4 July, which approves the legal regime of entry, stay, exit and expulsion of foreigners from national territory, establishes the following as family members: 'the following are considered to be family members of the resident (a) the spouse; (b) the minor or incapacitated children dependent on the couple or one of the spouses; (c) the minors adopted by the applicant when not married, by the applicant or the spouse, as a result of a decision by the competent authority of the country of origin, provided that the law of that country recognises the adopted persons' rights and duties identical to those of natural parentage and that the decision is recognised by Portugal; (d) adult dependent children of the couple or one of the spouses, who are single and are studying at an educational institution in Portugal g) Minor siblings, provided that they are under the resident's guardianship, in accordance with a decision taken by the competent authority in the country of origin and provided that this decision is recognised by Portugal. 2 - The following are also considered to be family members for the purposes of family reunification of unaccompanied minor refugees: a) direct ascendants to the first degree; b) their legal guardian or any other relative if the refugee has no direct ascendants or it is not possible to locate them. (Law No. 23/2007 of 4 July).

As we can see, a wide range of relatives are considered as family members, which, from the migratory point of view, is extremely favourable for migrants, as they can apply for family reunification, thus minimising the increase in transnational families. Therefore, the impact of Portuguese migration laws on migrants is very large compared to other countries in Europe. In fact, Portugal, like Germany, has an inclusive approach towards immigration, which is why it was well-ranked in 2015 by the Migrant Integration Policy Index (Mipex), which gathers data from 33 countries in several areas, including family reunification, employment, education, labour market access and participation '[despite] the crisis and austerity, PT maintained its investment in integration and even worked to increase its reach and effectiveness. PT continues to climb ahead on MIPEX: +1 point from 2007 to 2010 during the start of the crisis; immigrants benefited from more realistic family reunion requirements and more targeted support to pursue jobs, training and recognition procedures. PT rose another +1 point from 2010 to 2014; more immigrants can access protections against domestic violence and expanded targeted employment programmes, e.g. Mentoring for Immigrants Programme. Moreover, PT's integration policies have been given a new overall focus after the crisis. The new mobility and social realities reconfirmed that PT is a country of emigration (both for PT and non-EU citizens now working abroad) and a country of integration (both for non-EU families settling long-term and PT citizens living in a more diverse society). As a result, the High Commissioner for Immigration and Intercultural Dialogue (ACIDI) was transformed into the High Commissioner for Migration (ACM). This shift adds new goals on the mobility, return and integration of PT citizens working abroad to its well-established work on integration and dialogue in PT with immigrant residents and youth and increasingly with local communities' (Migrant Integration Policy Index, 2015).

It should be noted that the Migrant Integration Policy Index compares countries according to their integration laws and policies and that this ranking of favourable (80-100) for family reunion mainly reflects laws and policies regarding the labour market and the right to family reunion.

However, over time Portugal has been able to adapt to European guidelines on integration policies for immigrants. Thus, in the 1990s, Portugal increased a process of extraordinary regularisations with three distinct periods that allowed many migrants a regularisation; in 2006, 'the nationality law strengthened the ius soli principle, i.e. the right to citizenship for children born in Portugal if the parents were legally resident in the country for a period of five years' (Grassi and Vivet, 2015, pp.85-108); In 2007, "the new migration law was approved, which facilitated the regularisation of the processes, namely with the introduction of the 'long-term resident status', and established the right of children and their parents to have a 'residence permit' when they were enrolled in school up to secondary level" (*Idem*, pp.85-108).

Moreover, as Grassi and Vivet point out,

> in Portugal, any citizen with a valid residence permit is entitled to family reunification with family members living outside the country. This is a point on which Portugal differs from many other European countries, and which suggests a family-friendly policy in the approach to migration management (*Ibidem*, pp. 85-108).

As we can see, Portuguese migration law favours family reunification, which, to a certain extent, mitigates the trauma of a transnational family. It is true that not everyone is subject to regrouping. It is true that there is still a limited concept of what can be understood as a family member. However, it is also true that Portugal has a more inclusive or friendly immigration policy in comparison to some European countries.

However, when it comes to refugees and asylum seekers, this Portuguese 'friendly law' changes dramatically, despite the fact that transnational families have devastating effects on this category of vulnerable people. This is because we cannot forget that most migrants leave their country of origin by choice, in search of new life opportunities, with the exception of refugees and asylum seekers. This vulnerable group of people is forced to abandon their country of origin, their family, and their affective ties with their country of origin because they are victims of persecution against the most elementary human rights.

In comparison with other migrants who have a much faster process for regularisation in the receiving country, along with family reunification, the process is very difficult for refugees and asylum seekers. In fact, refugees and asylum seekers must first prove that they are victims of the most basic human rights, an almost impossible task for those who leave their country of origin often with only the clothes on their back, as can be confirmed "[the] 28 Member States of the European Union (EU) granted protection status to nearly 333 400 asylum seekers in 2018, down by almost 40% from 2017 (533 000). In addition, the EU Member States received over 24 800 resettled refugees" (Eurostat, 2019).

Final Consideration

In today's migratory process, the existence of transnational families is inevitable. We must learn to live with this transnational phenomenon, and in particular, the family in its traditional conception must readapt to the new reality of the twenty-first century since migration is a global phenomenon that will not stop in time or space but will proliferate in the world.

It is true that in the twenty-first century, the traditional family (heterosexual couple united by marriage) is not exclusive to contemporary society. At present, we have many other forms of families. However, the great change within the family has been attributed to women. She has gained visibility and freedom with access to education and the labour market. On the other hand, in modern trends regarding the conceptualization of the family, feelings and affection are valued, regardless of the blood connection, for example, in the case of adopted children, stepchildren, stepmothers and stepfathers.

Today, the family is no longer a father, a mother and children. There are new family scenarios, de facto unions (no marriage contract), single-parents, same-sex families (homosexual couples with children), recomposed families (arising after divorces or separations), extended families (including grandparents, uncles and cousins), large families (those with three or more children), and finally, transnational families resulting from the migration process.

Just as the concept of family has evolved, host states should also draw some lessons from transnational families, mainly because a migrant who is part of a family is a good person, a person who is part of a society and not on the margins of society. Therefore, host states should adopt public policies to provide each and every migrant with access to information and communication technology. These means are fundamental for better integration into the host society, for the minimisation of family homesickness and for the maintenance of ancestral and family culture and experiences. No man or migrant is an isolated being, and the migrant integrated into a transnational family and a host society is undoubtedly a social being.

References

Bacigalupe, G. and Parker, K. 2016. 'Conexões Transnacionais através de Tecnologias Emergentes' *in Nova Perspectiva Sistêmica*, Rio de Janeiro, dezembro, nº 56.

Bógus, L.M.M. and Silva, J.C.J. 2017. 'Fluxos migratórios contemporâneos: Condicionantes políticos e perspectivas históricas' in *Fluxos Migratórios e Refugiados na Atualidade*, 7ªsére relações Brasil-Europa da Fundação Konrad Adenauer Stiftung. Viewed 6.22.22. https://www.academia.edu/35838186/ Fluxos_Migrat%C3%B3rios_Contempor%C3%A2neos_Condicionantes_Pol %C3%ADticos_e_Perspectivas_Hist%C3%B3ricas

Borsa, J.C. and Feil, C. F. 2008. 'O papel da mulher no contexto familiar: uma breve reflexão'. Viewed 1.9.22 at https://www.psicologia.pt/artigos/textos/A0 419.pdf

Bryceson, D. and Vuorela, U. 2002. *The transnational family: new European frontiers and global networks*, Oxford, Berg Publishers.

Cogo, D. 2017. 'Comunicação, migrações e gênero: famílias transnacionais, ativismos e usos de TICs', São Paulo, *Intercom — RBCC*, v.40, n.1, jan/abr. Viewed 2.11.22 from https://medium.com/revista-subjetiva/famílias-migrantes- e-famílias-transnacionais-f840e7718cbb

Constitution of the Portuguese Republic. 1976. Viewed at 3.23.22. https://portal. oa.pt/cidadaos/direitos-dos-cidadaos-instrumentos-fundamentais/constituicao- da-republica-portuguesa/

Eurostat 2019. Statistics. Viewed 8.23.22 from https://ec.europa.eu/eurostat/ documents/2995521/9747530/3-25042019-BP-EN.pdf/22635b8a-4b9c-4ba9 -a5c8-934ca02de496

Francisco, E. 2017. 'Famílias Transnacionais de Origem Mineira: Trajectórias, Experiências e Estratégias de Vidas que Cruzam Fronteiras Nacionais (1984- 2014)', *Seminário Internacional Fazendo Gênero 11& 13th Women's Worlds Congress* (Anais Eletrônicos), Florianópolis, ISSN 2179-510x. Viewed 8.11.22 from http://www.en.wwc2017.eventos.dype.com.br/resources/anais/1499384643 _ARQUIVO_Textofazendogenero2017.pdf

Grassi, M. and Vivet, J. 2015. 'Cuidar das crianças entre Angola e Portugal: a parentalidade nas famílias transnacionais', *Sociologia – Problemas e Práticas*, nº 79, SPP, 79, 2015. Viewed 7.11.22 from https://journals.openedition.org/ spp/2250

IOM (2020). *World Migration Report 2020*. Law No. 23/2007 of 4 July. Retrieved 8.22.22 https://sites.google.com/site/leximigratoria/artigo-99-o-membros-da -familia

Levitt, P. and Glick-Shiller, N. 2004. 'Conceptualizing simultaneity: a transnational social field perspective on society' in, *International Migration Review*, v.38, n.03.

Machado, I. *et al.* 2008. 'Notas sobre a Família Transnacional' *in Revista Interdisciplinar da Mobilidade Humana* (REMHU), Ano XVI, nº 30.

Migrant Integration Policy Index 2015. Index Viewed 9.11.22 from http://www. mipex.eu/portugal.

Neves, A. *et al.* 2016. 'Mulheres imigrantes em Portugal: uma análise de gênero. Psicologia Social e Organizacional'. *Estudos de Psicologia*, Campinas, nº 33 (04), Oct-Dec. Viewed on 8.20.22. https://www.scielo.br/j/estpsi/a/4Q3Zh8 ByLXbthzXHdXqBC6r/?lang=pt&format=pdf

Risson, A. P. 2019. Mi*grantes e famílias transnacionais*. Viewed 9.19.22 from https://medium.com/revista-subjetiva/fam%C3%ADlias-migrantes-e-fam% C3%ADlias-transnacionais-f840e7718cbb

Schiller, G. N., Basch, L. and Blanc, C. S. 1995. 'From Immigrant to Transmigrant: theorizing transnational migration'. *Anthropological Quarterly*, v.68, n.1. Viewed 2.27.22 from https://eportfolios.macaulay.cuny.edu/lutton15/files/2015/02/Theorizing-Transnational-Migration.pdf

Schuler, F. de M.G. and Dias, C.M.S.B. 2016. *Famílias Transnacionais: Um estudo sobre filhos envolvidos na migração materna.* Viewed 5.18.22 from file:///C:/Users/Jos%C3%A9/Downloads/850-Texto%20Artigo-3360-1-10-20 160706%20(1).pdf

United Nations 2021. 'Global Perspective Human Reports'. *UN News*. Viewed 3.11.22 from https://news.un.org/pt/story/2021/01/1738822

Valderrama, C.B.F. de. 2006. *Migraciones: Nuevas movilidades en un mundo en movimiento*, Barcelona, Anthropos.

Vasconcelos. I. dos. S. 2010. 'Famílias Transnacionais na Fronteira Brasil/Venezuela' in *Revista Eletrônica de Ciências Sociais, História e Relações Internacionais*, V. 3, n°2.

World Report on Migration. 2020. *Migration and Migrants: Global Overview*. Viewed 3.11.22 from https://publications.iom.int/es/system/files/pdf/wmr-2020-po-ch-2.pdf

Chapter 2

What Role does the General Comments of Human Rights Instruments Have in the Community Structure of the Asylum-Seeking Refugee Child? UNCRC Article 22

Tanya Herring

Salem State University

Abstract

Member states of human rights instruments receive guidance from General Comments and Recommendations on interpreting procedural and substantive requirements of treaty obligations. The United Nations Convention on the Rights of the Child (UNCRC), Article 22, is a section of Child Law in an international context and sets out that State Parties shall take appropriate measures to ensure that a child seeking refugee status or considered a refugee receive appropriate protection and humanitarian assistance outlined in the Convention. This research investigates the seldom studied role of General Comments across human rights instruments and State obligations. It proposes furtherance of a State's positive obligation to the Committee on the Protection of the Rights of all Migrant Workers and Members of their Families (CMW) and the UNCRC Committee's Joint General Comment 4 (2017) and 23 (2017); and UNCRC Committee General Comments 6 (2005) and 14 (2013) to close protection gaps in international community structures for the accompanied and unaccompanied asylum-seeking refugee child. The chapter analyses case law of child refugee and asylum-seeking protections in contrast to gaps in defence against child-specific forms of persecution, including subjection to genital mutilation, under-age recruitment, sex-trafficking for prostitution, forced organ transplant, to include the European Court of Human Rights' adjudication in the CRC's first assessment in the case of *I.A.M. v Denmark* (2018) and the standards set out in *Rantsev v Cyprus and Russia* (2010).

Keywords: UNCRC, Child Law, Migrant workers, refugee/asylum-seeking child

***

Introduction

The Asylum-Seeking Child in Vulnerable Situations

Child law, in the international context, provides provisions for children displaced across borders that unquestionably are designed to protect children in vulnerable situations. International research supports the premise that policy and practice on relocation encounter a phenomenon of precarious child detention, abduction, trafficking-in-persons (Palermo Trafficking Protocol, article 3)[1], and a myriad of child-specific exploitations[2] (Save the Children, 2006; UN General Assembly Report, 2019). The Oxford Handbook of Refugee and Forced Migration links the trafficking of children to both in-country and cross-border migrations (Loescher, 2014). A host of global literature expands the discourse of migration to examine the long-term physical and psychological outcomes of cross-border and internally displaced children's (IDP) adverse childhood experiences (ACE) from detention and trafficking, as well as the proffered remedies to address social structures that impact and target ethnic groups (Jeremiah *et al.,* 2017; National Work Group for Sexually Exploited Children, 2008). This research investigates the seldom studied role of General Comments across human rights instruments and State obligations. It proposes furtherance of a State's positive obligation to the Committee on the Protection of the Rights of all Migrant Workers and Members of their Families (CMW), and the UNCRC Committee's Joint General Comment 4 (2017) and 23 (2017); and UNCRC Committee General Comments 6 (2005) and 14 (2013) to close protection gaps in international community structures for the accompanied and unaccompanied asylum-seeking refugee child.

---

[1] For a comprehensive and legally accurate definition of trafficking please see Art. 3 of the Protocol to Prevent, Suppress and Punish Trafficking in Persons Especially Women and Children (Trafficking in Persons Protocol), which supplements the UN Convention against Transnational Organized Crime (A/RES/55/25 of 15 Nov 2000).

[2] Children are often trafficked for child-specific forms of exploitation, such as illegal adoption, child labour, child prostitution, child pornography, and forced recruitment into armed forces or groups. Other forms of exploitation to which children are often exposed include domestic service, agricultural work, mining, forced and early marriage, and begging. It is important to note that any recruitment, transfer, harbouring or receipt of children for the purpose of exploitation is considered a form of trafficking regardless of the means used.

Human Rights Instruments and the General Comments

General comments are also referenced as 'general recommendations' expand over a large spectrum of human rights themes and cover a range of topics that constitute explanations, clarity, or interpretations of substantive as clarification or an interpretation of substantive provisions of the respective treaty. The focal principles of general comments Centre on the right to life. The general comments outline the treaty's interpretation of basic subsistence, such as food and shelter. It is also inclusive of issues surrounding violence against vulnerable persons, the rights of minorities and the disabled, and the continuing emergence of the general comments which focus on the right to life and food. It also encompasses a range of evolving issues of violence against vulnerable persons, the rights of the disabled and minorities, and other emerging human rights matters (International Human Rights Instruments, 2008; OHCHR Human Rights Treaty Bodies – General Comments, 2021).

The CRC Committee expounded its general comments with the intent to provide clarity on the normative context and content of the specific rights as indicated under the Convention on the Rights of the Child, the thematic content pertinent to the CRC, which is also inclusive of implementation guidance and measures for compliance. Unlike other human rights instruments' general comments, the CRC Committee General comments provide an authoritative interpretation to States Parties on expectations for implementation and the carrying out of obligations.[3] The full and consolidated listing of the CRC Committee's general comments has been published on the Office of the High Commissioner United Nations Human Rights website (OHCHR.org) or on the Child Rights International Network (CRIN) at: http://www.crin.org/resources/infoDetail.asp?ID=8043&flag=report. The CRIN's report also includes General comment No. 16 (2013) on State's Party obligation regarding the business sector on children's rights.

Article 43 of the CRC sets out the authority and provisions of the Committee on the Rights of the Child. Collectively with art. 44 and 45, art. 43 are part of the provisions for international monitoring:

> CRC Committee, *Treaty-specific guidelines regarding the form and content of periodic reports to be submitted by States Parties under article 44, para 1 (b), of the Convention on the Rights of the Child* (3 March 2015) CRC/C/58/Rev.3 Rule 77; CRC Committee, *General guidelines regarding the form and content of initial reports to be submitted by State Parties under article 44, para 1 (a) of the Convention* (30 October 1991) CRC/C/5.

---

[3] Child Rights net provides a fact sheet in English, French, and Spanish at: Child Rights Net – Legal Updates on Child Rights Law.

CRC Committee, *Revised guidelines regarding initial reports to be submitted by States Parties under article 12, para 1, of the Optional Protocol to the Convention on the Rights of the Child on the sale of children, child prostitution and child pornography* (3 November 2006) CRC/C/OPSC/2; CRC Committee, *Revised guidelines regarding initial reports to be submitted by States Parties under article 8, para 1, of the Optional Protocol to the Convention on the Rights of the Child on Involvement of children in armed conflict* (19 October 2007) CRC/C/OPAC/2.

The reporting structure is detailed under art. 44 in the form of eight clusters under four themes, 'factors and difficulties encountered', 'progress achieved', 'implementation priorities', and 'specific goals'. The standard reporting procedures for periodic reports, the States Parties have a requirement to submit a report and written replies to what is identified as a 'list of issues' (CRC art 44).[4]

Convention on the Rights of the Child, article 22

CRC art. 22 affirms the States' obligation for the best interest principle under CRC art. 3 affirms the protection and care of refugee children by providing implementation guidance with CRC Committee *General comment No. 6 (2005): Treatment of Unaccompanied and Separated Children Outside their Country of Origin*. CRC Committee *General comment No. 14*, adds further clarity to member State protection responsibilities as it explains that a child in circumstances and situations of vulnerability may not be the same from one child to the other.[5] Author Kristen Sandberg (2015; 2018) explains that one child's situation may not be the same as another child's vulnerable situation – "each child is unique, and each situation must be assessed according to the child's uniqueness". The CRC further obliges State parties to identify particular groups/subgroups of children as vulnerable for the purposes of implementing special measures for these groups, CRC Committee *General comment 14*.

CRC art 22 outlines the State obligation to child refugees or children seeking refugee status in their respective territory under the positive obligations under international human rights and humanitarian law. The three primary elements of art. 22:

---

[4] CRC Committee, *Working methods for the participation of children in the reporting process of the Committee on the Rights of the Child* (16 October 2014) CRC/C/66/2 para 8 and 15-28.

[5] UNCRC, General comment No 14 on the Right of the Child to Have His or Her Best Interests Taken as a Primary Consideration (art 3, para 1), 62nd session, UN Doc CRC/C/GC/14 (2013) ('General comment No 14') [76].

1) adequate protection and humanitarian assistance

2) cooperation with organisations linked to the UN when providing protection and assistance;

3) and, the establishment of an adequate environment of care for children, either by reunification with their family or by finding alternative state protection.

The child protection and assistance declaration are required to take place according to the relative domestic and international law. Accordingly, art. 22 refers to the 2018 Global Compact for Migration[6] as being guided by art. 1, the best interest principle as an international protection for asylum-seeking and refugee children to all children in the jurisdiction of a State Party that lack citizenship or migration status (Pobjoy, 2015). Following art. 3.1's guidance Global Compact for Migration (2018) states are called on to provide 'accurate, timely, accessible, and transparent information on migration-related aspects for and between states, communities and migrants at all stages of migration'… 'child-sensitive and gender-responsive support and counselling' and information' (para 19, c, d).

Gaps in the State obligations to international protection of an asylum-seeking child have judicial references discussed further within the text, *I.A.M. v Denmark*, No 3/2016, 25 January 2018. The case and others related under Art 22.1 does not draw a distinction between accompanied and unaccompanied children, therefore, the provisions of assistance and rendering of protection do not vary. However, there is an exception, whereas para. 2 avers accommodation for the unaccompanied child and children separated from family. The CRC Committee recognizes the heightened vulnerability of the unaccompanied child and includes legal empowerment/access to justice in the processing of decisions in its *General comment 6;* whereas states are obliged to provide an adequate standard of living as well as material assistance and support 'with regard to nutrition, clothing and housing'.[7]

CRC art. 22 provides a definition of a refugee. CRC Committee GC 6 refers to the 1951 Refugee Convention but indicates that the refugee status may be based upon child-specific forms of persecution that incorporates the CRC ruling of I.A.M. v Denmark where the assessment includes persecution of kin, under-age recruitment; tracking of children for prostitution; and sexual

---

[6] Global Compact for Safe, Orderly and Regular Migration (2018) Global Compact for Safe, Orderly and Regular Migration para 19(c) and (d).

[7] CRC General comment 6: Treatment of unaccompanied and separated children outside their country-of-origin para 68.

exploitation or subjection to female genital mutilation'.[8] Non-refoulment is addressed under CRC art. 22.1 refers to the enjoyment of rights not only in the CRC but also in other international human rights or humanitarian instruments to which the states are parties. Embraced within art. 22 are substantive references to the 1951 Convention relating to the Status of Refugees and its 1967 Protocol. Non-refoulment is a central tenet of international law content, and the Refugee Convention prohibits States Parties from expelling or returning "a refugee in any manner whatsoever to the frontiers of territories where his life or freedom would be threatened on account of his race, religion, nationality, membership of a particular social group or political opinion".

Prominently used as an authoritative interpretation under CRC Committee's GC 22, which provides States Parties guidance in the application of the fundamental children's rights principles, often referred to as general principles of non-discrimination, best interests, participation, and the right to life, survival, and development (CMW and CRC Committee Joint *General Comment* 4/23, para. 45-46). Each are also designating of non-refoulment to be a fundamental principle of the human rights of children in the context of migration (CRC Committee *General comment 6*).

The content of protection and assistance for asylum-seeking and refugee children have been litigated in regional human rights systems and added clarity to the obligatory protection and assistance. Precedent-setting cases at the EctHR have referenced CRC art 22 on State obligations for humanitarian assistance and protections whether a child is alone or accompanied by his or her parents (*Popov v France* 2012).[9]

Joint Stakeholders: Human Rights Committees and Treaty Bodies

The global community, as responsible stakeholders, have a bottom-up and top-down tenet role in forming structures that protect the human rights of unaccompanied asylum-seeking children. On the international human rights platform, Human Rights Committees are comprised of global representatives who serve as appointed independent experts guiding the monitoring and implementation of the ten human rights treaty bodies[10] that bind State parties.

---

[8] *CRC Committee, General comment 6: Treatment of unaccompanied and separated children outside their country of origin,* para 74.

[9] *Popov v France* (Application nos. 39472/07 and 39474/07) Judgment (European Court of Human Rights (EctHR) 2012 para 91.

[10] According to the United Nations Human Rights Office of the High Commissioner, as of 2021, there are ten human rights treaty bodies that monitor implementation of the core international human rights treaties:

The Office of the High Commissioner for Human Rights (OHCHR) described these treaty bodies as follows, "nine of these treaty bodies monitor implementation of the core international human rights treaties while the tenth treaty body, the Subcommittee on Prevention of Torture, established under the Optional Protocol to the Convention against Torture, monitors places of detention in States parties to the Optional Protocol" (OHCHR 2021).

Simply stated, these appointed independent experts emerge from a host of professions that reflect the State parties and serve as vital stakeholders in their community. These experts are keenly aware of critical human rights issues and render their expertise within the scope, functions, and implementation of core international human rights treaties. Hence, the effete of these treaties is highly contingent upon implementation goals and expectations set by State leadership from the top for social change across both natural and human endogenous factors. Analogously, the bottom-up is indicative of the treaty implementation and its application in contrast of endogenous to exogenous factors, which include migration (the shifting flow of people), economic shifts pushed by migration, and the government rules and decisions imposed by the treaty at the State level (Kaufman, 2004). Sociological scholars working in endogenous and exogenous factors argue that there are a multitude of thresholds that influence outcomes, change, and adaptation of government policies to control, anchor, or organize the implementation of human rights instruments (Swidler, 1986; 2001).

At the international top-level, the Human Rights Council operates as a separate entity from the OHCHR. The Human Rights Council has separate mandates derived from the General Assembly,[11] a principal organ of the United

---

Committee on the Elimination of Racial Discrimination (CERD)

Committee on Economic, Social and Cultural Rights (CESCR)

Human Rights Committee (CCPR)

Committee on the Elimination of Discrimination against Women (CEDAW)

Committee against Torture (CAT)

Committee on the Rights of the Child (CRC)

Committee on Migrant Workers (CMW)

Subcommittee on Prevention of Torture (SPT)

Committee on the Rights of Persons with Disabilities (CRPD)

Committee on Enforced Disappearances (CED)

[11] The only body in which all UN members are represented, the General Assembly exercises deliberative, supervisory, financial, and elective functions relating to any matter within the scope of the UN Charter.

Nations (UN), [12] whose powers, functions, and composition are set out in Chapter IV of the United Nations Charter[13]. Nonetheless, the OHCHR renders substantive support for the Human Rights Council sessions and the subsequent follow-up deliberations. The Human Rights Council forum's principal mandate is 'to prevent abuses, inequity, and discrimination, protecting the most vulnerable, while exposing perpetrators' (UNHR 2021). Hence, Special Procedures are characterized as an established mechanism of the Human Rights Council and can take the shape of a workgroup or a special rapporteur (an individual) (UNHR 2021). The outcomes of Special Procedures result in the examination, monitoring, advising, and submission of public reports that focus on human rights situations in identified territories, countries, and concern worldwide thematic mandates. As of 1 August 2017, there are 44 thematic mandates with 12 country mandates, which include a mandate for 'Ending immigration detention of children and providing adequate care and reception of them' (UNHR, 2021; UN General Assembly 20 July 2020, A/75/183).

This chapter links the international community structure with endogenous and exogenous factors to explain the State obligation, compliance, roles, or gaps in the roles of protecting accompanied and unaccompanied asylum-seeking children. Communities are people functioning amongst a problem of social changes, which is a constant in the central foci of sociological 'why' inquiries and how can the behaviours change (Maheshwari, 2016). The consensus of literature is expressed to describe social change, where change is the law and places great emphasis on foundations to migratory resistance of anyone, including children, due to geographical conditions, the composition of ideologies and diffusions of communities. The content then conducts an analogy of community structures through the lens of international law.

---

[12] The United Nations has six principal organs: The General Assembly, the Security Council, the Economic and Social Council, the Trusteeship Council, the International Court of Justice, and the Secretariat.

[13] United Nations, Charter of the United Nations, 24 October 1945, 1 UNTS XVI; The Charter was signed at San Francisco on 26 June 1945. The amendments included here are: Amendments to Articles 23, 27 and 61, 557 UNTS 143, adopted by the General Assembly Resolutions 1991A and B (XVIII) of 17 December 1963, entered into force on 31August 1965 for all Members; - Amendment to Article 109, 638 UNTS 308, adopted by the General Assembly Resolution 2101 (XX) of 20 December 1965, entered into force on 12 June 1968 for all Members; Amendment to Article 61, 892 UNTS 119, adopted by the General Assembly Resolution 2847 (XXVI) of 20 December 1971, entered into force on 24 September 1973 for all Members.

Beginning with State obligations to the Children's Rights Convention (CRC),[14] article 22, precedent-setting children's rights' case law, and binding instruments to include:

> a) the Committee on the Protection of the Rights of all Migrant Workers and Members of their Families (CMW) and the UNCRC Committee's Joint General Comment 4 (2017) and 23 (2017);[15] (*Joint General comment No 4 and 23: State obligations regarding the human rights of children in the context of international migration in countries of origin, transit, destination, and return*); b) UNCRC Committee General Comments 6 (2005) [16] (*General comment No. 6 (2005): Treatment of Unaccompanied and Separated Children Outside their Country of Origin*) and 14 (2013) [17] (*General comment No. 14 (2013) on the right of the child to have his or her best interests taken as a primary consideration*); and,
>
> c) the 20 July 2020 A/75/183 mandate focused on the immigration detention of children.

The Obligation

The commitment to fulfil the positive obligations set out in treaties is underpinned by the 1965 Vienna Convention on the Law of Treaties.[18] Around the world, community structures and processes rely heavily upon the preventions and protections for the refugee child and the respective States'

---

[14] UN General Assembly, Convention on the Rights of the Child, 20 November 1989, United Nations, Treaty Series, vol. 1577, p. 3; The Convention on the Rights of the Child was adopted and opened for signature, ratification and accession by General Assembly resolution 44/25 of 20 November 1989. It entered into force on 2 September 1990, in accordance with article 49.

[15] UN Committee on the Protection of the Rights of All Migrant Workers and Members of Their Families (CMW), Joint general comment No. 4 (2017) of the Committee on the Protection of the Rights of All Migrant Workers and Members of Their Families and No. 23 (2017) of the Committee on the Rights of the Child on State obligations regarding the human rights of children in the context of international migration in countries of origin, transit, destination and return, 16 November 2017, CMW/C/GC/4-CRC/C/GC/23.

[16] UN Committee on the Rights of the Child (CRC), General comment No. 6 (2005): Treatment of Unaccompanied and Separated Children Outside their Country of Origin, 1 September 2005, CRC/GC/2005/6.

[17] UN Committee on the Rights of the Child (CRC), General comment No. 14 (2013) on the right of the child to have his or her best interests taken as a primary consideration (art. 3, para. 1), 29 May 2013, CRC /C/GC/14.

[18] Rantsev v. Cyprus and Russia, Application no. 25965/04, Council of Europe: European Court of Human Rights, 7 January 2010.

compliance, where article 1(b) VCLT provides the defining role of ratification and accession as an international act of being bound by a treaty, articles 11-17.[19] To guide the implementation and contextual interpretation of a treaty,

---

[19] VCLT, article 11-17:

- Article 11
  Means of expressing consent to be bound by a treaty
  The consent of a State to be bound by a treaty may be expressed by signature, exchange of instruments constituting a treaty, ratification, acceptance, approval or accession, or by any other means if so agreed.

- Article 12
  Consent to be bound by a treaty expressed by signature
  1.The consent of a State to be bound by a treaty is expressed by the signature of its representative when:
  the treaty provides that signature shall have that effect;
  it is otherwise established that the negotiating States were agreed that signature should have that effect; or
  the intention of the State to give that effect to the signature appears from the full powers of its representative or was expressed during the negotiation.

- 2.For the purposes of paragraph 1:
  the initialling of a text constitutes a signature of the treaty when it is established that the negotiating States so agreed;
  the signature ad referendum of a treaty by a representative, if confirmed by his State, constitutes a full signature of the treaty.

- Article 13
  Consent to be bound by a treaty expressed by an exchange of instruments constituting a treaty
  The consent of States to be bound by a treaty constituted by instruments exchanged between them is expressed by that exchange when:
  the instruments provide that their exchange shall have that effect; or
  it is otherwise established that those States were agreed that the exchange of instruments should have that effect.

- Article 14
  Consent to be bound by a treaty expressed by ratification, acceptance or approval
  1.The consent of a State to be bound by a treaty is expressed by ratification when
  the treaty provides for such consent to be expressed by means of ratification;
  it is otherwise established that the negotiating States were agreed that ratification should be required;
  the representative of the State has signed the treaty subject to ratification; or
  the intention of the State to sign the treaty subject to ratification appears from the full powers of its representative or was expressed during the negotiation.
  2.The consent of a State to be bound by a treaty is expressed by acceptance or approval under conditions similar to those which apply to ratification.

VCLT article 3(3) further sets out the highly authoritative character of General Comments/recommendations where it notes that the treaty needs continuous contextual interpretation. The United Nations Convention on the Rights of a Child (CRC),[20] art. 43, establishes the role and authority of the Committee to set out the rules of procedure, and the continuous, and contextual interpretation of the CRC. Whereas art. 45 clarifies that the UNCRC is a treaty amongst states and that 45(c)(d) obliges States parties to grant the Committee the power to make suggestions, general recommendations, establish reporting obligations, and the implementation of the CRC.

The CRC's thematic areas in health, migration, and best interest continue to be globally remarkable issues of human rights committee's General Comments and State party implementation guidance, specifically *General Comment 4*,[21]

- Article 15
  Consent to be bound by a treaty expressed by accession
  The consent of a State to be bound by a treaty is expressed by accession when:
  the treaty provides that such consent may be expressed by that State by means of accession;
  it is otherwise established that the negotiating States were agreed that such consent may be expressed by that State by means of accession; or
  all the parties have subsequently agreed that such consent may be expressed by that State by means of accession.

- Article 16
  Exchange or deposit of instruments of ratification,
  acceptance, approval, or accession
  Unless the treaty otherwise provides, instruments of ratification, acceptance, approval or
  accession establish the consent of a State to be bound by a treaty upon:
  their exchange between the contracting States;
  their deposit with the depositary; or
  their notification to the contracting States or to the depositary, if so agreed.

- Article 17
  Consent to be bound by part of a treaty and
  choice of differing provisions
  1.Without prejudice to articles 19 to 23, the consent of a State to be bound by part of a treaty is
  effective only if the treaty so permits or the other contracting States so agree.

[20] The Convention on the Rights of the Child was adopted and opened for signature, ratification and accession by General Assembly resolution 44/25 of 20 November 1989. It entered into force on 2 September 1990, in accordance with article 49.

[21] UN Committee on the Rights of the Child (CRC), General comment No. 4 (2003): Adolescent Health and Development in the Context of the Convention on the Rights of the Child, 1 July 2003, CRC/GC/2003/4.

6,[22] and *23*, each detailed further in the chapter to exclaim the critical survival issues of health, migration, and best interest. Whether State parties heed their respective positive obligations by respecting, protecting, and fulfilling the rights of the CRC, inclusive of the adjoined General comments, is contingent upon the shall endeavour spectrum of the positive obligation. Response to the shall endeavour may have an adverse impact on the unaccompanied or accompanied asylum-seeking refugee child. The chapter's investigation evaluates divergence in the varying layers of the community's application of the CRC Committee's general comments and the CRC Article 22 in relation to an asylum-seeking child, the case of *I.A.M. v Denmark* (2018),[23] to include the standards set by *Rantsev v Cyprus'* 2010[24] European Court of Human Rights case to guide future strategies for actionable change. Both cases will be discussed in more detail further in the text.

The Dichotomy of the Positive Obligation, *Shall Endeavour*

Compliance with human rights treaty obligations is troublesome in that the language translates into questionable compliance (O'Flaherty and O'Brien, 2007; Oette, 2018). Could treaty language and interpretation be the root cause? International communities are consistently competing with cultural challenges, social structures, and social equality within the scope of natural and human endogenous factors (Kaufman, 2004). A potential root-cause influencing component is the language of 'shall endeavour' in treaty interpretation. Legal theorists Richard Gardiner (2008) and Serge Sur (1974), among others, support the concept that there is not any component of the law of treaties where the text-writer approaches more vicariously than the interpretation[25] (ILC 1966).

To gain a better understanding of endeavour, a review of the Vienna Convention on the Law of Treaties is silent on the interpretation of endeavour, but commercial contract case law serves as a guide. Actions of State parties in response to their human rights obligations can be compared to commercial contract law, which inserts a qualification that parties are concurring to 'try' to

---

[22] UN Committee on the Rights of the Child (CRC), General comment No. 4 (2003): Adolescent Health and Development in the Context of the Convention on the Rights of the Child, 1 July 2003, CRC/GC/2003/4.

[23] *I.A.M. (on behalf of K.Y.M.) v Denmark*, communication No. 3/2016, CRC/C/77/D/3/2016, UN Committee on the Rights of the Child (CRC), 25 January 2018.

[24] *Rantsev v. Cyprus and Russia, Application no. 25965/04*, Council of Europe: European Court of Human Rights, 7 January 2010.

[25] Report of the ILC on the Work of its 18th -Session: Draft Articles on the Law of Treaties with Commentaries (A/6309/Rev1), vol. II. Extract from the Yearbook of the International Law Commission.

achieve the particular obligation. However, this brings into question the lengths a party, or in this case, the member-States of the CRC Convention and its instruments, will pursue in 'trying' to achieve the obligation, refer to Figure 1. It is clear from the commercial contract case law that there is a spectrum of endeavours, with the best endeavours at one end and 'nothing' at the other. An example can be found in the civil law case of *Jet2.com v Blackpool Airports*, 2012,[26] where best endeavours had to be used even if the airport endured a commercial loss. A further interpretation can be made those circumstances have a key role when the issue of enforceability arises in determining a breach, as illustrated in the civil case of *Astor Management AG and others v Atalaya Mining PLC.*[27] Similarly, in *Phillips Petroleum Co UK Ltd v Enron Europe Limited, Court of Appeal (Civil Division)*,[28] where the court raised the question of the lengths a party must exercise in 'trying to achieve that obligation'. When placed in juxtaposition to the States' obligation, further clarity can be obtained from the European Court of Human Rights ruling in *Rantsev v Cyprus and Russia*, paras 64-65; paras. 264-268, where State positive obligations denote:

> Enactment of appropriate legislation,
> Introduction of review procedures for the operation of certain businesses known to be a cover for human trafficking,
> Establishment of punishments commensurate to the nature of the crime of trafficking,
> Introduction of measures to discourage demand,
> Assurance of the training of law enforcement for the identification of trafficking victims and for building trust amongst victims and law enforcement,

---

[26] *Jet2.com Limited w Blackpool Airport Limited* [2012] EWCA Civ 417, The Court of Appeal has ruled in favour of Jet2.com in a case concerning the construction of a 15 year old agreement relating to the use of Blackpool Airport by a low cost carrier; Blackpool Airport Limited ('BAL'), 95% owned by Balfour Beatty plc, had argued unsuccessfully before HHJ Mackie QC at trial that it was not obliged to keep Blackpool Airport open to accommodate Jet2.com's schedules beyond its promulgated opening hours. BAL had contended that the provisions of the agreement that obliged it to cooperate and use best endeavours to promote Jet2.com's low-cost services from Blackpool Airport and use all *reasonable endeavours* to provide a cost base that would facilitate Jet2.com's low-cost pricing did not require it to sacrifice its own commercial interests. BAL renewed that argument on appeal, namely that *best and all reasonable endeavours* entitled it to consider its own commercial interests before those of Jet2.com.

[27] *Astor Management Ag and Another V Atalaya Mining Plc and Others*, [2017] 1 Lloyd's Rep. 476.

[28] *Phillips Petroleum Co UK Ltd v Enron Europe Limited,* Court of Appeal (Civil Division), [1997] CLC 329.

Encouragement of research, information campaigns, awareness
  law enforcement, and
Vigorous investigation of allegations of human trafficking.
Plotting an obligator's endeavour spectrum on the graph, Figure 1
  reflects the categorical performance of the endeavour clause of the
  positive obligation.

Figure 2.1 The Spectrum of 'Shall Endeavours' is Charted on the Graph to Assess the
State's Actions and Omissions of its Treaty Obligations[29]

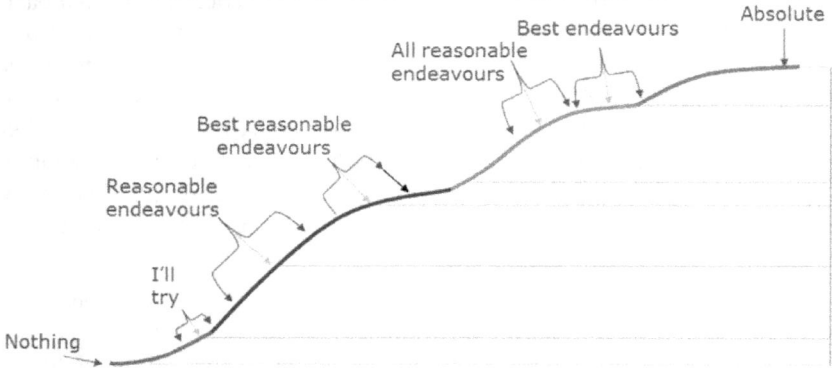

Absolute/Best Endeavours to the Positive Obligation

Absolute obligation entails the State's complete fulfilment of the obligation. An
example of absolute can be found in two court rulings.[30] First, in referring to
Siliadin v France,[31] where States are under an obligation to 'adopt laws to
combat trafficking and to strengthen policies and programmes to combat
trafficking', where the question could arise of 'shall endeavour', *Siliadin v
France.* The second tier would encompass the courts' ruling of *Rantsev v Cyprus
and Russia,* where a state's obligation for absolute compliance would be met.

---

[29] Graphic adopted from Ashurst Business Services LLC for educational purposes only.

[30] 'States are required to' are used, the reference is to a mandatory provision. Otherwise,
the language used in the legislative guide is 'required to consider', which means that
States are strongly asked to seriously consider adopting a certain measure and make a
genuine effort to see whether it would be compatible with their legal system.

[31] *Siliadin v. France,* 73316/01, Council of Europe: European Court of Human Rights, 26
July 2005

However, the term 'best endeavours' has been highly judicially scrutinized, as in the case of *IBM United Kingdom Ltd v Rockware Glass Ltd*[32] where it is judged by standards of reasonableness. Wherein the ruling conveys that the term 'best endeavours' has the most tangible of the 'endeavours' formulations. Usually, the best endeavour obligation, in contract law, is demonstrated through the obligor taking all reasonable steps or steps that are within their power to take. 'Best endeavours' obligation and 'absolute' appear to align with the mandatory measures and are reflected at the far-right peak of the spectrum as illustrated in Figure 2.1 (reading right to left – absolute red sections through to all reasonable endeavours, orange lined sections of the spectrum).

Best Reasonable Endeavours/All Reasonable Endeavours/ Reasonable Endeavours to the Obligation

The endeavour is 'less stringent' than the application of best endeavours where the party takes on one reasonable course of action, but not all courses of action are available to meet the obligation.[33] Referring to the realm of contract law again, all reasonable endeavours are frequently adopted as a compromise between best endeavours and reasonable endeavours. In the case of *Rhodia International Holdings Ltd and another v Huntsman International LLC*, the court ruled that 'an obligation to use reasonable endeavours was less stringent than one to use best endeavours. The commercial court held,

---

[32] This case is cited by: Cited – Overseas Buyers v Granadex ([1980] 2 Lloyd's Rep 608); The court considered the meaning of a promise by one party to use its best endeavours. Held: Mustill J said: 'it was argued that the arbitrators can be seen to have misdirected themselves as to the law to be applied. Cited – Rhodia International Holdings Ltd. Rhodia UK Ltd v Huntsman International Llc ComC (Bailii, [2007] EWHC 292 (Comm), Times 06-Apr-07, [2007] 2 Lloyds' Reports 325); The parties contracted for the sale of a chemical surfactants business. The claimant had contracted to use reasonable endeavours to obtain the consent of a third party for the assignment of a contract to supply energy to the business. The defendant. Cited – EDI Central Ltd v National Car Parks Ltd SCS (Bailii, [2010] ScotCS CSOH – 141). Cited – R and D Construction Group Ltd v Hallam Land Management Ltd SCS (Bailii, [2010] ScotCS CSIH – 96, 2011 GWD 2-85, 2011 SLT 326). Cited – Dhanani v Crasnianski ComC (Bailii, [2011] EWHC 926 (Comm)) The parties disputed the terms of a contract between them under which the defendant was to provide substantial sums for the claimant to invest.

[33] *Rhodia International Holdings Ltd. Rhodia UK Ltd v Huntsman International Llc*: ComC 21 Feb 2007. References: [2007] EWHC 292 (Comm); where the court summarised by a judge in *Rhodia International v Huntsman* summarised it nicely when he explained that an obligation to use reasonable endeavours probably only requires a party to take one reasonable course, not all of them, whereas an obligation to use best endeavours probably requires a party to take all the reasonable courses he can.

There might be a number of reasonable courses which could be taken in a given situation to achieve a particular aim. An obligation to use reasonable endeavours to achieve the aim probably only required a party to take one reasonable course, whereas an obligation to use best endeavours probably required a party to take all the reasonable courses she could. In that context, it might well be that an obligation to use all reasonable endeavours (Rhodia International Holdings Ltd and another v Huntsman International LLC [2007] EWHC 292].

In that context, an interpretation can be made that an obligation to use 'all reasonable endeavours' equates with using 'best endeavours'. In contrast, if the same obligation instrument uses 'both expressions', which is often seen in treaty instruments, for different obligations, then based upon *Rhodia International Holdings Ltd and another v Huntsman International LLC*'s ruling, it could be presumed an intention was to impose a different standard. The reasonable endeavour aligns with measures that indicate States have the latitude to consider absolute compliance or 'endeavour' to comply. In the case of *Rantsev v Cyprus and Russia*, the court ruled that Cyprus' legislation had prohibited trafficking and sexual exploitation. However, the Ombudsman criticized Cyprus' implementation in prohibiting trafficking and sexual exploitation of a child but ruled the laws were satisfactory. Moreover, the Council of Europe Commissioner found Cyprus' laws as 'suitable'. On Figure 1's graph and the concerns expressed regarding implementation in *Rantsev v Cyprus and Russia*, Cyprus would likely fit on the graph between 'best reasonable endeavours' and 'reasonable endeavours'.

'I'll Try' to 'Nothing' Obligation

The 'I'll try' endeavours present the most difficult posture of the three categories. There is a high degree of disagreement and uncertainty as to where reasonable endeavours is plotted on the graph and 'I'll try'. Circumstances and the difference of opinion weigh heavily in the determination between 'reasonable endeavours', 'I'll try', and 'nothing'. An example could easily be the Cyprus legislation situation. On one hand, Cyprus was criticised, but in totality, Cyprus did fulfil the 'reasonable endeavours' of the obligation.

Yet, the AIRE Centre voiced extreme concern as to what can be best described as the 'reasonable endeavours' by Cyprus was insufficient. The case notations reflect that AIRE Centre cited the wording to 'consider' or 'endeavours' to introduce certain measures as hortatory and often lacked practical and effective rights for the protection of victims. AIRE Centre's posture would place the States' 'reasonable endeavours' closer to the 'I'll try' or possibly to 'nothing' plot on the graph and viewed as non-compliant by the court with the treaty obligation. Consequently, determining whether a State breached an obligation is contingent upon the circumstances, situation, and case law.

The Due Diligence Obligation Standard

Examining the case of *Rantsev c Cyprus and Russia* as it cites *Larissis et al. v Greece*,[34] international law makes clear that States are under a legal obligation to investigate and prosecute trafficking with due diligence, imposing a positive duty as in the case of *Larissis et al. v Greece* and *Rantsev c Cyprus and Russia*. Due diligence obligations are obligations of conduct or means, thus leaving some discretion for the state in practice (ILA 2014). This discretion explains why the record of compliance with these obligations is not highly satisfactory. For many years, international human rights law has been thought to not be serious and is often referred to as 'soft law' (Guzman, 2010).[35]

Considering the trafficking of children, the state's duty is to combat not only trafficking but also the demand for the services of human trafficking. States are obliged to combat child human trafficking and exploitation that hinder human rights within their jurisdiction through the States' criminal laws.[36] There are a range and latitude of measures that states can adopt to combat the human trafficking of asylum-seeking children, accompanied or unaccompanied. The international obligations of states are frequently stated in general terms. Subsequently, parties to a legal instrument are permitted to adopt measures best suited to their respective national legal systems.

---

[34] *Larissis et al v Greece*, Apps nos140/1996/759/958–960 Council of Europe: European Court of Human Rights, 24 February 1998.

[35] International agreements come in a multitude of forms. Some have dispute resolution while others do not, monitoring provisions vary from significant to nonexistent, and some are highly detailed while others are frustratingly vague; For example, the International Covenant on Civil and Political Rights (ICCPR) provides for the submission of reports by the parties when so requested by the Human Rights Committee ('the Committee'), and the Committee is authorized to review and comment on these reports. See International Covenant on Civil and Political Rights, art 40(1)(b)(4), Dec. 16, 1966, 999 U.N.T.S. 171. The Genocide Convention, on the other hand, does not provide for any formal monitoring system. See Convention on the Prevention and Punishment of the Crime of Genocide, Jan. 12, 1951, 78 U.N.T.S. 277.

[36]The prohibition against exploitation of children is a general prohibition under human rights law: The 1989 UN Convention on the Rights of the Child, 1577 UNTS 3, arts 34–37(a); the 2000 UN Optional Protocol to the Convention on the Rights of the Child on the sale of children, child prostitution and child pornography, G.A. Res. 54/263, Annex II, 54 U.N. GAOR supp (no 49) at 6, U.N. Doc. A/54/49, vol III (2000), arts 3(1)(b) and (2).

In contradiction, multiple cases before the Inter-American Court of Human Rights, European Court of Human Rights, and the UN Human Rights Committee shine a different light on how States are being held in violation of their international legal obligations to human rights.[37] In *Rantsev* v *Cyprus and Russia*, in relation to trafficking, the European Court of Human Rights identified an obligation on State parties to investigate cases of trafficking. The Court placed emphasis on the requirements for investigations to entail the full spectrum of the trafficking allegation through to the recruitment and exploitation (*Rantsev v Cyprus and Russia*). The court's ruling for the States' positive obligation for investigation was to be 'full and effective' (*Rantsev v Cyprus and Russia, para 307, p 76*). The positive obligation extended to the various States potentially involved in human trafficking—States of destination, States of transit, and States of origin (*Rantsev v Cyprus and Russia, para 389, p. 71*). The same court ruling obliged States to 'take such steps as are necessary and available in order to secure relevant evidence' regardless of where the investigation leads in or outside the territory. The court ruled that, "in addition to the obligation to conduct a domestic investigation within the respective territory, Member States are also subjected to a duty in cross-border trafficking cases to cooperate effectively with the relevant authorities of other States concerned in the investigation of events which occurred outside their territories" (*Velásquez Rodríguez v Honduras, 1988*).[38]

The European Union was integrally involved in the decision on *Velásquez-Rodriquez*,[39] in 1988, which brought the due diligence doctrine to the forefront for acts by private entities. States' responsibility to prevent breaches of

---

[37] For state-party compliance with the European Convention on Human Rights, see Christian Tomuschat, Quo Vadis, 'Argentoratum? The Success Story of the European Convention on Human Rights - and a Few Dark Stains' (1992) 13 Hum. RTS. L. J. 401; For state-party compliance with the American Convention on Human Rights, see Annual Reports of the Inter-American Court of Human Rights.

[38] Velásquez Rodríguez v Honduras, Merits, Judgment, Inter-Am. Ct. H.R. (ser. C) no 4, ¶ 147(g)(i) (July 29, 1988); the first case decided by the Inter-American Court of Human Rights. The Velásquez Rodríguez case, together with the Godínez Cruz, Fairén Garbi, and Solís Corrales cases, all considered by the Court around the same time, form a trio of landmark cases targeting forced disappearance practices by the Honduran government during the early 1980s.

[39] Velásquez Rodríguez v Honduras, Merits, Judgment, Inter-Am. Ct. H.R. (ser. C) no 4, ¶ 147(g)(i) (July 29, 1988); the first case decided by the Inter-American Court of Human Rights. The Velásquez Rodríguez case, together with the Godínez Cruz, Fairén Garbi, and Solís Corrales cases, all considered by the Court around the same time, form a trio of landmark cases targeting forced disappearance practices by the Honduran government during the early 1980s

international obligations has been discussed in several legal decisions. In Chile, *Question of the Fate of Missing and Disappeared Persons,* led by Judge Abdoulaye Dieye in Senegal 1979, was the actual pioneer due diligence case (UN Doc A/34/583/Add.1 (1979), paras 172-175). Yet, the *Velásquez-Rodriquez,* the most memorable case, paved legal ground, and the case is often referenced as the Commission alleged that Honduras violated 'art. 4 —Right to Life, art. 5 —Right to Humane Treatment, and art 7 —Right to Personal Liberty, and in relation to art 1(1) — Obligation to Respect Rights.

The monumental impact on States' responsibility to due diligence can be attributed to the outcomes of *Velásquez-Rodriquez* (1988)[40] case, where the court ruled, "the state's failure to *prevent* the disappearance, to investigate it, and to *punish* the perpetrators was a violation of the obligation in the Inter-American Convention to 'ensure' the full exercise of rights and freedoms in the Convention, including the right to life".[41]

A comparison of the Convention on the Rights of the Child can be made to the General comment on the International Covenant on Civil and Political Rights (ICCPR)[42] torture prohibition, where it states, "It is the duty of the State Party to afford everyone protection through legislative and other measures as may be necessary against the acts prohibited by art 7, whether inflicted by

---

[40] *Velásquez Rodríguez v Honduras,* Velásquez Rodríguez Case, Inter-Am.Ct.H.R. (Ser. C) no 4 (1988), Inter-American Court of Human Rights (IACrtHR), 29 July 1988.

·American Court of Human Rights (IACrtHR), 29 July 1988; Loy. L.A. Int'l & Comp. L. Rev [vol 36:1913]; Inter-American Court decision of Velasquez Rodríguez, in 1988; The case notes: "The judgment on compensatory damages delivered by the Inter-American Court of Human Rights (hereinafter 'the Inter-American Court' or 'the Court') on July 21, 1989 in the Velásquez Rodríguez Case, in which it established at seven hundred and fifty thousand lempiras the compensatory damages that the State of Honduras (hereinafter 'Honduras') must pay to the next of kin of Mr. Angel Manfredo Velásquez-Rodríguez and decided that the Court would supervise 'execution of payment of [this] compensation ... and that only after it was settled [would] the case be closed.'; No Pecuniary damages; The Court ordered the State to pay $93750 to Ms. Emma Guzmán Urbina de Velásquez, the wife of Mr. Velásquez Rodríguez, for psychological damage and loss of income from losing her husband; The Court ordered the State to pay $281250 dollars to the three children of Mr. Velásquez Rodríguez: Héctor Ricardo, Herling Lizzett, and Nadia Waleska Velásquez, for psychological harm due to the forced disappearance of their father, and for loss of income from losing their father as a provider; $375,000 in costs and expenses; each cost by the State was directed to commence within 90-days and five consecutive months thereafter".

[42] The aim of the provisions of article 7 of the International Covenant on Civil and Political Rights is to protect both the dignity and the physical and mental integrity of the individual.

people acting in their official capacity, outside their official capacity or in a private capacity" (UNHRC 2021, CPR GC 20).

Research implies that asylum-seeking children are forced to engage in a multitude of low-range remunerative activities as well as petty crime, substance abuse, and prostitution. The UN Human Rights Committee (HRC) also indicates that whether the trafficking is internal or cross-border, the crime is inextricably connected to the involuntary or deceitful movement of people to achieve the end-object sexual, labor, child marriage, organ removal, or a multitude of other forms of exploitation (CCPR General comment no. 20).[43]

Guidance for States can also be found in the UN Doc. A/RES/63/156, GA Res. 63/156, 'Trafficking in Women and Girls', where it outlines,

> States have an obligation to exercise due diligence to prevent, investigate, and punish perpetrators of trafficking in persons, and to rescue victims as well as provide for their protection, and that not doing so violates and impairs or nullifies the enjoyment of the human rights and fundamental freedoms of the victims.[44]

There have been minimal cases to address where the State has been responsible for failure to provide due diligence. Also, there are two cases in Austria that have a correlation to the Rohingya critical case where the court emphasizes the 'State should have known' but failed to exercise due diligence. The first is in the case of *Goekce v Austria,* [45] where the State was found accountable for failure to provide protection and exercise due diligence by

---

[43] UN Human Rights Committee (HRC), CCPR General comment no 20; art 7 (Prohibition of Torture, or Other Cruel, Inhuman or Degrading Treatment or Punishment), 10 March 1992

[44] UN Doc. A/RES/63/156, 'Trafficking in Women and Girls' GA Res. 63/156 (30 January 2009).

[45] *Goekce v Austria, Sahide Goekce (deceased) v Austria,* Comm. 5/2005, U.N. Doc. A/62/38, at 432 (2007), Committee on the Elimination of Discrimination against Women, 2007, CEDAW, domestic and intimate partner violence, international law; Sahide Goekce's husband shot and killed her in front of their two daughters in 2002. Police reports show that the law enforcement failed to respond in a timely fashion to the dispute that resulted in Ms. Goekce's death. The complaint to the Committee on behalf of the decedent stated that Austria's Federal Act for the Protection against Violence within the Family provides ineffective protection for victims of repeated, severe spousal abuse and that women are disproportionately affected by the State's failure to prosecute and take seriously reports of domestic violence. The Committee found that although Austria has established a comprehensive model to address domestic violence, it is necessary for State actors to investigate reports of this crime with due diligence to effectively provide redress and protection. The Committee concluded that the police knew or should have known that Ms. Goekce was in serious danger and were therefore accountable for failing to exercise due diligence in protecting her.

actions of its organs (the police department and State prosecutor) in the instances of domestic violence and diminishing the importance of violence against women. Notably, in each application of the theory of a state's responsibility for vicarious liability, three principles are consistent: a) *respondent superior* (let the principal be liable), b) *Quifacit per alium facit per se* (he who acts through another does it himself), and c) socialization of compensation. In the Optional Protocol for the sale of children, art 9(3), States 'shall' "ensure that all child victims of the offences described in the present Protocol have access to adequate procedures to seek, without discrimination, compensation for damages from those legally responsible".[46]

References

Gardiner, R. K. 2008. *Treaty Interpretation.* New York: Oxford University Press.

Guzman, A.T. 2010. 'International Soft Law' 2 J. *Legal Analysis* 171, 179 Retrieved 1.11.22 from https://scholarshiplaw.berkeley.edu/facpubs

Global Protection Working Group. 2010. *Handbook for the Protection of Internally Displaced Persons.* Viewed 1.22.22 from https://reliefweb.int/report/world/handbook-protection-internally-displaced-persons-enar

National Working Group for Sexually Exploited Children and Young People. 2008. 'How is child sexual exploitation defined?'. *National Working Group for Sexually Exploited Children and Young People.* Viewed 3.13.23 from https://nwgnetwork.org/what-is-child-exploitation/

IOM (2018). 'Global Compact for Migration'. Viewed 2.12.22 from https://www.iom.int/global-compact-migration

International Law Association. 2014. 'Study Group on Due Diligence in International Law', First Report, 7 March. Viewed 1.11.22 from https://ila.vettoreweb.com/Storage/Download.aspx?DbStorageId=1429&StorageFileGuid=fd770a95-9118-4a20-ac61-df12356f74d0

International Law Commission. 1966. '*Interpretation of treaties*'. Viewed 2.12.22 from https://www.researchgate.net/publication/231814719_Interpretation_of_Treaties

International Human Rights Instruments (IHR) 2008. '*Compilation of general comments and General recommendations adopted by human rights treaty bodies.*' Viewed 1.12.22 from https://www.ohchr.org/Documents/HRBodies/TB/HRI-GEN-1-REV-9-VOL-I_en.doc HRI/GEN/1/REV.9(VOL.I) and HRI/GEN/1/REV.9(VOL.II) (2008)

Jeremiah, R. *et al.* 2017. 'Exposing the culture of silence: Inhibiting factors in the prevention, treatment, and mitigation of sexual abuse in the Eastern Caribbean'. *Child Abuse Neglect.* 2017 Apr, 66:53-63. doi: 10.1016/j.chiabu.2017.01.029

---

[46] *Rudul Shah v State of Bihar, (1983) 4 SCC 141; State of Andhra Pradesh v Challa Ramkrishna Reddy, (2000) 5 SCC 712; D K Basu v State of West Bengal, (1997) 1 SCC 416.*

Kaufman, J. 2004. 'Endogenous explanation in the sociology of culture'. *Annual Review of Sociology*, 30, 335-357. Viewed 3.12.23 from http://www.jstor.org/stable/29737697

Loescher, G. 2014. 'The Oxford handbook of refugee and forced migration'. *Political Science, International Relations, Comparative Politics*. Viewed 2.17.2 from http://10.1093/oxfordhb/9780199652433.013.0003

Maheshwari, V.K. 2016. 'The concept of social change'. *Social Change-Theoretical Rationale*. Viewed 1.11.22 from http://www.vkmaheshwari.com/WP/?p=2163

Oette L.(2018. 'The UN Human Rights Treaty Bodies: Impact and Future'. In: Oberleitner G. (eds) *International Human Rights Institutions, Tribunals, and Courts*. International Human Rights. Springer, Singapore. https://doi.org/10.1007/978-981-10-4516-5_5-1

O'Flaherty, M. and O'Brien, C. 2007. 'Reform of UN human rights treaty monitoring bodies: a critique of the concept paper on the high Commissioner's proposal for a unified standing treaty body'. *Human Rights Law Rev* 7:147–172.

Office of the High Commissioner for Human Rights. 2012. 'Human Rights Treaty Bodies – General Comments'. *Office of the High Commissioner, United Nations Human Rights*. Viewed 2.15.22 from https://www.ohchr.org/EN/HRBodies/Pages/TBGeneralComments.aspx

Pobjoy, J. 2015. 'The Best Interests of the Child Principle as an Independent Source of International Protection' *International and Comparative Law Quarterly*, 64(2), 327-363. doi:10.1017/S0020589315000044

Sandberg, K. 2015. The Convention on the Rights of the Child and the vulnerability of children *Nordic Journal of International Law* [84] 221-47, 229. ISSN 1891-8131.

Sandberg, K. 2018. 'Children's Rights to Protection Under the CRC', In Asgeir Falch-Eriksen & Elisabeth Backe-Hansen (ed.), *Human Rights in Child Protection Implications for Professional Practice and Policy*. Palgrave Macmillan. ISBN 978-3-319-94799-0.

Save The Children. 2006. 'Save the children cross-border project against trafficking and exploitation of migrant and vulnerable children'. *Save the Children UK*. Viewed 3.14.23 from https://resourcecentre.savethechildren.net/sites/default/files/documents/2708.pdf

Sur, S. 1974. *The interpretation of public international law* (Paris, LGDJ).

Swidler, A. 1986. 'Culture in action; symbols and strategies'. *American Sociological Review*. 41(2), 273-86.

Swidler, A. 2001. *Talk of Love: How culture matters*. Chicago, IL: Univ. Chicago Press.

United Nations. 1979. 'Documents of the conference'. (A/34/583/Add.1, paras. 172-175). *UN Document* (1979). Viewed 1.18.22 from https://treaties.un.org/doc/source/docs/A_CONF.62_121-E.pdf

United Nations. 2020. 'Ending immigration detention of children and providing adequate care and reception for them'. *UN General Assembly Report* (2020). Viewed 2.19.22 from https://www.undocs.org/A/75/183

United Nations. 2019. 'Estimated 17 million children displaced by violence, special rapporteur tells third committee as delegates tackle modern slavery, exploitation'. *UN General Assembly 3rd Committee, 74th Session, 35th meeting,*

GA/SHC/4275 25 (October 2019). Viewed 2.23.22 from https://www.un.org/press/en/2019/gashc4275.doc.htm

United Nations. 2021. 'Human Rights Treaty Bodes – General Comments'. *UNHR Office of the High Commissioner* (2021). Viewed 2.14.22 from https://www.ohchr.org/EN/HRBodies/Pages/TBGeneralComments.aspx

United Nations. 2010. 'Handbook for the Protection of Internally Displaced Persons – Action Sheet 7: Human Trafficking'. *UNHR* (32 March 2010). Viewed 1.11.22 from https://reliefweb.int/sites/reliefweb.int/files/resources/Handbook%20for%20the%20Protection%20of%20Internally%20Displaced%20Persons.pdf

Chapter 3

Minors and Forced Migration: Between Integration Plans and Repressive Policies

Isolde Quadranti

European Documentation Centre of University of Verona, Italy

Abstract

It seems that measures in favour of a social inclusion program for 'those already here' who are legal residents and a predominantly security approach focused on opposing illegal immigration can proceed on two parallel paths, neither communicating nor interfering with each other. What will be the consequences of proceeding in such a manner? This paper aims to provide possible answers by analysing the provisions of the EU Pact on Migration and Asylum and the Action Plan on Integration and Inclusion for both accompanied and unaccompanied minors. To this end, we will look at the laws of the European Court of Justice and the European Court of Human Rights and how they evolved concerning the detention of minors, reception conditions and so-called 'Dublin transfers,' and highlight the impact of restricting rights and measures judged to be contrary to the *best interest of the child*, on the minor's development and their social inclusion process in the country of arrival (if there is to be one). Lastly, from the Italian legal system point of view, we propose a reading of the Italian integration plan of 2017 for holders of international protection status, the fostering of social integration introduced by Italian Decree-Law no. 130 of October 21, 2020, converted with amendments into Italian Law 173/2020, and the failure to recognize the principle of social inclusion in the so-called 'Salvini Decree'.

Keywords: Minors, social inclusion, security approach, human Rights, EU Law, Italy

***

Introduction

According to the latest global data, the general trend of forced migration kept growing in 2020, to 82.4 million people (more than 1% of the world's population), of which about 42% are minors. In addition, long-standing situations have also inexorably increased; according to UNHCR statistics, these are situations that have gone on uninterruptedly for at least five years.[1] Whereas, in the '90s, an average of 1.5 million refugees would manage to return to their country of origin every year, in the last ten years, this average has dropped to about 385,000, reaching 251,000 in 2020 (out of a total 3.4 million 'displaced people returned').[2]

'Forced displacements, today, are not only widely more widespread, but also no longer a temporary and short-term phenomenon,' declared the United Nations High Commissioner for Refugees, Filippo Grandi, and as a result, 'people cannot be expected to live in a precarious condition for years and years, without having the opportunity to return home or the hope of being able to start a new life in the place they are in' (UNHCR 2020b).

This paradigm shift, which has been clear and constant in Europe since the so-called 'refugee crisis' of 2015, underscores the urgency to supersede emergency solutions limited to first reception Centres; it also requires that effective integration systems be put in place, as complex as that may be, to facilitate gradual inclusion in society and adherence to its values, without however forcing individuals to assimilate but considering their specific characteristics and vulnerabilities.

Observing the costs of 'non-immigration and non-integration,' the Economic and Social Committee also pointed out in 2018 that integration, a prerequisite for achieving 'the full potential of migration requires an approach which, among other things, makes better use of the skills of the migrant population (...) and minimize the related and long-lasting risks and avoidable socio-

---

[1] According to 2020 data from the United Nations High Commissioner for Refugees (UNHCR), the number of fleeing people has doubled in ten years. As before, almost half are internal displacements (internally displaced persons amount to 48 million, while 26.4 million refugees, 4.1 million asylum seekers and 3.9 million Venezuelans are displaced abroad; other cases involve for the most part (80%) people fleeing to bordering countries, including Turkey (3.7 million refugees), Colombia (1.7 million, including Venezuelans who fled abroad), Pakistan (1.4 million) and Uganda (1.4 million). These percentages do not account for the so-called environmental migrants, increasingly numerous due to the effects of climate change, to the point that 200-250 million people will move for causes related to climate change by 2050, based on UNHCR data.

[2] In 2018, there were at least 15.9 million refugees in a protracted situation, of which 5.8 million for over 20 years.

economic costs,' requires a two-way action from both the society receiving the immigrants and the immigrants themselves, independently of their status and origin, and that, at the same time, we cannot overlook the fact that 'special policies are required for people with particular vulnerabilities (such as refugees), and a community-based rather than one-size-fits-all approach may yield best results' (European Economic and Social Committee 2018, para. 5).

In the case of applicants for international protection and those who have multiple vulnerabilities, such as unaccompanied foreign minors (UAFMs) and human trafficking victims, we must consider the causes of said vulnerabilities in addition to effectively recognizing their rights and providing them with concrete protection measures (La Spina, 2020).

Although the EU Member States could learn measures and policies from each other to support migrant integration, success depends on how well their levels of governance interact and coordinate, including central bodies and local institutions as well as non-profit organizations. A multilevel action is needed based on local welfare programmes that will consider the different contexts and specific characteristics of the individuals involved and their full integration into the host communities.

Europe's Integration Plan of 2021-2027 and Minors

What was stated by the Economic and Social Committee in 2018 is shared by the European Commission in the more recent Action Plan on Integration of 2021-2027 (European Commission 2020a), attached to the Pact on Migration and Asylum of September 2020 (European Commission 2020b), whose explicit target consists in promoting social cohesion and building societies that are more inclusive for all. Integration — understood as 'a dynamic, two-way process of mutual accommodation by migrants and by the societies that receive them' (Council of the European Union, 2004), not as a one-sided assimilation process — is recognized therein as a 'cornerstone' of migration and asylum management to be implemented both internally and externally while respecting the values shared by and characterizing European society.[3]

---

[3] This interpretation is in line with the definition of integration contained in the Presidency Conclusions of the Thessaloniki European Council of June 19 and 20, 2003, according to which integration policies are to be understood 'as a continuous, two-way process based on mutual rights and corresponding obligations of legally residing third-country nationals and the host societies' (European Council 2003: para. 28-43), and with the 'Common Basic Principles for Immigrant Integration Policy in the EU.' Adopted by the EU Justice and Home Affairs Council on November 16, 2004, at the instigation of the

Right from the start, we should make it clear that the 'all' referred to by the integration measures are just those migrants who hold a regular residence permit, including refugees. This is linked to the fact that the legal notion of integration is limited by EU legal immigration policy,[4] whereas, in other cases, the protection of fundamental rights is recognized, but not the integration measures (Caggiano, 2020).

The Action Plan defines a diverse set of tools and progressive measures in the fields of employment, education, health and housing, which together provide guarantees for the stable establishment and rooting of individuals. This last aspect characterizes and distinguishes the concept of inclusion, where the individual is repositioned within an ordinary situation that will benefit all the parties involved, including regional and local communities and foreigners.

The above policy provides a broader perspective than the one outlined in the 2016 plan (European Commission, 2016) because, in addition to non-EU citizens who have just arrived, it is also aimed at the so-called 'second-generation migrants.'[5]

Furthermore, the Action Plan reveals that inclusion will be the central theme of the global EU strategy on the rights of *minors*. Adopted by the Commission six months later, namely on March 24, 2021 (European Commission, 2021), the strategy is set up as a framework policy for global EU action so that minors may have equal access to the same rights and protection mechanisms, regardless of origins, abilities, social and economic conditions, legal status and place of residence.[6]

Thessaloniki European Council, these Principles laid the foundations for the 'open coordination method' which is the basis of the European governments in the field of integration.

[4] On this subject, see the reference only to legally residing third-country nationals contained in the definition of integration established by the 2003 Thessaloniki European Council (European Council 2003).

[5] In other words, according to the broader interpretation adopted by the European Migration Network, a person born and resident in a country in which at least one of the parents ('mixed' couples) entered as a migrant. The term is also used in literature for those who experienced migration in their childhood or adolescence, or, conversely, strictly speaking, to designate foreigners or naturalized citizens born in the country where both foreign parents reside.

[6] Again, dated back to March 2021, Principle 11 of Chapter III of the Action Plan aimed at giving concrete form to the European Pillar of Social Rights reaffirms that all minors have the right to good quality early childhood education and care at sustainable costs and that minors from disadvantaged backgrounds are entitled to specific measures aimed at promoting equal opportunities (European Commission, 2021b).

Among the goals outlined in the Action Plan for each intervention area, some concern minors explicitly or include them, such as high quality and inclusive access to early childhood education and care and more straightforward quicker recognition of degrees obtained from non-EU countries.[7] There also some that are not exclusively or primarily addressed to minors but may regard them or affect their condition in indirect albeit significant ways, such as equal access to health services, including psychological help, according to national laws and practices, and adequate low-cost housing, including public housing, as well as the promotion of individual rather than collective housing for asylum seekers, in particular for families.

To date, these provisions have not been adequately or, at the very least, sufficiently implemented. As we shall see below, this is due to different but related reasons. As determined by the European Union Agency for Fundamental Rights (FRA), and also as far as international protection beneficiaries are concerned, integration 'remains a challenge in the EU' (FRA, 2020b).

Although in matters of immigration and asylum, the EU recognizes as a priority the target of integration and inclusion — understood as a prerequisite for greater social cohesion, cultural diversity, stability and security. The EU makes no provision for harmonising national laws and regulations of Member States to promote the integration of legally resident third-country nationals (Article 79, para. 4 of the TFUE). Hence it follows that, like the preceding Agenda for the Integration of Third-Country Nationals of 2011 (European Commission, 2011) and according to the open method of coordination, the Action Plan contains specific recommendations for the EU States to promote and monitor the various steps of the complex integration process, including with the support of EU funds, as the document mentions, but without identifying unitary strategies.

Since the EU provides only support and coordination for integration, the clauses of pertinent acts of secondary law (including Article 7 (2.1) of Council Directive 2003/86/EC on the Right to Family Reunification) should recognize that it is at the discretion of the Member States to introduce internal measures

---

[7] The UNHCR generally recommends as a priority, starting with asylum seekers, in addition to refugees, teaching the language of the country of arrival when planning reception systems services and integration measures (UNHCR, 2017b). The Global Compact on Refugees also considers access to education among the areas that need special attention. Accordingly, the states and institutions involved are called upon to implement measures such as facilitating refugees' access to the national education system with adequate resources and skills, promoting the processes of recognition of academic degrees and professional qualifications. Offering available for the legal entry of categories of refugees relocated from third countries, including students.

for migrants and international protection beneficiaries, albeit within limits set by the targets of the EU Directive in question and the application of proportionality when choosing the measures suitable to achieve the target pursued. As the interpreter and protector of EU law, the Court of Justice verifying the above takes on particular importance when we consider that, although the data regarding foreigners legally residing in the EU may reveal a stabilization trend,[8] the Member States are experiencing a widespread 'tightening of integration conditions', which do not promote the inclusion of migrants in society but, on the contrary, become tools to limit their rights (as in the case of family reunification) and obstacles to accessing social benefits or even causes for deportation.[9]

We should also point out that the Pact on Migration and Asylum, which is a document valid for five years both politically and as a program and to which the Action Plan is attached, appears incapable of solving many relevant matters even though the Commission presented it with the intent to redesign the shared asylum system because aware of its inadequacy and went so far as to include nine regulation proposals and a roadmap for it to be approved by the Council and Parliament; in addition, it does not seem willing to change the security-oriented approach of fighting illegal immigration and secondary movements of asylum seekers that have characterized the EU migration and asylum policy up until now.[10] Besides its security focus, the EU Pact on Immigration and Asylum, promoted in 2008 on the initiative of the French EU Presidency, was characterized by an imbalance between there being integration requirements for migrants and no duties for the EU States (Caggiano, 2020). Even this new Pact, while presenting a series of recommendations addressed to the EU States, did 'not pursue a genuine Migration and Asylum Union' and, rather than ensuring solidarity for individuals, seems to legitimize national policies to accelerate and outsource procedures at the expense of respecting individual rights and asylum application guarantees (Carrera, 2021).

The direction taken — judged in legal literature as the legislative process result of 'a broken balance between politicization and rationality', which not even a 'stronger judicial control [can] fully compensate' (Cornelisse and

---

[8] According to the latest data from the European Commission, there are 23 million foreigners legally resident in the EU in 2020, amounting to about 5.1% of the population (https://ec.europa.eu/info/strategy/priorities-2019-2024/promoting-our-European-way-life/statistics-migration-europe_en).

[9] On this point, see Caggiano, 2020, paras. 5-12.

[10] Also referring to what is already happening in the Italian context, these critical issues had already been noted in the general comments initially made on the Plan, including ASGI 2021; Borraccetti 2021; De Pasquale 2021; Favilli 2020.

Reneman, 2021) — collides once again with choices favourable to a more outstanding balance between security needs and guarantees for liberty and justice. This approach persists even though applications for EU asylum, after reaching a maximum of 1.28 million during the so-called 'refugee crisis' of 2015, have gone down sharply, all the way to 698,000 in 2020, recording a 34.0% decrease from 2019 (Eurostat 2021)[11] and, as of the end of 2019, the number of refugees did not exceed 0.6% of the EU population. (European Commission, 2021).

Critical Issues for Minors in the Pact on Migration and Asylum Despite Repeated References to the Principle of 'Best Interests of the Child'

According to the European Union Agency for Fundamental Rights (FRA), respect for fundamental rights in border areas is, still in 2021, 'one of the top human rights challenges in the EU'. On March 9, 2021, the Commissioner for Human Rights of the Council of Europe reported a 'further deteriorated' general situation in the Mediterranean, which is a cause for 'great alarm'.[12] 'Actions of fundamental importance that cannot be further postponed' are needed (Commissioner for Human Rights 2021; for comment, see Delle Santi, 2021)[13] to deal with violations of the 'non-refoulement' principle (Article 78(1)

---

[11] According to Eurostat 2021 data related to 2020 (Eurostat 2021), Germany continues to be the EU State with the highest number of asylum applications in absolute terms (142,450, equal to 1 out of 4 of the applications submitted in the EU States) and which hosts the highest number of refugees (1.2 million); it is also the only EU State ranking in the first 10 'refugee-hosting countries.' Next come Spain (21%), France (20%), Greece (9%) and Italy (5%). On the other hand, overall asylum applications in the 27 EU Member States, Norway and Switzerland decreased by 31% compared to 2019, down from 671,200 to 461,300. The highest number of applicants relative to the number of inhabitants was recorded in Cyprus (8,448 applicants per one million inhabitants), Malta (4,686) and Greece (3,532); on the opposite end, Hungary showed the lowest number (9 applicants per one million inhabitants), followed by Estonia (35), Poland (40), and Slovakia (1200). In 2020, among the EU States with over 10,000 first-time asylum applicants, only Austria experienced an increase of 17.5% over the previous year (UNHCR 2021a).

[12] Commissioner for Human Rights 2021. For a comment, Delle Santi, 2021.

[13] In 2020, the FRA also expressed 'serious concern about actions intimidating humanitarian workers and volunteers who support migrants in irregular situations' (FRA 2020, p.116), while the OSCE pointed out that 'in Italy, defenders working on the protection of migrants and refugees as well as women's rights are exposed to increased risks of online and offline threats and attacks' (OSCE 2021, point 56). Apparently, in 2019, about 780 minors (out of 2,800 migrants and refugees) remained at sea for over a day before state authorities authorized NGO ships to dock; in addition, just like in 2018, of the migrants who had left Libya by sea more rescued people landed in Libya (9,000) than in Italy (4,000) and Malta (3,400) (FRA, 2020). The 2018-2019 cases reported by international, national and NGO organizations of violations of the ban on refoulement at

of the TFUE; Articles 18-19 of the EU Charter of Fundamental Rights)[14] and actions and omissions against the duty of EU States to guarantee rapid landings in a 'place of safety' based on the consolidated principles and prescriptions of the UNHCR, as well as obstacles set against NGO search and rescue operations. Although some Member States have achieved significant progress, reception facilities remain far below the minimum standards established by Directive 2013/33 in several cases, especially at the external borders of the EU. As the FRA also pointed out, about hotspots in Greece and first reception Centres in Malta, Spain, France and Belgium, in recent years, even UAFMs have been exposed to situations such as overcrowding, insufficient essential services and temporary suspension of food following protests in reception Centres (FRA, 2020b).

The European Commission responds to the need to address the apparent differences between Member States in matters of migration and asylum by producing new elements in its reform proposal, but, at the same time, it keeps in place the current criteria in force or revises them only partially. Such is the case for the mechanisms determining the competent State and the instruments of solidarity of those supporting the use of legal access routes linked to international protection but not legal entry channels for work-related reasons, except for the mobility of highly qualified individuals.

The Action Plan also strengthens controls and introduces procedures to go through, compulsory in some cases, before admission to a Member State (European Commission, 2020d).

By extending and formalizing relocation procedures already applied in Italian and Greek hotspots, migrants would be detained in border areas and large-sized facilities upon their arrival. When intercepted in the territory of one of the EU Member States, this is for a maximum period of ten days. The reasons would include completing identification procedures and assessing whether they are a possible danger to society, deportation or rejection, based on a standard debriefing form borne by the competent authorities of the Member States, or channelling into asylum procedures.

Up until now, EU law had considered indoor detention in border areas as a residual hypothesis, in line with ECtHR jurisprudence concerning cases of

---

the EU's external borders most frequently concerned Poland, Croatia, Hungary, Greece and the Spanish enclave of Ceuta and Melilla (FRA, 2020b).

[14] Although it does not justify the non-fulfillment of the prohibition by contemporary international practice, the EU legal system seems to show regulatory and institutional gaps preventing effective control over the Member States' compliance with the principle. (Starita, 2020).

violations of ECHR Articles 3 and 5,[15] precisely because it implies a reduction of individual rights; contrary to this, what is proposed would greatly expand situations that should have been only exceptional up to now.

As repeatedly stated by ECtHR, the absolute nature of the prohibition of torture and subjection to inhumane or degrading treatment does not allow the Member States not to make sure that the human dignity of the detainees is respected, even in extreme cases, such as handling sudden and substantial migrant flows at the external borders of the EU while the country of arrival is experiencing an economic crisis [16] and 'even treatment which is inflicted

---

[15] On December 15, 2016, the Grand Chamber of the ECtHR ruled on *Khlaifia and others v. Italy* (App. No. 16483/12). While excluding violations pursuant to Articles 3 and 4 of ECHR Protocol No. 4, which had instead been recognized by the Second Section of 9/1/2015, it condemned Italy for the first time for illegitimately detaining migrants inside hotspots. Namely, that of Lampedusa, citing severe and substantial violations of **ECHR Articles 5(1), (2) and (4) (§§ 55-108, §§ 109-122 and §§ 123-135 of the judgment). The relevant issues are the absence of a legal basis for detention in the aforementioned centers, which the Italian Government established in compliance with the European Commission Road Map of** 9/15/2015, and the lack of complete and understandable information on the legal situation of the applicants, the assumptions made in their case and the duration of the detention period. The legal basis would be introduced only in 2017 with the so-called Minniti Law; however, it did not regulate hotspots activities. According to the ECtHR, the breach of the information requirement constituted a violation of the right to an effective remedy, in compliance with ECHR Article 13 (on this decision, among others, see Bonetti 2017). In the case of *O.S.A. and others v. Greece* (App. No. 39065/16), the ECtHR finds that 'Greece violated the detained applicants' right to challenge the lawfulness of their detention (Article 5(4) of the ECHR) since remedies were practically inaccessible.'

[16] On this, see ECtHR (GC), M.S.S., para. 223; Aden Ahmed v. Malta, 23 July 2013, Application No. 55352/12, § 90. Concerning the more recent cases involving the detention conditions of minors in Italian and Greek hotspots (*Khlaifia v. Italy,* and *J.R and others v. Greece,* 25 January 2018, App. No. 22696/16), legal literature has criticized the fact that the Court did indeed maintain that 'a crisis cannot in itself be used to justify a breach of Article 3'. Still it seemed to assign greater relevance to 'the general context in which those facts arose' and therefore, the difficulties experienced by the State when dealing with migratory flows, thus, deeming that the minimum severity threshold provided for by ECHR Article 3 had not been exceeded, despite the extreme vulnerability of the applicants, UAFMs and single mothers with children, in addition to the serious shortcomings of the centers as far as minimum services. Likewise, the Grand Chamber recognized only the violation of ECHR Article 5.4 in the case *Kaak and others v. Greece* (3 October 2019, App. No. 34215/2016), on the right to appeal to a court, since the applicants couldn't pursue domestic remedies, also in reference to the situation of the minors transferred to the Vial hotspot on Chios island. Considering the brief duration of the detention period, which was at most thirty days, and the transfer of minors to a facility

without the intention of humiliating or degrading the victim, and which stems, for example, from target difficulties related to a migrant crisis, may entail a violation of Article 3 of the Convention.'[17]

As indicated by the ECtHR in the case *Khan v. France,*[18] the authorities are required to do everything that could 'reasonably' be expected of them to take charge of the minor, even when there are many target difficulties, namely, for this case, the number of people present and the complexity of a quick identification process of UAFMs.

In the case mentioned above, the Court considered the shanty town's unsanitary, dangerous and precarious conditions where the twelve-year-old minor lived as equivalent to degrading treatment in breach of ECHR Article 3.

There is fear that the Pact will be used negatively by the Member States, 'as indirectly bringing supranational legitimacy to some of their national policies that international and regional human rights bodies have widely criticized by international and regional human rights bodies for leading to the rule of law and human violations running contrary to EU's constitutional principles' (Carrera, 2021). Furthermore, according to the new Article 41 of the amended proposal for a regulation establishing a standard international protection procedure for the EU and repealing Directive 2013/32/EU, a twelve-week extension is provided for the accelerated procedure application for the analysis of asylum applications, both in terms of admissibility and the matter itself. More in detail, to expedite the border asylum procedures the Member States are required to apply, the cases have been included regarding citizens from third countries for whom favourable decisions are fewer than 20% according to the latest annual average data from Eurostat (European Commission, 2020e). It was pointed out that this provision contrasts with the prohibition of discrimination between refugees (Article 3 of the Geneva Convention) and the need to ensure an individual and specific examination of each asylum request. The provision contained in Article 53 of the proposed regulation establishing a common international protection procedure for the EU is a regressive push —

---

that has become semi-open since 2016 and is considered a safe zone, the Court did not rule for a violation of Articles 3 and 5(1). In opposition to the above, the unsanitary severe detention conditions of minors and promiscuity with adults reported by the European Committee for the Prevention of Torture and Inhuman or Degrading Treatment or Punishment (CPT) could have led to a conclusion similar to the one reached by the Court in **2011,** when Greece was condemned for the detention of a minor in conditions that were defined to be 'abominable' at the time, but lasted **'only' two days** (on this, see De Vittor, 2020; Mentasti, 2019).

[17] ECtHR, *Khlaifia,* §184; Kaak, § 63.

[18] ECtHR, *Khan v. France,* 28 February 2019, App. No. 12267/16.

especially for legal systems like that of Italy, which differentiate between denial of protection and deportation measures —according to which the refoulement decision would be appealed 'before the same judge within the same judicial proceedings concerning the decision rejecting the application for international protection' (ASGI, 2021).

As for accompanied and unaccompanied minors, the reform proposal presented by the European Commission aims to 'strengthen the guarantees and protection standards provided for by EU law for migrant minors' and provides that the Member States put in place specific procedural guarantees for a better assessment and implementation of the best interests of the child, also by cooperating among each other (Quadranti, 2021). To this end, it mentions the involvement of the authorities responsible for the protection of the child and the provision of adequate assistance during the procedure for determining their status, including legal assistance, as well as the presence of qualified personnel specially trained to listen to the child and adequately convey information concerning them, considering age, maturity and personal development. Furthermore, always in accordance with the New York Convention, they should watch over their physical and mental health and social development and make sure that they have timely and non-discriminatory access to education and integration services.

An additional guarantee for UAFMs is the assistance and participation of a representative guardian in the procedures and decision-making process of determining the competent Member State. These relevant and sensitive functions are further enhanced by the will expressed in the plan to ensure a more incisive role for the European protection network (European Commission, 2020c). Despite the reforms and progress made by the national protection systems of at least some of the EU States, the FRA still points out numerous gaps in the implementation of reform laws in recent years, together with the lack of adequate training for guardians and of a 'support from a guardian who could effectively promote their best interests for many UAFMs arriving at the external borders of the EU (FRA, 2020b).

This paper will examine whether and how these targets are set forth by the more specific measures outlined in the Pact.

Reception of Minors and Administrative Detention Situations

Despite the lack of homogeneous data adequately captured and published at the national level on the detention in Europe of minors seeking asylum or who are in an irregular situation,[19] studies and reports made by international bodies, including the FRA and by NGOs, have denounced that this is a widespread measure. Moreover, in recent years, it has even been increasing in some EU Member States, including France, Greece, Malta, Poland, and Slovenia, albeit with differences in duration, at times including or excluding UAFMs, at least in the law.[20]

Since June 2021, thousands of people, among them several families, tried to reach the European Union territory from Belarus[21]. In response to this crisis, in which Europe accused Belarus of using the migrants as an arm of pressure, Poland, especially since November 2021, built border fences, refused to allow access to the border area between the two countries to an international organization, that aimed to investigate the migration crisis, and to humanitarian organizations, in the absence of their help, migrants, including those with special needs, have not got the protection to which they are entitled.

As declared by the Office of the United Nations High Commissioner for Human Rights, the police returned migrants automatically to Belarus without an individual study of their case and systematically detained those who were

---

[19] Some EU Member States do not tally minors detained together with their parents, as they are not the direct recipients of the detention order; nonetheless, they are deprived of their freedom to avoid separating them from their parents. Integrating them in Eurostat statistics and the assessment mechanisms of the implementation of the Return Directive is one of the solutions proposed to improve data collection on minors' detention (PICUM, 2020).

[20] In Malta and Greece, minors may be detained for months in anticipation of a so-called Dublin transfer. The ECtHR has ruled against them in numerous cases (over 200 per month in the second half of 2019) of UAFMS held in police stations and immigration detention facilities considered temporary solutions before transferring the minors to centers appropriate for their age. There were numerous cases in 2019 of UAFMs detained in Malta, where all those who arrive irregularly by sea are systematically detained. The same situation occurred in Poland and Slovenia, which detained almost ten times more UAFMs than accompanied minors. In France, where administrative detention is forbidden for UAFMs, but it is provided for families with minors, albeit as a last resort, there was a rise from 208 minors in 2018 to 276 in 2019. The situation in the French overseas department of Mayotte is even more severe, as in 2019 it became 'the part of the EU that detained most children for immigration purposes,' including UAFMs 'arbitrarily attached to accompanying adults and detained with them' (FRA 2020b: 122).

[21] In January 2022, the number of migrants staying in Belarus significantly reduced consequently to the repatriation flights realized above all for Iraqi/ Iraqi-Kurdish migrants (3,817 of them repatriated from Belarus and 112 from Lithuania) and due to the IOM Assisted Voluntary Repatriation and Reintegration Program, which assisted 381 migrants to returned from Belarus to their countries of origin (IFRC, 2022).

not returned [22]. The same atmosphere, dominated by the emphasis on security and fuelled by narratives hostile to migrants, justified the decision of Latvia's Parliament to approve a series of amendments to limit the circulation of migrants in the country for a period that could last for one year 'not to give migrants a chance to think that arriving there, after waiting six months and then continue their journey to German' (as explained by the President of the Parliamentary Commission for the Defence and the National Security). Temporary derogations from EU asylum and return rules, support pushbacks, a significant increase in detention, not more used as an exceptional measure of last resort and for a limited period and prolonged registration periods constitute a serious threat that undermines fair asylum procedures.

The support expressed by Member States for activating the temporary protection provided by Directive 2001/55/EC (which has never been activated so far) due to the mass influx of persons who fled Ukraine as a consequence of the war led to the decision adopted unanimously by the Council to enable immediate and temporary refuge Ukrainian nationals. The decision establishes as well as third-country nationals or stateless persons benefiting from international protection in Ukraine, and their family members will benefit from temporary protection if they resided in Ukraine before or on 24 February 2022[23]. Will this attitude and support for Ukraine and its citizens lead to more general changes in openness inside the 'fortress Europe' and a decrease in serious human rights violations against refugees and asylum seekers at Europe's borders? The writer is not at all convinced.

With regard to Italy, although the detention of minors has been forbidden, in 2020, media and NGOs reported cases of UAFMs detained in Trapani, and that 'vulnerable people, including unaccompanied children, were detained under inadequate conditions before being sent back to Italy,'[24] and at the border between France and Italy.

---

[22] According to a report published in January 2022 by the International Federation of Red Cross and Red Crescent Societies, in Lithuania 3,200 people have been held in five centers, pending asylum application processes, with the number of cumulative arrivals being equal to 4,332. Since August 2021 until January 2022, 8,200 people were pushed-back from the Lithuanian borders. Always in January 2022, 1,675 migrants were in detention centers of Poland, 972 of whom being in detention centers for families and the rest in those for men, run by the border guards (IFRC, 2022).

[23] Council Implementing Decision (EU) 2022/382 of 4 March 2022 establishing the existence of a mass influx of displaced persons from Ukraine within the meaning of Article 5 of Directive 2001/55/EC, and having the effect of introducing temporary protection, in *OJ* L 71, 4.3.2022, p. 1-6.

[24] FRA, 2020a, pp. 19-20.

Even though all the EU governments have signed the New York Declaration for Refugees and Migrants,[25] pledging to resort to the detention of minors because of their immigration status 'only as a measure of last resort, in the least restrictive setting, for the shortest possible period, under conditions that respect their human rights and in a manner that takes into account, as a primary consideration, the best interest of the child, and we will work towards the ending of this practice,' once again the praxis diverges from the declaration of intents.

While failing to prohibit in absolute terms the administrative detention of minors, even UAFMs, the ECtHR pointed out that, in this case, detention must not only be necessary but regular (i.e., fall within one of the reasons indicated by the regulation itself) and complete with an actual weighting of its appropriateness but also implemented only in extreme cases. Therefore, the State must show that it has verified the non-existence of other, less coercive measures.[26]

In response to the variety of cases regarding the detention of minors submitted to its jurisdiction, the Court has outlined in ever more precise terms the positive protection and assistance requirements that Member States should meet in compliance with ECHR Article 3. To verify that the minimum severity threshold provided for by Article 3 has been exceeded, according to a now consistently held case law,[27] it is necessary to proceed with an individual weighting of three combined factors: age, conditions and length of detention (Klötgen, 2017; Quadranti, 2021).

It is an overall evaluation of these three factors that can lead to the recognition of a violation of ECHR Article 3.

---

[25] On this, among others, see Ruozzo, 2017.

[26] The European Council Guidelines for the Member States on implementing of 'various types of alternatives, including family-based care arrangements for children' (CoE, 2019) date back to 2019.

[27] Starting with the ECtHR case *Mubilanzila Mayeka and Kaniki Mitunga v. Belgium*, 12 October 2006, Application No. 13178/03, and, more frequently, the decision on the *Rahimi v. Greece* case of 2011 (5 April 2011, Application No. 8687/08), the Court has been emphasizing the particular vulnerability of UAFMs and its incompatibility with an administrative detention characterized by a series of factors leading to situations of stress and anxiety (as in the following ECtHR cases: *R.K v. France*, 12 October 2016, Application No. 68264/14; *Popov v. France*, 19 January 2012, Applications Nos. 39472/07 and 39474/07; *Kanagaratnam* and others v. Belgium, 13 December 2011, Application No. 15297/09; H.A., 13 September 2019. Application No. 14165/16); *Sh.D. and others v. Greece*, 13 June 2019, Application No. 14165/16; *Haghilo v. Cyprus*, 13 June 2010, Application No. 47920/12.)

Thus, in the 2019 sentences against Greece, for the cases *H.A.* and *Sh.D and others*, and Cyprus for the *Haghilo* case,[28] the psychological and physical damage suffered by a UAFM detained for weeks in a police station was considered as degrading treatment in violation of ECHR Article 3, as well as a measure in contrast with Articles 13 and 5(1). According to the Court, the unjustified and prolonged isolation of the applicant — together with his condition of vulnerability and the inability of the State to provide a satisfactory explanation for its failure to place him in a reception Centre, however temporarily, besides the massive presence of police personnel and lack of recreational activities — is a sufficient factor to establish that the minimum severity threshold of suffering was exceeded, in violation of Article 3.

In the case of accompanied minors, the Court went so far as to assert that maintaining the family unit does not prevent the recognition of a violation of ECHR Article 3.[29] In the case of *Muskhadzhiyeva*, the ECtHR recognized the detention of minors accompanied by the mother in inadequate detention facilities as a violation of Article 3 (only for minors), but, in contrast, manifestly unfounded the alleged violation of Article 8 due to a permanence together even if in a detention facility[30].

The need to find a balance between protecting human rights and the immigration policies of the Member States utilizing the so-called 'protection *par ricochet*' — based on the indirect requirements for the Member States to comply with the rights protected by the Convention as well as the evolving and teleological interpretation of the norms made by the ECtHR — also arises for situations of interference in family life[31] caused by detention.

---

[28] ECtHR, *Tarakhel v. Switzerland and Italy*, 4 November 2014, Application No. 29217/12.

[29] ECtHR, *Popov v. France*, 19 January 2012, Application Nos. 39472/07 and 39474/07.

[30] ECtHR, *Muskhadzhiyeva* v. *Belgium*, Application No. 41442/07. Also in case *R.R.* v. *Hungary* (2nd March 2021, Application No. 36037/17) considering the vulnerability of applicants, mother father and one son, the physical conditions of the container in which the family stayed in, the unsuitable facilities for children, irregularities in the provision of medical services, and the prolonged stay in the area amounted to a violation of Article 3 in respect of the applicant mother and the children. (Rogozik, 2021).

[31] As for the more restrictive notion of family life applied to cases concerning migrants, the Court includes relations between spouses as well as unwed couples living together, and with underage children, but not with adult children and different relatives, unless there are 'further elements of dependency, involving more than the normal, emotional ties' (according to constant jurisprudence starting from the ruling of the European Commission for Human Rights on *S.S. v. the United Kingdom*, 10 December 1984, App. No. 10375/83, § 196). As opposed to what was stated above, said emotional ties are included in the broad concept of private life, namely, the 'network of personal, social and

Although ECHR Article 8 — which can be suspended, as opposed to Article 3 — does not in principle preclude measures of administrative detention for families with minors, these must be provided for by law once the existence is ascertained of the private and family life affected by the provision of the State. They must be shown to be necessary and proportional to meet the requirements of imperative needs as indicated in Article 8(2). To limit the impact on family life, the requirement of proportionality presupposes that the State should prove that it has sought measures alternative to detention with sufficient diligence, like in the case of the balancing made on the basis of Article 5.1 (Klötgen, 2017).

Similar hermeneutic principles and procedures were also applied in the recent July 22, 2021, ruling on the *M.D., and A.D.* case,[32] concerning the situation of a mother and four-month-old minor detained for 11 days (until the execution of the provisional measure according to ECHR Article 39) in administrative detention Centre no. 2 of Mesnil Amelot, which Centre is known to the media for its practices of refoulement to unsafe countries, on top of degraded reception conditions.[33] The Court recognized that both the minor and the mother had been treated in a manner exceeding the minimal threshold of ECHR Article 3, considering the minor's young age, duration of the detention and mother-daughter bond, which included breastfeeding interactions, and the *'emotions qu'ils partagent.'*

By ruling that a violation of Article 3 had occurred concerning both mother and daughter, the Court recalled its previous case law[34] held that it did not have to decide separately from the examination of the appeal pursuant to ECHR Article 8. Instead, the Court recognized the violation of Articles 5(1) and 5(4), as the national authorities acted without considering the amendments to the *Code de l'entrée et du séjour des étrangers et du droit d'asile* (CESEDA), which limit the circumstances for which detention may be considered for an individual with minors and when such measures may be extended. According to the Court, the existence of less restrictive and more short-term measures had

---

economic relations that make up the private life of every human being' that the migrant has with the host society. However, in the case of children recently become adults who have remained in the family of origin, the Court considered these relationships to be relevant for family and private life (starting with *El Boujaïdi v. France,* 26 September 1977, App. No. 25613/94, § 33), or even family life alone (as in *Maslov v. Austria,* 23 June 2008, App. No. 1638/03).

[32] ECtHR, *M.D. and A.D. v. France,* App. No. 57035/18, 22 July 2021.

[33] As seen in the joint 2018 report of 6 NGOs referred to by the ruling in para. 38-40.

[34] ECtHR [GC], *Centre de ressources juridiques au nom de Valentin Campeânu v. Romanie,* 17 July 2014, App. 47848/08.

not been verified in the present case, nor was the presence of the minor given sufficient consideration, in addition to that of the mother, when choosing the initial placement and when detention was prolonged by 28 days.[35]

The reasoning of the ECtHR seems to recognize that minors in a situation of detention should be considered minors first and foremost, no matter their status or condition of illegal residence.[36] Therefore, the situation of extreme vulnerability to which they are exposed should be taken into account — in addition to the proven adverse effects that detention has on their development, however long that may be and whatever the conditions of the place where they are deprived of their freedom (PICUM, 2020) — and their rights protected, by applying the critical/fundamental principles set forth by the New York Convention, starting with the best interests of the child, which is not only an important interpretive rule but also a substantive law and procedural regulation.[37]

EU law does not ban the detention of child migrants either, whether they are seeking asylum or in an irregular situation;[38] however, it may only be used

---

[35] However, note the presence of a dissenting opinion (Judge Mourouu-Vikström) in connection to the breach of Article 3 as well as Articles 5(1) and 5(4).

[36] However, legal literature has criticized the ECtHR for seemingly making contradictory decisions in the more numerous cases of right to family life where a residence permit for family reunification was denied. In assessing the necessity and proportionality of the restrictive measure put in place by the State to pursue its general objective of immigration control, the Court privileged more frequently the prerogatives of said State to the detriment of the applicants' rights. A telling example is the *Berisha v. Switzerland* case (30 July 2013, App. No. 948/12), where it accepted that the family unity of the children was compromised at the expense of their best interests as a result of a denied residence permit due to the parents' unlawful conduct (on this, see Favilli and Ferri:, 2020, pp. 310-306; Del Guercio, 2010).

[37] According to the interpretation of the principle contained in General Comment No. 14 of the UN Committee on the Rights of the Child (CRC) of 2013, also invoked by the European Asylum Support Office 2019, 13.

[38] On the basis of the Reception Conditions Directive 20133/33/EU, Article 2(h), the term 'detention' means a 'confinement of an applicant by [an EU] Member State within a particular place, where the applicant is deprived of his or her freedom of movement.' Article 8(2) specifies that migrants can be detained for Immigration-related reasons, either as asylum applicants, to ensure transfer under the Dublin Regulation procedure, or to facilitate their return, 'when it proves necessary and based on individual assessment of each case, Member States may detain an applicant, if other less coercive alternative measures cannot be applied effectively'. In the case *R:R. v. Hungary* (App. No. 36037/17), the ECtHR emphasized the obligation for the EU Member State under the Reception Conditions Directive to consider the vulnerability of pregnant women and minors (Rogozik, 2021)

under exceptional circumstances, including repatriation and Dublin transfers, and upon initial reception. In addition, it should take as little time as possible, and it should be proven that all alternatives have previously been evaluated.[39] In fact, as mentioned by the CJEU in the *Haqbin* case, when there is an issue involving a vulnerable person under Directive 2013/33 — a UAFM in this case —the Member States should have more significant consideration for their specific situation and the principle of proportionality, holding the best interests of the child in the highest regard. This determines a smaller margin of discretion than the State would otherwise enjoy and imposes an exceptionally high standard of protection.[40]

The proposal for reform of the EU rules exempts only unaccompanied foreign minors and accompanied minors under the age of 12 from extended border detention and the procedure applied therein, provided they are not deemed dangerous to national security or the public order of the State (European Commission 2020e, art. 41, para. 3 and 5).[41] These border measures discourage arrivals, primarily from low recognition-rate countries, without substantially resolving long-standing issues of first-arrival countries. Therefore, it is not convincing when the Commission asserts that the exemption from these procedures only for specific categories of minors, albeit deserving special protection due to their age or 'state of contingent abandonment,' should be interpreted as evidence that the European institutions are willing to ensure that the interests of the child are protected 'in every situation' (European Commission 2020e). The proven harmful effects of detention on a minor's life and development, regardless of its location and duration, coupled with the lack of evidence as far as consequences in terms of increased repatriations and

---

[39] Nevertheless, according to the report of FRA (2020), detention conditions of children 'remained poor or even deteriorated in 2019.'

[40] CJEU (Grand Chamber), *Haqbin*, 12 November 2019, Case C-233/18. This is the first ruling of the EU Court of Justice on the compatibility of the sanctions that can be adopted by Member States against applicants for international protection in the event of severe reception violations center rules as per the provisions of Article 20, para. 4 and 5, and Directive 2013/33. Considering Article 1 of the Charter, the Court believes that these rules prohibit a Member State from effectively sanctioning the revocation of material reception conditions, due to which the most basic needs are compromised, thus violating human dignity (on the illegitimacy of Italian revocation rules in light of the *Haqbin* case, see Bonetti, 2020).

[41] In 2016, while agreeing on the advisability of making the accelerated examination procedure mandatory in some instances, the EU Commission, Parliament and Council expressed different opinions on which situations should be mandatory, especially for UAFMs. In this last case, the position of the Parliament was opposed to that of Council (European Commission, 2020c).

decreased disappearances of minors, should always lead one to look for alternative solutions within the childhood protection system (PICUM, 2020).

In addition, as evidenced by the FRA, to ensure 'more complete fundamental rights compliance' at the EU borders, the Member States should implement effective and independent mechanisms for 'the monitoring of border – surveillance activities and not only (...) the pre-entry screening procedure itself.'

When it comes to repatriation measures, which several Member States have not officially banned yet when applied to minors, albeit less frequently,[42] the Commission hopes that thanks to the Pact, the proposal to recast Directive 2008/115/EC will be promptly adopted, which directive was introduced on September 12, 2018[43] (European Commission, 2020b). Even in the case of UAFMs and families with minors, the proposal reiterates what is contained in the so-called Return Directive, allowing the use of detention[44] when less coercive measures cannot be applied. Although this is not in contrast with Article 6 of the Charter of Fundamental Rights of the European Union nor with the ECHR case law cited earlier, in order to make sure that the alternative measures cease to have just a marginal role, it would be desirable to require that the Member States always put in place suitable procedures and facilities, at least when cases of greater vulnerability are involved.[45]

The Dublin System Reform and Minors

The Dublin system, currently based on the Dublin III Regulation, governs responsibility allocation among the EU Member States and four EFTA

---

[42] The European Parliament also expressed its total opposition to the repatriation of minors unless it could be demonstrated that it is in their interest (European Parliament,2020).

[43] European Commission, 2018.

[44] The CJEU specified that the term 'detention,' in the case of the Return Directive 'is the same as defined under the Reception Conditions Directive 20133/33/EU in Article 2(h)': CJEU (GC), Joined cases C-924/19 PPU and C-925/19 PPU, FMS and others, 14 May 2020, ECLI:EU:C:2020:367, para. 224-225. In the case of both accompanied and unaccompanied minors, the so-called Return Directive provides for the adoption of ad hoc rules only as far as treatment methods (Article 17 (2, 3, and 4). In its judgment of *TQ* of January 14, 2021 (C-441/19, *TQ v. Staatsscretaris van Justitie en Veiligheid*), the CJEU ruled in favor of a more effective protection system for vulnerable individuals, establishing that, in the case of UAFMs returned to their country of origin, adequate reception conditions in the said country should always be verified entirely the repatriation decision is made, regardless of the minor's age (Fratea, 2021).

[45] On this, see Pistoia, 2020; De Bruyker, 2015.

'associate' States (Iceland, Norway, Switzerland and Liechtenstein)[46], setting out which country is responsible for processing an individual's asylum application lodged in one of the Member States by a third-country nation. Starting from the Dublin Convention[47], the primary aim of the system has been to establish the most straightforward, linear and effective model possible in order to ensure rapid and certain identification of the competent state and, consequently, to prevent pursuing multiple claims in several Member State (i.e. the phenomenon of applicants in orbit) and to mitigate secondary movements of applicants. This general system affects the hierarchy of the 'objective criteria' established by the regulation: firstly, the preservation of family ties established in the country of origin (only the spouse and the partner if the law of the member state assimilates married couples to unmarried couples and unmarried minor children); secondly, the recognition of priority to legal situations already established in a state of the Dublin area (first the one where the applicant holds a residence permit or visa), thirdly and, if no other criterion is applicable, the 'place of first arrival' where the first application has been lodged (see Arts. 3(2) and 8-16 Regulation Dublin III). This last criterion, which operates for a period of twelve months after the illegal crossing of the border, is actually the elective connecting factor in most cases since the first two categories concern marginal situations compared to the overall volume of applications for international protection.

Furthermore, under the 'sovereignty clause' of Art. 17(1), each Member State may examine any applications lodged with it, especially, but not exclusively, on human rights or compassionate grounds (recital 17 Regulation Dublin III) and under the 'humanitarian clause' of Art. 17(2) Member States may agree to derogate from the criteria to protect family unity.

However, the practice has proved that precisely these mechanisms and criteria are at the origin of the crisis of the system inadequately fulfilling its task. Actually, the same rules create disparities in the distribution of burdens between States that damage the functioning of the Common European Asylum System and, at the same time, inflict severe hardship for protection seekers through a strict 'no-choice' policy and an underestimating consideration for the applicants' circumstances (European Parliament 2016: 10).

Despite the failure of the 'Dublin system,' the amendment proposal for Regulation EU/604/2013 has little consideration for the more advanced reform

---

[46] The UK was bound by the Dublin Regulation until 31 December 2020.

[47] The Dublin Convention has been replaced by the Council Regulation No 343/2003 (Dublin II regulation) bringing the matter within the scope of the EU area of freedom, security, and justice.

text introduced by the LIBE Committee of the European Parliament in September 2017, which the Chamber approved in November of the same year (European Parliament 2017). This latter text took more into consideration the applicants' 'real ties' with a State, meaning the will of individuals, in addition to the need to distribute the applications according to the disparate quotas imposed on the national asylum systems.[48]

The reform proposal retains the principle of irregular first-country entry in order to determine which State is responsible for examining asylum applications, once again at the expense of Member States' sharing responsibilities, which is essential for the effective implementation of the solidarity principle when it comes to the matter of asylum.[49]

On the other hand, the amendments proposed by the Parliament promote factors that suggest a local rooting to recognize the competent State, such as obtaining a diploma in a Member State and extending family ties, including siblings. At the same time, proven bonds formed during the trip should also be considered (European Commission, 2020c).

Although the above should be seen as a step forward in recognizing the life projects of individuals as well as factors fostering their path of inclusion in the State of reception, we need to realize that the burden of proof in the case of asylum seekers is in practice very limiting and easily in conflict with the right to family unity, which the Member States recognized as an essential criterion in the application of Regulation 604/2013. The proposal provides for a simplification of the rules in question only in the case of UAFMs, in order to raise the level of protection and accelerate the process of determination of the competent State,[50] besides reiterating that the presence of family or a relative

---

[48] Distancing itself from the last amendment proposal made by the Commission in 2016 (European Commission 2016), the EU Parliament had proposed that applicants without 'real ties' to a particular State would be relocated to one of the four Member States with fewer applications at the time, as determined by an automated system. On the reform limits and attempts of the Common European Asylum System, an expression of the EU States lacking a shared political will, among others, see Morgese, 2020; Fratea,, 2019; Maiani, 2017.

[49] Due to the unsustainability of involuntary transfers and the poor results achieved by relocation, and the fact that the latter seems insufficient even if EU countries are made to pay fines for not taking in refugees, legal literature has explored other avenues (see Morgese 2020); however, these are always limited by their reliance on the political will of the Member States.

[50] To reduce the time needed to determine the competent State and avoid secondary movements causing a high number of untraceable UAFMs, the general criterion provides that the competence is rooted where the minor requested international protection for

in another State who can take care of the child is a binding criterion of competence. In fact, in the presence of 'coherent, verifiable and sufficiently detailed' circumstantial evidence, formal evidence such as original supporting documents and DNA tests should no longer be needed to establish competence for the purpose of examining an international protection request (European Commission, 2020c).[51] In other cases, the reunification of family members, relatives, or persons connected by other bonds of kinship is explicitly indicated as a reason for a Member State to decide to waive the competence criteria established by the legislation and assume the responsibility of examining a registered international protection application in place of another Member State (European Commission, 2020c).

Whereas the Dublin III Regulation (Article 17 (1)) and previous Dublin II Regulation did not connect the use of the 'sovereignty clause' to specific reasons,[52] restricting it to this type of humanitarian reasons reduces the circumstances for which a Member State can be held responsible for not availing itself of the margin of appreciation and implementing the 'Dublin transfer' of people requesting protection based on a mechanical application of the competence criteria established by European legislation, leading to a serious violation of the applicant's fundamental rights. In fact, the Court of Strasbourg, starting with the leading case *M.S.S.*,[53] has been called upon to rule on several occasions regarding a possible indirect breach of ECHR Article 3 by a Member State initiating a Dublin proceeding, for having exposed an applicant to risks caused by asylum system deficiencies in the Member State of destination. The ECtHR reached the same conclusion even when the situation did not reveal any systemic deficiencies in the asylum process and reception system,[54] based

---

the first time, unless there is evidence that this is against his or her best interests (European Commission, 2020c).

[51] Provision is made for the Commission to implement acts pursuant to TFEU Article 290 to establish specific rules regarding the identification of family members and the assessment of the bond that unites them to the minor and order to establish specific rules regarding the identification of family members and the assessment of the bond that unites them to the minor as well as their ability to take care of them. Legal literature has highlighted the need to simplify the proof of existence of such bonds more generally, not only for UAFMs. On this, see Favilli, 2020.

[52] According to Article 17.1, 'each Member State may decide to examine an application for international protection lodged with it by a third-country national or a stateless person, even if such examination is not its responsibility under the criteria laid down in this Regulation.'

[53] ECtHR, *M.S.S. v. Belgium and Greece* [GC], 21 January 2011, Application No. 30696/09.

[54] Which deficiencies were found in the Greek reception system in the *M.S.S. v Belgium* case.

on which, according to Article 3(2) of the Dublin III Regulation, the State Member that initiated the process continues to verify the criteria for the possibility to designate another State Member as competent.[55]

Thus, in the *Tarakhel* case,[56] considering the extreme vulnerability of the parties involved and holding 'serious doubts' about the capability of the Italian State to guarantee it, the Court maintained that the Swiss authorities could not proceed with the transfer for as long as the Italian authorities did not provide individual guarantees regarding the presence of fit reception conditions vis-à-vis the age of the child and the protection of the family unit.

In interpreting Article 17.1 of the Dublin III Regulation in the *C.K., H.F., and A.S.* case of 2017, the CJEU also adopted the ECtHR's modus operandi, based on the assessment of the risks that an individual can suffer during the transfer, thus departing from its previous case law interpreting Regulation no. 343/2003 (Dublin II), where it had limited the ban to proceed with a transfer only if systemic deficiencies existed.[57] Therefore, the CJEU made it clear that the principle of mutual trust between the Member States in the matter of immigration can and should be restricted by the requirement to respect fundamental rights.[58] According to the recitals 32 and 39 introduced by the Dublin III Regulation III, when applying Article 17.1, the Member States are

---

[55] However, according to well-established CJEU jurisprudence, this assessment is not up to the country that should take charge of the applicant (see, most recently, CJEU, Order of the Court, 13 November 2019, Bundesrepublik Deutschland v. Adel Hamed and Amar Oma, Joined Cases C-540/17 and C-541/17, ECLI:EU:C:2019:964)

[56] ECtHR, *Tarakhel v. Switzerland and Italy*, 4 November 2014, Application no. 29217/12,§ 2. In this case, the applicants had invoked asylum system deficiencies in Italy due to difficulties in accessing reception facilities and lengthy identification procedures, as well as the facilities being insufficient and incapable of providing adequate living conditions (Palladino, 2016). Besides blocking Switzerland from going ahead with the transfer, the Court's decision served as a warning to Italy to significantly strengthen its protection and reception system in full compliance with common European standards.

[57] CJEU (GC), 21 December 2011, N.S. and others, joined cases C-411/10 and C- 493/10, ECLI:EU:C:2011:865, para. 60.

[58] As pointed out by Panella, 2018; Reginelli, 2020. After this ruling, the CJEU seems to have taken backsteps as far as higher individual protection levels vis-à-vis state interests in matters of immigration, for example, by considering states exclusively competent in the matter of humanitarian visas, not the EU as a whole (on this, among others, see Nascimbene and Andró, 2017). At any rate, the ECtHR also opted for a restrictive interpretation in the case *M. N. and others v. Belgium,* where it excluded that submitting a humanitarian visa request to the diplomatic representation of a third country could entail an extraterritorial application of the Convention and therefore make the State liable for a possible violation of ECHR Article 3 (ECtHR, *App. No.* 3599/18, *5 May 2020).*

committed to respecting the Charter of Fundamental Rights of the European Union, identical to ECHR Article 3, and pertinent case law of the Courts, by which, even when there are no reasons to seriously believe that systemic deficiencies exist in the Member State responsible for examining the asylum application, which condition is referred to in Article 3.2, an asylum seeker can be transferred within the Dublin regulation only if this does not involve a real and established risk that the party involved will be treated in an inhumane and degrading way.

Resettlements and Humanitarian Admissions by Way of Safe and Legal Access Channels in Favour of Vulnerable Persons

In 2016, the year when the New York Declaration for Refugees and Migrants was unanimously adopted by the General Assembly (General Assembly 2016), the UNHCR invited the EU to follow 'a bold, imaginative and workable approach to overcome fragmentation and manage refugee movements effectively under accordance with international law (…) through a comprehensive EU asylum and refugee policy of the future, both in its internal and external dimensions' (UNHCR, 2016).[59] Surely, this meant that, in the future, the EU would expand 'legal pathways for refugees,' like the Declaration; later, the Global Compacts on Refugees and for Safe, Orderly and Regular Migration would express the same wish on a global scale (General Assembly 2018),[60] but not only, since 'resettlement is a tool to provide protection and a durable solution to refugees rather than a migration management tool'. It can never be 'an alternative to providing access to territory for asylum seekers' (UNHCR, 2016). Considering the small number of actual cases[61] and the voluntariness at the basis of a transfer from a third country to an EU State, expressed by the Member States in resettlement cases and humanitarian admission by willing communities

---

[59] The Council of Europe Commissioner for Human Rights also reported in March 2021 that, faced with a widening gap between resettlement needs and availability of places, the 47 Member States are called upon to contribute to making sure that the 'laudable resettlement actions' taken in collaboration with the UNHCR and OIM start increasing again after the sharp slowdown caused by the Covid-19 health crisis. Member States that are not yet taking part in these actions are urged to hurry and start doing so (Council of Europe Commissioner for Human Rights, 2021b).

[60] Not all EU States signed the Global Compacts (including Italy), despite the consensus expressed by the EU concerning New York Declaration (on this, see Borraccetti, 2020).

[61] The considerable impact that the pandemic had on resettlements during 2020, when they were suspended starting in March and for several months, made it so that the Commission's recommendation on legal pathways would keep the commitment in favor of 29,487 individuals planned for 2020 also for 2021 (European Commission, 2020f).

and/or private parties, either solution can only complement the forms of protection recognized at the international and European level.

The reform proposal, in both the Pact and the Recommendation on legal pathways to protection (European Commission, 2020f), recognizes the importance of increasing and strengthening legal ways to enter Europe based on TFEU Article 78 for holders of international protection and anyone worthy of protection which meets the requirements of both EU and third-country States. Furthermore, explicit reference is made to the twofold target of protecting human lives while also regulating flows and combating migrant smuggling and human trafficking.

As critically evidenced in legal literature, by looking at the beneficiaries of the recommendation, we can see how far we still are — due to the lack of political will, starting with the Council[62] — from including work reasons in legal access pathways and the EU doing more for regular migration, except, in keeping with the past, its will to encourage the mobility of highly qualified workers.[63] Furthermore, no right is provided for the resettlement of individuals; there is no ad hoc regulation to recognize the rights of the candidates, and last but not least, there are no legally relevant consequences for the Member States failing to implement the mechanism.[64]

Regarding minors, the Recommendation includes the broader criterion of 'possible vulnerabilities' (to which the situation of minors belongs) to guarantee the quality of resettlements; this is parallel to the provisions for cases of relocation between the EU States, according to which the transfer of UAFMs should be considered as a priority unless it is preventively assessed that it would harm the best interests of the child. A payment of 10,000 EUR is also

---

[62] The European Parliament's resolution of May 20, 2021, expressed a different position, inclined to favor access to the EU also for workers with medium or minimal training, as legal labor migration is an 'indispensable factor for a global policy on migration and asylum' (European Parliament, 2021).

[63] As critically pointed out by Borraccetti, 2020; Favilli, 2020; Carrera, 2020. However, the European Parliament's resolution of May 20, 2021, showed its willingness to favor access to the EU also for workers with medium or minimal training, considering legal labor migration as an 'indispensable factor for a global policy on the subject of migration and asylum' (European Parliament, 2021).

[64] Moreover, the proposal does not consider the possibility for the consular authority of the chosen State to provide short-term humanitarian visas in the applicant's country of origin (Borraccetti, 2020). By the same token. The European Commission had not followed up on the Parliament's request of 2018 to present a proposal for the establishment of a European humanitarian visa (European Parliament 2018), judging it to be 'not politically sustainable' (Morgese, 2020).

provided in support of Member States for each person resettled from priority regions or particularly vulnerable groups, including through the Asylum, Migration and Integration Fund (AMIF) (European Commission, 2020f).

We emphasize in a positive way the recommendation addressed to the Member States to accelerate the integration process, including in resettlements, by establishing, expanding and possibly anticipating integration measures to facilitate the social inclusion process (European Commission, 2020, point 12).

Minors often benefit from other forms of legal access routes included in the terms 'humanitarian admission' and 'community and private sponsorship' used by the European Commission. Falling within these definitions are the humanitarian corridors managed by the Sant'Egidio Community, Italian Caritas, Federation of Evangelical Churches in Italy and Tavola Valdese, which the Recommendation also makes accessible to the family members of those who benefit from the protection (point 12). The Commissioner for Human Rights has recently reported on the efficacy of these communities in giving a new opportunity to over 3,000 people in Italy, France, Belgium and Andorra (Council of Europe Commissioner for Human Rights, 2021). Italy's pilot project '*Pagella in tasca – Canali di studio per minori rifugiati*' [Report card in your pocket – Study channels for refugee minors] is specifically aimed at protecting UAFMs with refugee status and focused on developing the right to education. With the support of INTERSOS and UNHCR, the purpose of this project is to promote entry into Italy with a student visa of 35 UAFMs aged 16 to 17 who fled violence in Darfur by taking refuge first in Libya and then Niger. In this case, the reception and social inclusion process is based on the involvement of volunteering foster families and guardians, as well as private social organizations.[65]

The predictable mass exodus following the return to power of the Taliban in Afghanistan in August 2021, and the US President's decision to complete the evacuation of the country no later than August 31, have recently shown the central importance of an urgent need for humanitarian corridors, but also, at the same time, the EU's difficulty in speaking with one voice. However uncertain of the number of Afghan nationals who will manage to reach Europe and, even more so, the EU's ability to organize a shared reception plan, the

---

[65] For more information on the project, go to: https://www.intersos.org/pagella-in-tasca-canali-di-studio-per-minori-rifugiati. The University Corridors for Refugees (UNICORE) project is also based on the motivation to study as the primary criterion for identifying beneficiaries, aimed at refugee university students and promoted by the UNHCR, the participating Universities and several national and locally based partners (https://universitycorridors.unhcr.it). 2021 saw the third edition of the UNICORE project, which allows refugee students in Ethiopia to arrive in Italy with a study visa to continue their studies in the 24 partner universities.

creation of humanitarian corridors for women and minors who may be victims of human rights abuses and violations was one of the options put on the table. However, the EU States were once again divided on the proposal, as not all of them were inclined to agree with the judgment by the President of the European Commission that it is a 'moral obligation for the EU' to take on the current crisis. Although the migratory emergency will be primarily regional, as it always is, political fears of a scenario like the '2015 refugee crisis' seem, to date, insurmountable obstacles to a prompt EU definition of methods and schedules for legal and safe access routes.[66]

'The Sooner Integration Starts the More It is Likely to Succeed'; Positive and Negative Aspects of the Italian Reception System for Asylum Seekers and Refugees

The first and only Italian national integration plan for holders of international protection was set up by the Ministry of the Interior on September 26, 2017, to 'guarantee an orderly civil coexistence' since, as emphasized by the Minister of the Interior Marco Minniti at that time, 'a more integrated society is also a safer society.'[67]

The plan, legally based on Article 2 of the Italian Constitution and Article 4 bis of the Immigration Consolidating Act,[68] outlines integration as a complex

---

[66] The Extraordinary Council of the Ministers for Home Affairs of August 31 produced only a generic acknowledgment of the need 'to support and provide adequate protection to those in need, in line with EU law and our international obligations, and to bring the practices of Member States closer in the reception and processing of Afghan asylum seekers,' setting the primary target 'to strengthen the support to the countries in Afghanistan's immediate neighborhood to ensure that those in need receive adequate protection primarily in the region' e 'to effectively protect the EU external borders and prevent unauthorized entries, and assist the most affected Member States' (Council of the European Union 2021). The day before, the Council of Europe Commissioner for Human Rights had called on the 47 Member States to 'make an unequivocal commitment to deal with the arrival of people fleeing the dire situation in Afghanistan in line with their human rights obligations,' while criticizing the measures announced or undertaken by various EU States related to 'closing borders, building walls and fences, restricting asylum applications or refoulements' (Commission for Human Rights. Council of Europe 2021).

[67] Given Article 1, para. 1 of Legislative Decree 18/2014, every two years, or even earlier in case of need, the National Coordination Table at the Ministry of the Interior should prepare national plans to favor the integration of international protection beneficiaries.

[68] Article 4 bis contains a very similar definition of integration to the one found in the common basic principles of the EU (European Council, 2004), at least as far as its constitutive elements. Integration is referred to therein as a two-way process that has economic, social and cultural dimensions, implies respect for the values of the

process that goes from initial reception to the achievement of personal independence. Moreover, in line with those mentioned within International and European guidelines, one of its basic principles is to improve the governance of the integration system by focusing 'specific attention' on individuals with greater vulnerability, including UAFMs and refugee women who have been the victims of human trafficking (Italian Ministry of the Interior, 2017). Thus, as far as UAFMs having access to education,[69] it is highlighted therein that the system should consider the reasons for the high dropout rate and get expert outside help to cope with it.

The lines of action outlined in favour of the social inclusion and independence of international protection beneficiaries concern language training, information on individual rights and duties, and employment orientation. It should be noted that not only the regions perform central functions in these areas, but also the local authorities, mainly thanks to the action of the regional legislation that followed the reform of Title V of the Italian Constitution. As previously mentioned, the European Action Plan itself highlights the crucial role of local and regional authorities in education, training and inclusion. As far as minors are concerned, the Council of Europe Strategy for the Rights of the Child 2016-2020 also focuses on the impact of local action to ensure measures for minors to access rights and procedures, supporting 'integration by adopting practical measures to reduce access barriers and accelerating the integration of refugee children in the school system.' However, as there is no systematic approach in this area, there is a risk that we will see a plethora of local solutions with varying quality leading to non-uniform results.

It is interesting to note that Italy's national plan was introduced just over six months after the so-called emergency landings[70] and the Decree-Law 'Minniti-

Constitution, and is based on the interaction between immigrants and Italian citizens and their mutual effort.

[69] The right to education of international protection holders is governed by Article 26 of Legislative Decree no. 18 of February 21, 2014, implementing Directive 2011/95/EU. Refugee minors and holders of subsidiary protection are granted access to study according to the procedures that apply to Italian citizens. Adults with the same status can access the general education system within the limits and in the manner established for legally residing foreigners. The law also identifies validation and accreditation systems for degrees obtained abroad by refugees even in the absence of certification by the State in which the degree was obtained.

[70] Following the EU-Turkey statement of March 18, 2016, and the closing of the eastern Mediterranean route, almost 85% of the landings on coasts reached Italy in the first half of 2017 (83,752 out of 99,864 overall arrivals in the first six months of 2017, according to UNHCR Italy data); a substantial increase (of 18%, compared to the first half of 2016), but

Orlando' (DL no. 13 of February 17, 2017) set in place to accelerate international protection proceedings and fight illegal immigration. The decree, based on the repression of the migratory phenomenon in an emergency perspective, was aimed at accelerating repatriation and simplifying judicial proceedings; however, this came at the expense of the guarantees offered by two levels of jurisdiction and the hearing the asylum applicant. In the security-minded approach of the National Integration Plan, one could already sense these dissonances between commitments in favour of 'those who are already here' and limitations to the entry of 'those arriving,' in addition to a reduction of their rights.

Even though a decrease in the total number of admissions should go hand in hand with legislative tools and reforms providing a more efficient and effective system to support the inclusion process and strengthen the presence of legal and safe channels, an opposite mechanism was triggered at the end of the so-called 'emergency landings' with the entry into force of the so-called Safety Decree (Decree-Law no. 113 of October 4, 2018), later amended into Law no. 132 of December 1, 2018. This had a major impact on the Italian legal system due to the numerous and substantial changes in introduced procedures.[71]

The novel legislation, aimed at reforming national and international humanitarian protection,[72] prioritized the fight against irregular immigration and the reorganization of reception. It led, first of all, to the abrogation of the (general) permits for humanitarian reasons, replacing them with special permits limited to tightly prescribed circumstances, which left unprotected a series of cases previously attributable to humanitarian protection, including those of applicants who had achieved adequate social integration in Italy (Ferri, 2021). Decree 113/2018 was followed by increased rejections of asylum applications and reduced readmission agreements with countries of origin, thus causing an increased presence of irregular population, including those whose repatriations could not be enforced because of the risk that their fundamental rights would be violated in the countries of origin.

---

not so great as to justify terms such as 'siege,' which were circulating at that time for political communication and propaganda.

[71] The Association for Legal Studies on Immigration promptly ruled on the unconstitutionality of Law-Decree113/2018 (see ASGI 2018). For a reading of the legislative changes with a view to their comparison and (in)compatibility with EU law and the ECHR, see Caggiano 2020, pp. 311-324.

[72] According to Article 6 of Directive 2008/115/EC, 'Member States may at any moment decide to grant an autonomous residence permit or other authorization offering a right to stay for compassionate, humanitarian or other reasons to a third-country national staying illegally on their territory.'

In addition to the novel legislation making immigration 'precarious' (Caggiano, 2020), significant changes to the reception system and new deterrent measures for asylum seekers contributed to the worsening of the situation (such as Italian law joining in the adoption of an accelerated procedure for border and transit areas and the list of safe countries of origin). The drastic and highly discriminatory reduction of access to the protection system for asylum seekers and refugees to only beneficiaries of international protection and UAFMs resulted in fewer service programmes and financial resources made available, to the point that legal literature hypothesized the actualization of a systemic reception problem equal to that the ECtHR had recognized there to be in Greece.[73] The elimination of social inclusion measures for asylum seekers, such as Italian language courses and psychological assistance, and the limitation of social assistance services, impacted the inclusion route, postponing its start to when international protection would be recognized.

As for minors, the new legislation did not change the residence permits granted to UAFMs, reorganized from Article 10 of Law no. 47/2017[74] as per minors and family reasons (in the case of UAFMs under guardianship on in foster care), the non-deportability of minors under the age of eighteen except for 'reasons of public order or State security' (art. 19 of the Immigration Consolidating Act), and the absolute prohibition against refusing entry at the border for UAFMs specified by Law 47/2017 (new para. 1-*bis* in art. 19 of the ICA). However, it was pointed out that changes not specifically addressed to UAFMs, starting with the abrogation of the permit for humanitarian reasons, had an extremely significant impact on their status, especially after attaining majority, when their legal status (whether they were previously in the Siproimi-Sprar system as minors seeking/not seeking asylum, refugees or holders of subsidiary protection) and the eventual continuation of the administrative process in their favour would affect their chances of having the right to reception, in which facility and for how long.[75]

---

[73] On this point, see Reginelli, 2020.

[74] Law no. 47/2017 improves the legal status of UFMs attaining majority, introducing new types of residence permit for family reasons (Art. 10).

[75] As pointed out by ASGI–INTERSOS 2018, many UAFMs applied for asylum, even if they were not eligible for international protection, as they had a reasonable expectation of obtaining humanitarian protection. Measures were included to suspend the asylum process for people convicted of a crime or considered socially dangerous, including minors. Moreover, the new legislation, with Article 1, para. 1, point n-a, intervened by repealing the provisions of Article 13 of Law no. 47/2017, later restored by Legislative Decree no. 130/2020, providing that the Directorate General of Immigration and Integration Policies of the Ministry of Labor failing to issue a positive opinion for the

Two years after the so-called 'Salvini Decree,' Decree-Law no. 130 of October 21, 2020, amended into Law no. 173 of December 18, 2020, intervened on all the management phases of the migratory phenomenon, addressing with mixed results the critical issues of the previous reform in compliance with those mentioned above constitutional and international requirements. Our analysis[76] shows that the new Reception and *Integration System (SAI, in Italian) now provides access to protection seekers, admitting them to the first two reception levels. This includes new integration processes after the second SAI reception* (art. 5), which fosters individual autonomy by emphasizing language education, employment orientation and essential public services, as well as knowledge of the fundamental rights and duties sanctioned by the Italian Constitution. The increased number of cases where 'special protection' permits can be issued is undoubtedly positive and of interest for our purposes, especially the one provided for in Art. 19, based on the respect for family life, considering the effectiveness and nature of the family ties that interested parties have in Italy,[77] as well as their private lives. The relevant criteria are the length of residence and effective social integration in Italy, collectively with cultural and social family ties in the country of origin.

Therefore, the special protection granted for social integration appears to align with the most recent ECtHR case law on ECHR Article 8 concerning cases of deportation and including illegal residents, where autonomous and independent importance has been attributed to private life and family life.[78] At

---

conversion of the residence permit of UAFMs upon turning eighteen could not legitimize the refusal to renew the permit and that a silence procedure is applied to such proceedings.

[76] Legislative Decree 130/2020 introduced essential innovations, but also partial changes not devoid of critical issues, in connection to residence permits, border controls, the principle of non-refoulement, administrative detention, and procedures before Territorial Commissions. On this point, see ASGI 2020 (containing a series of changes proposed for critical issues in view of the conversion into law); Reginelli, 2020; Zorzella, 2021.

[77] As restated in the national integration plan, 'family reunification and the possibility of rebuilding a minimum family nucleus creates the basis for true integration' and uncertainty about the safety of family members and the absence of news from them 'can represent a strong obstacle to integration' (Ministry of the Interior, 2017).

[78] Article 8 is an instrument of protection for foreigners even in deportation cases that result in the collapse of social and/or family relationships developed in the host country. The cases of settled migrants for whom deportation has been ordered following a criminal conviction are more frequent. They show more rulings in favor of the applicants, especially when second-generation migrants are involved. As to the less conspicuous case law of foreigners without a regular residence permit, the ECtHR recognized a family life violation only in exceptional circumstances. The applicants lacked a legitimate expectation to have their will to stay recognized and due to the precariousness of their

the same time, as others already pointed out, Article 19 does not contain a direct reference to ECHR Article 8 and is not 'exhausted' in it. The smaller number of targets the State can claim based on Article 19 to legitimize a squeeze on the rights of the individual (national security, public order and safety and health protection) makes this a special regulation for defending civil liberties, in addition to its link with the previous humanitarian protection and reference to other supranational sources, such as the Charter of Fundamental Rights of the European Union.[79]

Conclusion

As far as the recipients of the legal notion of integration are regularly resident migrants and not irregular migrants, the latter being the focus of the European Pact on Migration and Asylum, a legitimate question seems to be whether an integration policy can be successful within a framework of legality based on solutions that keep being about compromise and the containment and limitation of entries, the likes of which are proposed by the Pact. A similar security-based perspective also appears in the case of vulnerable subjects, such as minors seeking asylum UAFMs, still failing in many respects to implementing greater protection of rights, which the reform proposal recognizes as a general priority. Such a dyscrasia, also found in national policies, as we have seen, seems to be in contrast with the observation that 'The sooner integration starts, the more it is likely to succeed.'[80] We are not just referring to factors that delay regularity from being recognized, including the waiting periods for the issuing of residence permits; as we have seen, there are measures (such as language courses, psychological assistance and training courses) that fail to be recognized during initial reception, which affects rights and social integration processes as well as development in the case of minors. Bringing forward this process as much as possible means promoting regular entry channels into a

---

presence. However, a full application of the principle of best interest of the child can lead to an opposite conclusion, such as in the leading case of *Rodrigues da Silva v. The Netherlands* (31 January 2006, App. No. 50435/99). As for deportation cases, including of illegally residing foreigners, it has been pointed out that the more recent jurisprudence of the ECtHR attributed autonomous and independent importance to private life with respect to family life, as in the case of *But v. Norway* (App. No. 47017/09, 14 December 2012). On this, among others, see Ferri 2021: 96-107.

[79] Ferri, 2020. The latter emphasizes the relevant influence of EU law on Article 19 of the Consolidating Immigration Act, since para. 1.1 thereof provides for criteria to assess the risk of a violation of the right to privacy that coincides with those of Article 17 of the Directive on family reunification.

[80] See European Court of Auditors, 2018.

country to protect the rights of the parties involved considering their vulnerabilities; as seen in the case of the necessary Dublin Regulation reform, it also means defining processes that consider the wills, needs and perspectives of these individuals from the very beginning. Not placing obstacles in the way of a complex inclusion process is equivalent to ensuring 'maximum expansion of the guarantees' offered by a 'systemic and non-fractional assessment of rights,'[81] which includes the right to a private and family life, thus nurturing the family and social ties built in the host country.

The inclusion process is not without delays and possible setbacks. Not only should social inclusion measures be brought forward, but possible difficulties should also be considered, by implementing support measures in the most delicate phases, such as that of attaining a majority in the case of UAFMs, to which the European Action Plan makes a reference. As most unaccompanied foreign minors are 16-17 years old on arrival, this means that the process of integration and transition to autonomy is compressed into a limited and difficult period of time. Effective minor accompaniment and orientation starting right from their arrival is, therefore an essential requirement. Moreover, Europe has taken steps to ensure that the offer of assistance is extended beyond the immediate transition to adulthood based on clear and specific requirements. For example, the administrative continuation car occurs in Italy if ordered by the Court for Minors up to the age of twenty-one, recognizing the fact that unaccompanied foreign minors who attain majority require extended support to achieve autonomy as part of their social inclusion process.

Considering that the European Pact on Migration and Asylum sets forth a program, one wonders which migration and asylum policy scenarios opened up in the EU one year after its presentation on September 23, 2020. The implementation of the Pact will depend on the approval of the EU Parliament and Council. As several perplexities and critical issues have been observed so far, which may even be opposed to each other (such as the opinions expressed by the LIBE Committee and the Visegrad Group in the immediate aftermath of the pact presentation), the assumption that the contents of the proposal cannot be more than 'an uphill start for a reform process' appears to be a convincing one; this is further supported by the fact that there is no continuity with the regulations in force and underlying policies. Following the proposal's adoption, case law expressed the fear that there will be a 'compromise on the compromise' (on which, among others, see De Pasquale, 2021; Zotti, 2021). This

---

[81] Constitutional Court Judgment no. 202/2013, point 5. Regarding a mismatch between the position taken by the Supreme Courts and the work of the legislator, see Favilli and Ferri, 2020.

seems to be reflected in the 'non-answers' given almost a year later at the European Council in Brussels in June 2021 and two months later at the Extraordinary Council of Home Affairs Ministers on Afghanistan. A change of direction is urgently invoked from several sides, together with the radical revision of an approach to migration based on containment and deterrence. The unheard plea made to Europe to facilitate the evacuation of Afghan men, women and minors who believed in the values of freedom to express themselves and study is joined by a slightly earlier Doctors Without Borders report based on data from the NGO-run mental health clinics of Chios, Lesbos and Samos, which are the headquarters of the Greek hotspots (*Medecins Sans Frontières* 2021). Two-thirds of the 180 people treated by the Organization for episodes of self-harm or attempted suicide were minors; in one case, the child was only six years old. Lack of information on their status, continuous exposure to violence, separation from family, and denial of essential needs are among the causes of mental suffering that make people, and minors in the first place, even 'more invisible.'

References

ASGI. 2021. 'Il nuovo Patto europeo su migrazione e asilo. Le criticità alla luce del contesto italiano.' Accessed on 8.01.2021. https://www.asgi.it/wp-content/uploads/2021/01/PolicyNote_Patto_8gen21-2.pdf

ASGI-INTERSOS. 2018. "Quali percorsi per i minori non accompagnati in seguito all'abrogazione del permesso per motivi umanitari?" *Scheda per i tutori e gli operatori che seguono minori non accompagnati*. Accessed on 12.12.18. https://www.asgi.it/wp-content/uploads/2018/12/Scheda-Percorsi-dei-MSNA-in-seguito-allabrogazione-del-permesso-per-motivi-umanitari.pdf

Bonetti, P. 2020. 'Il richiamo della Corte al Belgio (dignitose condizioni di accoglienza per i richiedenti asilo) vale anche per l'Italia.' *Quaderni costituzionali*. no. 1:173-176.

Borraccetti, M. 2020. 'Le vie legali di accesso all'Unione nel nuovo Patto su asilo e migrazione della Commissione europea.' In *Annali AISDUE*. II, a cura di A.A.VV.,357-378. Napoli: Editoriale Scientifica https://www.aisdue.eu/category/annali-aisdue/

Caggiano, G. 2020. *Scritti sul diritto europeo dell'immigrazione*. Terza edizione. Torino: Giappichelli: 151-185.

Carrera, S. 2021. 'Whose Pact? The Cognitive Dimensions of the EU Pact on Migration and Asylum'. In *The EU Pact on Migration and Asylum in light of the United Nations Global Compact on Refugees. International Experiences on Containment and Mobility and their Impacts on Trust and Rights.*, edited by Carrera Sergio and Geddes Andrew, 1-24. San Domenico di Fiesole: European University Institute. Accessed 2.2.22 at https://www.asileproject.eu/wp-content/uploads/2021/03/EU-pact-migration-asylum-global-compact-refugees.pdf

COE. 2019. 'Practical guidance on alternatives to immigration detention: Fostering effective results.' COE. Accessed 2.13.22 from http: https://rm.coe.

int/practical-guidance-on-alternatives-to-immigration-detention-fostering-/ 16809687b1

Cornelisse, G. and Reneman, M. 2021. 'Border procedures in the Commission's New Pact on Migration and Asylum: A case of politics outplaying rationality?' *European Law Journal*, 23, March 2021: 1-18.

Council of Europe Commissioner for Human Rights. 2021a. 'A distress call for human rights The widening gap in migrant protection in the Mediterranean'. Follow-up report to the 2019 Recommendation by the Council of Europe Commissioner for Human Rights. Accessed 1.11.22 from https://rm.coe.int/ a-distress-call-for-human-rights-the-widening-gap-in-migrant-protectio/ 1680a1abcd

Council of Europe Commissioner for Human Rights. 2021b. 'Council of Europe member states should not undermine human rights protections in response to Afghans seeking safety'. 30 August 2021. Accessed 1.11.22 from https://www. coe.int/en/web/portal/-/council-of-europe-member-states-should-not- undermine-human-rights-protections-in-response-to-afghans-seeking-safety

Council of the European Union. 2004. 'Common Basic Principles for Immigrant Integration Policy in the EU.' 2618th Council Meeting Justice and Home Affairs. Brussels 19 November 2004. 14615/04. accessed 11.11.22 from https:// ec.europa.eu/migrant-integration/?action=media.download&uuid=29C7FD 4E-BA62-D4EA-18A8C8B34E873190

Council of the European Union. 2021. 'Statement on the situation in Afghanistan.' 31 August 2021. Accessed 3.13.22 from https://www.consilium.europa.eu/it/ press/press-releases/2021/08/31/statement-on-the-situation-in-afghanistan/

De Pasquale, P. 2021. 'Il Patto per la migrazione e l'asilo: più ombre che luci.' In *Annali AISDUE*. II, a cura di AA.V., 379-394. Napoli : Editoriale Scientifica. Accessed 1.11.22 from https://www.aisdue.eu/category/annali-aisdue/

De Vittor, F. 2020. 'Migrazioni, frontiere e tutela dei diritti dello straniero: il controllo dei confini nella giurisprudenza recente della Corte europea dei diritti dell'uomo.' *Diritto Costituzionale*. no. 2: 81-112.

K della Corte di Strasburgo e nell'ordinamento dell'Unione europea.' In *La tutela dei diritti umani in Europa. Tra sovranità statale e ordinamenti sovranazionali*, Caligiuri A., Cataldi G., Napoletano N., a cura di, 387-413. Padova: Cedam.

European Commission. 2005. Communication from the Commission to the Council, to the European Parliament, the European Economic and Social Committee and the Committee of the Regions of 1 September 2005. '*A Common Agenda for Integration – Framework for the Integration of Third-Country Nationals in the European Union.*' COM(2005) 389 final, September 1, 2005. Accessed 1.11.22 from https://eur-lex.europa.eu/legal-content/EN/ TXT/PDF/?uri=CELEX:52005DC0389&from=EN

European Commission. 2016. Communication from the Commission to the European Parliament, the Council, the European Economic and Social Committee and the Committee of the Regions. '*Action Plan on the integration of third country nationals.*' COM(2016) 377 final, June 7, 2016. Accessed 1.11.22 from https://eur-lex.europa.eu/legal-content/EN/TXT/PDF/?uri= CELEX:52016DC0377&qid=1628686548584&from=EN

European Commission. 2018. Proposal for a Directive of the European Parliament and of the Council 'on common standards and procedures in Member States for returning illegally staying third-country nationals (recast).' A contribution from the European Commission to the Leaders' meeting in Salzburg on 19-20 September 2018. COM(2018) 634 final, 12 September 2018. Accessed 4.14.22 from https://eur-lex.europa.eu/legal-content/EN/TXT/HTML/?uri=CELEX: 52018PC0634&qid=1633382883065&from=EN

European Commission. 2020a. 'Action Plan on Integration and Inclusion 2021-2027.' Communication from the Commission to the European Parliament, the Council, the European Economic and Social Committee and the Committee of the Regions. COM(2020) 758, November 24, 2020. Accessed 1.11.22 from https://ec.europa.eu/home-affairs/sites/default/files/pdf/action _plan_on_integration_and_inclusion_2021-2027.pdf

European Commission. 2020b. 'Communication from the Commission to the European Parliament, the Council, the European Economic and Social Committee and the Committee of the Regions 'on a New Pact on Migration and Asylum.' COM(2020) 609 final. September 9, 2020. Accessed 4.21.22 from https://eur-lex.europa.eu/legal-content/EN/TXT/PDF/?uri=CELEX:52020DC 0609&from=EN

European Commission. 2020c. Proposal for a Regulation of the the European Parliament and the Council, 'on asylum and migration management and amending Council Directive (EC) 2003/109 and the proposed Regulation (EU) XXX/XXX [Asylum and Migration Fund]'. COM (2020)610 final. September 23, 2020. Accessed 1411.22 from https://eur-lex.europa.eu/legal-content/EN/TXT/ PDF/?uri=CELEX:52020PC0610&qid=1626902279645&from=EN

European Commission. 2020d. Proposal for a Regulation of the European Parliament and of the Council 'introducing a screening of third country nationals at the external borders and amending Regulations (EC) No 767/2008, (EU) 2017/2226, (EU) 2018/1240 and (EU) 2019/817.' COM (2020)612 final. September 23, 2020. Accessed 5.21.22 from https://eur-lex.europa.eu/legal-content/EN/TXT/PDF/?uri=CELEX:52020PC0612&qid=1626776958935&from=EN

European Commission. 2020e. 'Amended proposal for a Regulation of the European Parliament establishing a common procedure for international protection in the Union and repealing Directive 2013/32/EU.' COM (2020)611 final. September 23, 2020. Accessed 5.11.22 from https://eur-lex.europa.eu/legal-content/EN/TXT/PDF/?uri=CELEX:52020PC0611&from=EN

European Commission. 2020f. Commission Recommendation (EU) 2020/1364 of 23 September 2020 'on legal pathways to protection in the EU: promoting resettlement, humanitarian admission and other complementary pathways.' COM(2020)6467 final. September 23, 2020. Accessed 5.11.22 from https://eur -lex.europa.eu/legal-content/EN/TXT/?qid=1633382677858&uri=CELEX%3 A32020H1364

European Commission. 2021. 'EU strategy on the rights of the child'. Communication from the Commission to the European Parliament, the Council, the European Economic and Social Committee and the Committee of the Regions. COM(2021) 142 final. March 24, 2021. Accessed 1.11.22 from https://eur-lex.europa.eu/legal-content/EN/TXT/PDF/?uri=CELEX:52021D C0142&from=EN

European Council. 2008. 'Joint Proposal for a Council Regulation amending Regulation (EU) No 442/2011 concerning restrictive measures in view of the situation in Syria', COM(2011)645, October 10, 2011 Accessed 7.18.22 from. https://eur-lex.europa.eu/legal-content/EN/TXT/PDF/?uri=CELEX:52011PC 0645&from=EN

European Court of Auditors. 2018. 'The integration of migrants from outside the EU (Briefing paper).' No. 4. https://www.eca.europa.eu/en/Pages/DocI tem.aspx?did=45990

European Parliament. 2016. 'The reform of the Dublin III Study for the LIBE Committee' published by D.G. for Internal Policies Policy Department for Citizen's Rights and Constitutional Affairs. Accessed 4.12.22 from https://www. europarl.europa.eu/RegData/etudes/STUD/2016/571360/IPOL_STU(2016)57 1360_EN.pdf

European Parliament. 2021. 'Resolution on new avenues for labour migration', 20 May 2021, 2020/2010(INI) - P9_TA(2021)0260. Accessed 8.1.22 from https:// www.europarl.europa.eu/doceo/document/TA-9-2021-0260_EN.html

Eurostat. 2021. 'Asylum Statistics.' Eurostat. Accessed 6.19.22 from https://ec. europa.eu/eurostat/statistics-explained/index.php?title=Asylum_statistics# cite_note-1

Favilli, C. 2020. 'Il patto europeo sulla migrazione e l'asilo. «C'è qualcosa di nuovo, anzi d'antico».' In *Questione e Giustizia.* Accessed 1.11.22 from https:// www.questionegiustizia.it/articolo/il-patto-europeo-sulla-migrazione-e-l-asilo-c-e-qualcosa-di-nuovo-anzi-d-antico

European Parliament. 2017. 'Report on the proposal for a regulation of the European Parliament and of the Council establishing the criteria and mechanisms for determining the Member State responsible for examining an application for international protection lodged in one of the Member States by a third-country national or a stateless person (recast)' (COM(2016)0270 – C8-0173/2016 – 2016/0133(COD)). November 16, 2017. Accessed 5.21.22 from https://www.europarl.europa.eu/doceo/document/A-8-2017-0345_EN.html/

European Parliament. 2018. 'Resolution European Parliament resolution of 11 December 2018 with recommendations to the Commission on Humanitarian Visas (2018/2271(INL)).' *OJ* C 388, November 13 2020 : 11–17. P8_TA(2018)04 94. Accessed 1.11.22 from http: https://eur-lex.europa.eu/legal-content/EN/TXT/ PDF/?uri=CELEX:52018IP0494&qid=1633436362150&from=EN

European Parliament. 2018. 'Resolution with recommendations to the Commission on Humanitarian Visas', 11 December 2018, 2018/2271(INL) - P8_TA(2018)0494. Accessed 3.13.22 from https://www.europarl.europa.eu/doceo/document/A -8-2018-0423_EN.html

European Parliament. 2020. 'Resolution on the implementation of the Return Directive', 17 December 2020, 2019/2208(INI) - P9_TA(2020)0362. Accessed 1.11.22 from https://www.europarl.europa.eu/doceo/document/TA-9-2020- 0362_EN.html

Favilli, C. and Ferri, M. 2020. 'Il diritto alla vita privata e familiare ai sensi dell'art. 8 CEDU e la sua applicazione nell'ordinamento italiano'. In *IUS Migrandi. Trent'anni di politiche e legislazione sull'immigrazione in Italia,* a cura di, Giovannetti Monia and Zorzella Nazzarena, 299-345. Milano: Franco Angeli.

Ferri, M. 2021. La tutela della vita privata quale limite all'allontanamento: l'attuazione (e l'ampliamento) degli obblighi sovranazionali attraverso la nuova protezione speciale per integrazione sociale. *Diritto, Immigrazione e Cittadinanza.* No. 2 : 78-128. Accessed 4.22.22 from https://www.diritto immigrazionecittadinanza.it

FRA. 2020a. 'Children in migration 2019'. *Annual review* 1.1.2019 - 31.12.2019. Accessed 1.12.22 from https://fra.europa.eu/sites/default/files/fra_uploads/fra-2020-children-in-migration_en.pdf

FRA. 2020b. 'Fundamental Rights Report.' FRA. Accessed 3.13.22 from https://fra.europa.eu/en/publication/2020/fundamental-rights-report-2020

FRA. 2021. 'Fundamental Rights Report.' FRA Accessed 3.13.22 from https://fra.europa.eu/en/publication/2021/fundamental-rights-report-2021

Fratea, C. 2019. 'Obblighi di solidarietà ed effettività della tutela dei migranti: quale spazio per un ripensamento del sistema Dublino?.' In *Temi e questioni di diritto dell'Unione europea. Scritti offerti a Claudia Morviducci*: 703-716. Bari : Cacucci. Accessed 1.11.22 from https://www.aisdue.eu/p2s2_04-fratea/

Fratea, C. 2021. 'Rimpatrio del minore straniero non accompagnato: solo una lettura sistematica della Dir. CE 2008/115 assicura il rispetto del principio del superiore interesse del fanciullo.' *Famiglia e diritto.* no 6 : 576 – 585.

General Assembly UN. 2016. 'The New York Declaration for Refugees and Migrants.' 13 September 2016. No. A/71/L.1 Accessed 6.17.22 from https://www.ohchr.org/EN/Issues/Migration/Pages/NewYorkDeclaration.aspx

General Assembly UN. 2018. 'Global Compact for Safe, Orderly and Regular Migration.' 19 December 2018, No. A/RES/73/195. Accessed 1.19.22 from https://refugeesmigrants.un.org/sites/default/files/180528_draft_rev_2_final.pdf

General Assembly UN. 2018. 'Global Compact on Refugees'. 17 December 2018. No. A/RES/73/151. Accessed 11.4.22 from https://www.unhcr.org/the-global-compact-on-refugees.html

IFRC. 2022. 'Belarus and neighbouring countries - Europe Region: Population Movement Emergency appeal No. MGR65001. Operation update'. 22 January 2022. Accessed 7.12.22 from https://reliefweb.int/report/belarus/belarus-and-neighbouring-countries-europe-region-population-movement-emergency-2

ISMU. 2021. 'XXVI Rapporto sulle migrazioni 2020.' Accessed 1.18.22 from https://www.ismu.org/presentazione-xxvi-rapporto-sulle-migrazioni-2020/

Klötgen, P. 2017. 'Présence de mineurs en centre de retention: les conditions posées par la Cour européenne des droit de homme'. *Revue critique de droit International.* no. 2: 226-237

La Spina, E. 2020. 'La vulnerabilidad de las personas refugiadas ante el reto de la integración.' Cizur Menor: Aranzadi

Maiani, F. 2017. 'The reform of the Dublin system and the dystopia of «sharing people»'. *Maastricht Journal of European and Comparative Law* 24, no. 5: 622-645. Accessed 10.11.22 from https://journals.sagepub.com/doi/full/10.1177/1023263X17742815

Mentasti , G. 2019. 'Hotspots, trattenimento e diritti: una sentenza della Corte di Strasburgo condanna la Grecia per violazione dell'art. 5 par. 4 della convenzione.' *Sistemapenale.* Accessed 12.11.22 from https://www.sistema

penale.it/it/scheda/hotspot-trattenimento-diritti-sentenza-corte-strasburgo-condanna-grecia-violazione-art-5-pa-4-cedu

Ministero dell'Interno. Dipartimento per le Libertà civili e l'Immigrazione. (2017). 'Piano nazionale d'integrazione dei titolari di protezione internazionale'. 'National Integration Plan for Persons Entitled to International Protection.' Accessed 12.12.22 from https://www.interno.gov.it/sites/default/files/piano _nazionale_integrazione_eng.pdf

Morgese, G. 2020. 'La riforma del sistema Dublino: il problema della condivisione delle responsabilità'. *Diritto pubblico*. no. 1 : 97-115.

Nascimbene, B. and Andrò, I. 2017. 'La tutela dei diritti fondamentali nella giurisprudenza della Corte di Giustizia: nuove sfide, nuove prospettive.' *Rivista Italiana di Diritto Pubblico Comunitario*. no. 2. Accessed 1.11.22 from http://www.eurojus.it/wp-content/uploads/2017/01/Relazione-11.11.20161.pdf

OSCE. 2021. 'The Situation of Human Rights Defenders in Selected OSCE Participating States. The Final Report of the First Assessment Cycle (2017-2019). Accessed 10.10.22 from https://www.osce.org/files/f/documents/2/3/493867.pdf

Palladino, R. 2016. 'La tutela dei migranti irregolari e dei richiedenti protezione internazionale.' In 'CEDU e ordinamento italiano. La giurisprudenza della Corte europea dei diritti dell'uomo e l'impatto nell'ordinamento interno (2010-2015),' a cura di Angela Di Stasi, 167-2013. Padova: Cedam.

Panella, L. 2018. 'L'evoluzione della giurisprudenza della Corte europea dei diritti dell'uomo in materia di immigrazione e la posizione della Corte di giustizia dell'Unione europea'. *Studi sull'Integrazione europea*, no. 3 : 599-624

PICUM (Platformo for International Cooperation on Undocumented Migrants). 2020. 'Detenzione di minori stranieri nell'UE.' . Accessed 11.1.22 from http://picum.org

Pistoia, E. 2020. 'Rafforzamento della politica dei rimpatri e uso più esteso della detenzione.' *Diritto Pubblico*. no. 1: 117-139.

Quadranti, I. 2021. 'The Right to Education of Unaccompanied Minors and the Persistence of an Education Gap in their Transition to Adulthood'. In '*The Rights of Unaccompanied Minors: Perspectives and Case Studies on Migrant Children*,' edited by. Yvonne Vissing, Sofia Leitão, 163-185. Berlin: Springer. Accessed 12.19.22 from https://www.springer.com/gp/book/9783030755935

Reginelli, D. 2020. "I trasferimenti Dublino verso l'Italia dopo il decreto sicurezza: tra 'carenze sistemiche' e previe garanzie individuali". *Federalismi. Focus Human Rights*. 28 dicembre 2020. Accessed 12.28.22 from https://www.federalismi.it/nv14/articolo-documento.cfm?Artid=44684

Rogozik, M. 2021. 'Conditions of confinement in the transit zone RR v Hungary (Application No. 36037/17). *European Human Rights Law Review*. no. 4 : 455-457.

Starita, M. 2020. 'Il principio del no-refoulement tra controllo dell'accesso al territorio dell'Unione europea e protezione dei diritti umani.' *Diritto pubblico*, no. 1: 142-163.

UNHCR. 2016. 'Proposal for a Regulation of the European Parliament and of the Council establishing a Union Resettlement Framework and amending Regulation (EU) No 516/2014 of the European Parliament and the Council. UNHCR's Observations and Recommendations', November 2016. Accessed 1.11.22 from https://www.refworld.org/docid/5890b1d74.html

UNHCR. 2017a. 'Better Protecting Refugees in the EU and Globally': UNHCR's proposals to rebuild trust through better management, partnership and solidarity, December 2016, Accessed 1.11.22 from https://www.refworld.org/docid/58385d4e4.html

UNHCR. 2017b. 'Focus group sul tema dell'integrazione'. Report finale. UNHCR. Accessed 1.11.22 from https://www.unhcr.org/it/wp-content/uploads/sites/97/2020/07/Focus-group-integrazione.pdf

UNHCR. 2020a. Global Trends. UNHCR. Accessed 1.11.22 from https://www.unhcr.org/unhcr-global-trends-2020-media-page-60be2dd14

UNHCR. 2020b. '*1 per cent of humanity displaced: UNHCR Global Trends report*', UNHCR. Accessed 1.11.22 from https://www.unhcr.org/news/press/2020/6/5ee9db2e4/1-cent-humanity-displaced-unhcr-global-trends-report.html

Zotti. A. 2021. Le politiche dell'Unione europea in materia di migrazione e asilo: le (non) novità del 2020. In *Ventiseiesimo rapporto sulle migrazioni*, a cura di Fondazione ISMU. Accessed 9.5.22 from http://ojs.francoangeli.it/_omp/index.php/oa/catalog/book/633#downloadTab

Chapter 4

Use of Information-Communication Technologies Among Unaccompanied Migrant Youth in Liminal Places[1]

Blaž Lenarčič

Science and research centre Koper, Slovenia

Zorana Medarić

Science and research centre Koper, Slovenia

Abstract

In recent years, the role of information-communication technologies (ICT) in the lives of children on the move has attracted considerable scholarly attention. ICTs play an important role in the lives of migrant children at different stages of their migration process - in the pre-departure stage, during the journey, and upon arrival at the destination. ICT facilitates the preparation process and the journey itself, enables them to stay in touch with their social networks, and facilitates the integration process in the destination country. This chapter draws on qualitative research with unaccompanied migrant children in Slovenia to reflect on ICT's role for unaccompanied migrant children in their everyday lives in places of transition, such as the asylum home. In particular, the aim is to reflect on the supportive role of ICT in accessing information and to explore how they use this technology to stay in touch with family and friends in their countries of origin and beyond, build new relationships, and orient themselves in the transition countries. The empirical data derived from the Migrant Children and Communities in a Transforming Europe (MiCREATE) research project, funded by the EU Horizon 2020 Research and Innovation Programme, which runs from 2019 to 2022. It adopts a child-centred

[1] The chapter is published with the financial support of the European Union's Horizon 2020 Research and Innovation programme under grant agreement No 822664 and of the Slovenian Research Agency (ARRS) through the research programme Constructive Theology in the Age of Digital Culture and Anthropocene (P6–0434).

perspective that recognises children as social actors and agents whose views are relevant and should be acknowledged and taken into account in matters that concern them. This chapter presents the main findings from the field and their theoretical implications.

Keywords: ICT, migrant youth, liminal places, transition

***

My mark is 'no fear.' I must arrive, even if I die, I don't care, I must arrive, I must arrive to the end of it. I must make my dream come true. Fall to the front and not fall down to the back. /.../ Phone, GPS, food, go! (Unaccompanied minor)

Introduction

In recent years, the role of information-communication technology (ICT) in the lives of refugees and other migrants has attracted considerable scholarly attention. This technology plays an important role in their lives at different stages of their migration process - in the pre-departure stage (preparation process), during the journey (navigation, communication), and after arrival at the destination (to stay in touch with their social networks and facilitate the integration process in the destination country). Although ICT is involved in many children's daily activities and is therefore important in their lives as well as in youth culture (Ito *et al.*, 2010; Boyd, 2014, 2008), there is little literature that addresses the use of this technology by unaccompanied limin. Therefore, this chapter aims to reflect on the supportive role of ICT in accessing information and to explore how unaccompanied migrant youth use this technology in their everyday lives in places of transition.

What follows is an empirical qualitative study of the role that ICT has for unaccompanied migrant youth in Slovenia in transition placed in an asylum home. As Manjikian (2010) argues, temporal constraints, such as departures, deadlines, waiting for status decisions, etc., and spatial constraints, like movement restrictions, are the root of refugees' 'in-betweenness.' Considering that ICT is not limited by time-space obstacles, examining in-betweenness through the use of these technologies can shed further light on the daily lives of unaccompanied migrant youth who, according to Kohli (2014), undertake at least three different journeys. Namely, the journey through geographic space, from their country of origin to the country of destination, the journey through time as they grow older, and the psychological journey of who they are, what happened to them, and how they got to where they are. They are in a constant state of transition and liminality, no longer at home and not yet there, and at the same time, with often a clear goal of a better future, no longer looking back.

At this point, it is important to emphasise that ICT also has the capacity and potential to bring certain risks to refugees and migrants. Indeed, the consequences of certain digital data and information breaches can become threats, as they can be used to identify and target people based on their ethnicity, immigration status, vulnerability, etc. In this context, for example, studies (Atalan, Akgül, Güney, 2021; Caravita *et al.*, 2019) show that migrant children are more likely to experience ethnic-based cyberbullying. In addition, UNICEF highlights in its report Children in a Digital World that children living in camps are at 'a heightened risk of violence and abuse' because they use ICT as a means of communication, entertainment, and access to information. However, despite the importance and lack of studies dealing with unaccompanied minors as victims of online violence and other threats, this is not the focus of our research. In this chapter, we focus mainly on the benefits that ICT brings to unaccompanied migrant youth in liminal places.

Liminal Places in Migration Context

As Crawley and Jones (2020) note, refugee and migrant journeys are typically portrayed as linear movements between two places, with the academic and political gaze directed primarily towards the places people leave and those they eventually arrive to. However, transit migrations are much more than linear trajectories from the country of origin to the country of destination. Collyer (2010) introduces the notion of a fragmented journey, illustrating that it is divided into several separate stages involving different motivations, legal statuses, and living and employment conditions. Schapendonk (2012) comes to similar conclusions, arguing that for migrants, transit situations can slowly but surely turn into home-like situations and these, in turn, into transit situations. And the same is true for their intentions and strategies, which change over the course of their journey. 'It is often not the case that entire journeys are planned in advance, but one stage may arise from the failure of a previous stage, limiting future options and draining resources' (Collyer, 2010, p.275).

During the time they are unable to move, migrants are often housed in refugee camps, alien centres, or asylum homes in different countries, waiting in uncertainty as to if and when they will be able to continue to their final destination. This transitional period can last from a few weeks to several years. These places not only provide the physical setting in which migrants temporarily live but also create new opportunities, encounters, and relationships. Refugee camps, asylum homes and alien centres can be seen as places of transition, as liminal places. A place 'that is on the 'border,' a space that is somewhere in between /.../; at the boundary of two dominant spaces, /.../ not fully part of either /.../' (Dale and Burrell, 2008, p. 238). And because of their purpose and context, liminal places produce, as Agier (2016) argues, the experience of a gap from the 'official' social world. On this basis, Waardenburg *et al.* (2018) identify three important characteristics of liminal places and their impact on refugees: waiting (for the outcome of the asylum application, onward travel, etc.), loss of social status (old hierarchical and social statuses no longer apply), and the absence of a sense of community (living with people of different origins).

ICT can play an important role in the migration context, alleviating the stress of separation and connecting migrants with themselves as well as friends and family in the country of origin, the refugees they met on the journey and the country they want to live in, and others they wish to. ICT also changes 'perceptions of physical distance and social isolation, as well as influence the elaboration of the sense of belonging' (Fortunati, Pertierra and Vincent, 2012, p. 5). At the same time, cyberspace itself can also be seen as a liminal space (Lenarčič, 2020), particularly because it allows migrants to be in constant contact with the people and culture of their countries of origin. This means that the migrant connected to cyberspace (Diminescu, 2008) is physically present in the new cultural environment but at the same time also present in the home country, which means that he or she is here and there (in between), in a sort of intermediate space.

For the topic that we are dealing with in this paper, the important phenomenon is transit migration, which has become a significant research topic in recent years (e.g., Noussia and Lyons, 2009; Collyer, 2010; Schapendonk, 2012; Agier, 2016; Waardenburg *et al.*, 2018; Mueller, 2019; Albanski, 2020; Crawley and Jones, 2020; Genova and Zontini, 2020). Transit migrants are best described as '/.../ irregular migrants who have left their homes, travelled without documents or means of legal entry, but have not yet arrived in a place where they will settle. They live in an ongoing state of non-arrival' (Paynter, 2018, p.41). One of the main groups identified as transit migrants is unaccompanied children and youth, who need to build their identities as they go through multiple liminal stages while negotiating their identities and moving from childhood to adulthood. And on the other hand, as Albanski (2020) points out, unaccompanied migrant children live in a state of limbo that can persist virtually for an indeterminate period of time. In reality, this means that in many cases, they live across borders as unaccompanied or undocumented minors without full legal recognition, experiencing permanent temporariness and uncertainty. The problem of unaccompanied migrant youth in Slovenia is presented and explained in more detail in the following section, which provides the context for further analysis of the research topic.

Unaccompanied Migrant Children in Slovenia

We refer to an unaccompanied migrant child as a

> minor who arrives on the territory of an EU Member State unaccompanied by the adult responsible for him or her by law or by the practice of the EU Member State concerned, and for as long as he or she is not effectively taken into the care of such a person, or a minor who is left unaccompanied after he or she has entered the territory of the Member States (EU Directive 2011/95/EU, Article 2(I)[2]).

At this point, it is also important to emphasise that unaccompanied migrant children are often 'vulnerable' and 'traumatised' given the distress they face. Although the EU has issued several directives and regulations related to the migration and asylum procedures of unaccompanied children with the aim of uniform application across the continent (e.g., Action Plan on Unaccompanied Minors 2010–2014[3]), individual Member States have applied the directives or regulations differently. However, it should be noted that these documents are not binding legal acts, so many EU Member States still do not have specific laws or a comprehensive legal framework that would explicitly outline the rights and needs of unaccompanied migrant children. For example, as Žakelj *et al.* (2017) state, on the basis of the argument that Slovenia is only a transition state, authorities do not recognise the need for systematic improvements in the field of implementation of rights. This argument stems from the relatively small number of unaccompanied minors in Slovenia who actually remain in the country after applying for international protection[4]. According to the Ministry of Interior (2020), 70% of all minor children who applied for international protection in Slovenia came to Slovenia without their parents or other legal representatives. The vast majority of unaccompanied minors who applied for international protection were boys (Table 1).

---

[2] https://eur-lex.europa.eu/legal-content/EN/TXT/PDF/?uri=CELEX:32011L0095&from=EN

[3] https://eur-lex.europa.eu/LexUriServ/LexUriServ.do?uri=COM:2010:0213:FIN:EN:PDF

[4] The Dublin III regulation is the EU law setting out which Member State is responsible for an individual`s asylum application. This is usually the country where asylum seeker first arrives in the EU, however in the case of unaccompanied migrant children the regulation gives the responsibility to proceed with the request for international protection to the Member State where unaccompanied children have a 'family member' (defined as a parent, spouse or child) or a 'sibling' who is 'legally present' in the country. This State has an obligation to take the responsibility for examining an application of an unaccompanied child.

Table 4.1: Age and gender of unaccompanied minors who applied for international protection in 2020

Age	Boys	Girls
0–13 years	23	3
14–15 years	97	1
16 17 years	424	2
Total	**544**	**6**

Source: Ministry of Interior (2020)

The data presented in Table 2 show that most unaccompanied minors applying for international protection in Slovenia in 2020 came from Afghanistan, followed by Egypt and Pakistan.

Table 4.2: Unaccompanied minors by country of origin in 2020

Country of origin	Number of applicants
Afghanistan	205
Pakistan	86
Algeria	5
Morocco	69
Bangladesh	48
Egypt	111
Syria	6
India	2
Ivory Coast	1
Iraq	6
Libya	1
Sudan	1
Nepal	2
Yemen	1
Kosovo	5
Turkey	1
Total	**550**

Source: Ministry of Interior (2020).

In Slovenia, the Government Office for Support and Integration is responsible for the reception and accommodation of asylum seekers, among whom are unaccompanied minors. The legislation provides that applicants for international protection, after the preliminary procedure, are accommodated in the Asylum Home in Ljubljana or, more typically, in its branch in Logatec, where the unaccompanied minors and families are usually housed, and submit the application. Before applying for international protection, they are accommodated in the pre-reception area of the Asylum Home or in a separate building or container homes in Logatec, where they are detained.

Once the application for international protection is filed, the unaccompanied minors are accommodated in the Asylum Home or its branch in Logatec or in the Student Dormitory in Postojna. The latter is organised as a kind of institutional care, where a part of the dormitory is used to accommodate unaccompanied minors. As reported by Nabergoj and Regvar (2020), the number of unaccompanied minors in the dormitory in Postojna increased from 19 to 22 by the end of 2020. Because the number of children is higher than the reception capacity, only unaccompanied children under the age of 16 are accommodated there, while the rest are in Logatec.

The Constitution of the Republic of Slovenia guarantees freedom of movement to all asylum seekers (Article 32). Therefore, asylum seekers may leave their accommodation during the day. However, at night they have to respect the Decree on Asylum Centre House Rules, which stipulates that unaccompanied minors may be absent from 6 a.m. to 9 p.m. on weekdays and from 6 a.m. to 11 p.m. on weekends and public holidays. In Slovenia, unaccompanied migrant children who reside here have the right to access education. According to the International Protection Act[5] (Article 88), the right to elementary education for asylum seekers must be guaranteed for no longer than three months after filing an application. Therefore, most of the children accommodated in the Asylum Home in Ljubljana attend the Livada elementary school; the children accommodated in the Logatec branch are divided between two local elementary schools, and the children accommodated in the Postojna dormitory attend the elementary school for adults organised by Ljudska Univerza Postojna.

As mentioned above, Slovenia is not considered a final destination country for unaccompanied minors seeking international protection. In practice, this means that most of them leave the country quite quickly and continue travelling towards their final destinations in northern and western European countries. This has also been observed by Nabergoj and Regvar (2020), who argue that the absconding rate of unaccompanied minors in Slovenia is very high, which seems to be mainly due to the fact that the children have family in other member states or Slovenia generally is not their destination country. The authors rely on official statistics from the Migration Directorate, which show that in 2019, 668 unaccompanied minors applied for asylum, of which 656 absconded before the decision was made, establishing an absconding rate of 98%. According to the data presented by the authors, the absconding of unaccompanied minors continued in 2020. Namely, of 550 unaccompanied

---

[5] http://www.pisrs.si/Pis.web/pregledPredpisa?id=ZAKO7103#

minors who applied, 536 absconded before the first-instance decision was made, maintaining a similar absconding rate of 97.5%.

The Logatec facility, where our research took place, consists of several former military buildings in a green area on the outskirts of the town. The site is guarded, and there is a gate and gatehouse where all visitors must register. The grounds are guarded by day and night. There are several container homes set up in the pre-reception area where migrants are housed before they apply for international protection. Many of them do not apply for international protection, often staying only a few days and continuing their journey. These facilities are simple. There are up to 8 bunk beds in a container with no other furniture. There are also separate buildings making up a common dining area and a sanitary area. At certain times migrants are offered breakfast, lunch and dinner. While waiting for their applications, migrants are not allowed to leave the container area. Once they apply for their status, they are transferred to a building where there are rooms for 4 to 6 people, a common room, a small kitchen area, and access to Wi-Fi. Although this facility is better equipped and more comfortable, it offers little personal space for the migrant youth.

The living conditions in the places of transition allow for very limited privacy. Therefore, the personal and intimate nature of ICT, especially smartphones, plays a role in their imaginations, as Pérez and Salgado (2019) put it, similar to their bedrooms at home. Therefore, it can be said that the living conditions of the liminal places play an important role in the attachment of unaccompanied migrant minors to ICT, which is perceived as a private and customizable place, an oasis of intimacy and individual identity. During our fieldwork, we often observed young migrants sitting alone with headphones, immersed in their 'own world,' trying to isolate themselves from others to improve their sense of privacy and security. In the context of privacy, it is also important to highlight the question of the security of their possessions, particularly their smartphones. For example, during our fieldwork, one informant stated through the interpreter,

> They would like to have all their things and stuff safe. If you leave your phone, if you leave anything, that you are sure that you will come back and you will find it. But when it is too many people in the room, a lot of things disappear. The loss of a cell phone, which besides being a communication device also contains important information (data, photos), is usually experienced as a stressful event. ...as often an enormous amount of information of important emotional significance is packed inside their mobile devices (Pérez and Salgado, 2019, p. 11).

Use of ICT Among Unaccompanied Migrant Youth

It is well documented in the existing literature that ICT is considered among basic life needs by refugees and migrants (Frouws *et al.*, 2016; Gough and Gough, 2019; Kutscher and Kreß, 2018; Pérez and Salgado, 2019) as they rely significantly on social media and various apps to obtain information about and plan their journey. Therefore, smartphones are crucial for them (Frouws *et al.*, 2016; Kutscher and Kreß, 2018; Gough and Gough, 2019; Pérez and Salgado, 2019). This became evident at the very beginning of our fieldwork. During each visit to the asylum seeker's home, we were approached by migrants asking for help in acquiring or borrowing a smartphone, a charger, questions about the availability of Wi-Fi, etc. Many of them came from the border areas and reported that the police had taken away their belongings, including their smartphones, or simply destroyed them. This practice is very common along the so-called Balkan route, often as part of pushback strategies (Zavratnik and Zrilić, 2018).

The crucial role that ICT plays for migrants and refugees has also been recognised by the European Union, which refers to the combination of cell phones, the Internet, and social media as a 'game changer' for migrants, as these tools help them plan their journey and provide information on quality of life, which significantly affects migrants' expectations and aspirations (EPSC, 2017). However, Mancini et al. (2019), in their comprehensive literature review on cell phone use among refugees, note that the field of digital migration studies appears fragmented, unsystematic, and lacks analytical focus, particularly with respect to migrants living in or seeking to move to Europe. The reason for the lack of a systematic framework, they argue, is due to several aspects (e.g., the unpredictability of a migrant crisis, the emergency and risk conditions during the move, the illegal nature of migration, and the uncertainty of the reception path in the country of arrival) that have made the experiences of refugees barely accessible to systematic studies. As a result, ICT use among unaccompanied migrant children is seldom specifically addressed. In one of these rare studies, Kutscher and Kreß (2018) argue that ICT among young refugees in Germany is placed on par with basic requirements such as food and is regarded as indispensable during their precarious journey to Europe and for their daily lives.

This chapter aims to analyse the way ICT is used by unaccompanied youth in Slovenia while they are accommodated in a place of transition, such as an asylum home. For unaccompanied migrant youth, ICT, such as smartphones, can be seen as a kind of 'built-in survival kit' that provides various opportunities, such as (Mancini et al., 2019): establishing contacts in the destination country and in the home country, search for help when needed, navigation, various information to manage risks and opportunities during the journey and when crossing the border, keeping in touch with family and friends in the home country, connecting with services and institutions in the new countries, and in general improving their knowledge and skills to integrate in the new context. In addition, ICT can also provide a sense of stability and control (Gough and Gough, 2019), as well as the opportunity to take action: for example, by expressing their experiences on the journey.

This results in the following interrelated, but for the purposes of this article separate, domains of ICT use among unaccompanied migrant youth in places of transition in Slovenia: ICT practices in everyday life, ICT for maintaining and developing social relations, ICT use related to travel, and ICT for self-empowerment and self-assertion.

Methodological Explanations

A combined methodological approach of participant observation and individual or group interviews with a total of 17 unaccompanied migrant youth was conducted in August and September 2020. They were all male, 16 and 17 years old, and came from Afghanistan, Algeria, Morocco, Bangladesh, Pakistan, Western Sahara, and Egypt. Because of their ages, we refer to them as unaccompanied migrant youth. Participant observation represents the 'field entry' phase, in which a combination of passive and moderate participation approaches were used (Fine and Sandstrom, 1999). Field notes included personal, methodological, and theoretical reflections. This phase enabled the development of a certain degree of familiarity and trust to be established with the youth, which facilitated the collection of interviews. Interviews were recorded, transcribed verbatim, and analysed in accordance with the rules of qualitative data analysis (Mesec, 1998; Denzin & Lincoln, 2011). The aim of the interviews was wide in scope - to gain insight into the specific lived experiences of migrant youth, to capture their subjective understandings and perspectives on their own lives, and their experiences of migration, integration, and general well-being (Mayeza, 2017) while staying at the reception facilities. Part of this broad scope included gaining insight into their use of ICT in their daily lives. Two interviews were conducted in English, while interpreters were used for the other interviews. As mentioned earlier, the fieldwork took place at the Logatec facility. The young people interviewed were all asylum seekers and had applied for international protection in Slovenia, yet they all continued their journey to other European countries. The unaccompanied youth accommodated in Logatec who did not have smartphones upon arrival were given them by a local NGO (Infokolpa) but often simply borrowed them from each other when they needed them. While talking about their well-being in Logatec, the young asylum seekers most often complained about the Wi-Fi, which was either non-existent in certain areas or too slow. As will be shown further in the chapter, this attitude is quite understandable, as Wi-Fi access is central to their further journey and maintaining social contacts.

Information-Communication Technology as a Means to Pass the Time

In places of transition like Logatec, time passes slowly, especially when migrants are confined to the container area where not many activities are possible. Smartphones play an important role here, filling the day and helping to pass the time. Even in the pre-reception area where there is no Wi-Fi, migrant youth watch movies they have previously downloaded or listen to music. Taking and sharing photos was also frequently observed. As Witteborn (2015) says, these technologies are widely used among asylum seekers to entertain themselves during monotonous days in the shelters. An interpreter explained what a young migrant said about his smartphone:

> *He says if he'd be out of a smartphone, he'd be crazy by now because they're using the time in the night with the telephone, you know. Talking to girls and ... In the beginning, he didn't have the telephone and he didn't know what to do, he was bored. He was just walking there up and back again and then again up and then back ... and he's thankful to the one that brought the telephone.*

Browsing and posting on social media networks is one of the regular activities of young people to pass the time. For example, when asked about the importance of Facebook to him, one informant replied:

> *Just, you know, I cannot sit being bored here. I use that (Facebook). It makes the time go by faster.*

Facebook and other social networks are also valuable sources of information about the country in which the youth migrants are currently residing, as well as various advice about the migration process. Frouws *et al.* (2016) emphasise the connection potentials of social networks and applications such as WhatsApp or Viber between potential migrants, migrants on the move, and those who have already reached their destination. On several occasions, we were shown short videos shared on Facebook depicting different situations migrants face, for example, in one case, the experience of being held in the detention centre in Postojna. As the young migrants in Slovenia also noted, migrants with direct experience of life in Slovenia can provide the most valuable information:

> *Yes, they contact their friends on Facebook. Legal guardian, they don't know anything. Also, their friend, who is new here, he doesn't know anything. /.../ But who had lived before, who experienced, who lived here, they may advise what to do.*

Smartphones and social media were also used for more practical purposes, such as communicating with the aim of obtaining money. On several occasions, young migrants in asylum homes discussed transferring money via Western Union, which they had organised through ICT with the help of their families or someone they had met along the way. ICT was also used for practical orientation to help them find their way around their new surroundings, for example, by looking up using Google Maps where stores, bus stops, etc. were located.

Gough and Gough (2019: 94) also highlight the sense of control and agency that smartphones offer to those in situations over which they have little control: 'The smartphone thus becomes the most important object in asylum seekers' lives because it allows for feelings of control and opportunity, enabling them to exercise a level of agency in a situation that they otherwise have very little control over.' One of the informers vividly described the importance of his smartphone: '*without telephone, I would kill myself,*' simply emphasising the relevance of this small device in his current life in transition.

Information-Communication Technology and the Maintenance and Development of Social Relations in Transition

One of the most important roles of ICT is maintaining social ties with family and friends. Migrants own and regularly use smartphones including to stay connected during their migration journey (Frouws *et al.*, 2016) and to send details of their location to friends or family members, providing the 'distant proximities' (Rosenau, 2003) that make life bearable. During participant observation, researchers often loaned the young asylum seekers their own phones or Wi-Fi so they could connect with their families. This co-presence (Zhao, 2003) enables a transnational lifestyle that re-constructs family intimacy. Those who did not own phones often indicated that they would use them to connect with their families:

> *If I had a mobile, then I'd definitely talk to my family, maybe with my friends, definitely I would talk and plus it would help me to cope with the time, yes.*

Connecting with family and friends was a common way for those who had access to a smartphone to make the most of the long hours in the asylum home.

> *Interviewer: And you say, at night, you talk with your friends on Facebook, do you also talk to your family?*
> *Informant: Yes, I talk to my friends in Algeria and my family also.*

In addition to passing the time, regular contact and shared moments with family and friends bring familiarity and intimacy to their lives (Gough and

Gough, 2019). During the fieldwork, we were often asked to share our Wi-Fi on smartphones with migrant youth to be able to contact their families through Viber, WhatsApp, Messenger, or similar applications. On the other hand, some migrant youth deliberately refrained from contacting their families. This is the case, for example, of a Pakistani boy who explained that he chooses not to contact his family even if he can reach them by phone. When asked why this was the case, he explained that he did not want to give the family bad news, which meant that he did not want to let them know that he has not yet arrived at his final destination.

At this point, it is important to mention that in many cases, migrant youth manage their self-image in their interactions with family, relatives, and friends, or as Goffman (1959) puts it, the presentation of the self in everyday life. Namely, they try to show (only) the positive aspects of their lives and hide the problems they face. "Through the use of social media, migrant adolescents are able to present themselves far from the labels of 'unaccompanied foreign minors' or 'kids from the residence" (Pérez and Salgado, 2019: 11). It has often been observed that the photos posted by young migrant people on social media show a positive image of their current lives, for example, by posing in front of interesting buildings or tourist attractions or taking group photos with smiling faces. Such images serve the purpose of reassuring families and friends that they are doing well (Frouws *et al.*, 2016). At the same time, such self-presentation is also an important push factor for migration as it creates ideal-typical images of Western countries in developing countries (Appadurai, 1996), especially positive content posted online acts as pressure on peers to leave their home countries as well (Nimo-Ilhan, 2016).

During their travels, often lasting years, moving between different countries, migrants build many, sometimes very temporary, social relationships, which ICT helps sustain over time. This was the case of a Palestinian migrant who spent two years in Bosnia and one year in Croatia before coming to Slovenia. During our fieldwork, he would sometimes show on his smartphone some videos sent to him by the foster family in Bosnia with whom he was staying. He often said that they accepted him as their own son. They kept in touch and communicated regularly via smartphones.

> *'Look,' he said. He showed us a short video of police violence against migrants that showed two migrants and four police officers. 'My Bosnian family sent this to me. They live right on the border and they filmed it from the window of their house.'*
> (Field notes)

During the fieldwork, we tried to talk to a young Arabic-speaking boy who did not know English, while none of us spoke Arabic. The problem was quickly solved by using Google translate. Soon we had a discussion on the smartphone, and any question written in English was immediately converted into the Arabic language. Similarly, migrant youth used the possibilities for translating websites. ICT thus also plays an important role as a communication aid. Other functions, such as location sharing or Google Maps, were used, for example, to determine the location of a meeting with a friend who lives in the asylum centre in Ljubljana. Moreover, ICT can be seen as one of the coping strategies in the context of forced migration, including in cases where there is a lack of information and connections to relatives and the uncertainty and challenges associated with this (Kutscher and Kreß, 2018).

ICT for Planning the Journey, Self-Empowerment and Self-Assertion

ICT also plays an important role in the well-being of migrant youth in transition. It enables migrant children to exercise agency and self-empowerment through various activities such as storytelling or posting online (Pottie *et al.*, 2020). One example of such activity is vlogging - posting short videos on YouTube. A young asylum seeker from Western Sahara shared his vlog, which he started two years ago when setting out for Europe. Every few months, he posts a video intended for his friends and other interested viewers, documenting his journey, commenting, and offering advice. He shares videos of his journey, including walking through the forest, camping, and finally arriving at the destination. This platform allows him to express himself and gives him the feeling of having achieved something, which is reflected in the titles of the vlogs, such as: 'Finally arrived at the gates of Europe, EU Slovenia, after 15 days of suffering in the forest.' In the vlogs, he portrays himself as a tough, brave and successful young man pursuing his dream of a better future. He also sees his future in video making. In this way, social media can influence migrants and refugees in their decision-making by offering information, stories, and images about destinations and routes, etc. (Frouws *et al.*, 2016).

The time spent in the asylum home was also used by the youth to plan the rest of their journey, again using applications and social media such as Facebook, Twitter, WhatsApp, Skype, Viber, Google Maps, and some other map applications. One informant showed the map application with his route to Slovenia signed and showed the exact point where he was caught and taken to the asylum home. He also explained what his future plans to travel across the borders are and showed the route he plans to use. Some young people were in contact with smugglers who organised their trips, referring to the future transport as 'TAXI'. A young asylum seeker from Pakistan explained that he planned to leave the next day for Milan and later to Paris:

The boss will call me at 2 p.m. And then we'll see.

In addition to information about destinations and routes, ICT is a source of information for solving concrete issues and current problems of young people in transition. For example, a young couple from Morocco who was expecting a child was looking for information about different organizations in Slovenia or Italy that could help them organise their lives after the birth of their child.

From another perspective, ICT offered a source of empowerment for young asylum seekers, including through the trade business that developed around the purchase of SIM cards, smartphones, etc., for migrants who were detained and not allowed to leave the premises. In fact, the asylum home is divided into two parts. The movement restricted part for those who have not (yet) applied for international protection and the part for those who have already applied and have more freedom of movement. Since there is no possibility of buying anything in the facility, trade developed between the two groups. Applicants for international protection often went to a shop in the village and, for a fee, bought food, drinks, cigarettes and very often cell phones, SIM cards, etc., for those who had no possibility to go out. In this way, they earned some extra money and gained a special status among their peers.

It is also important to emphasise what Mancini *et al.* (2019) argued in their review study, that ICT can become both a vehicle of hope for migrant youth, reinforced by transnational digital connections through co-presence, but also a vehicle of despair, as they can communicate bad news such as deaths, wars, and reports of the loss of fellow refugees.

Conclusion

Dekker *et al.* (2018) refer to today's refugees as 'smart' refugees who use smartphones to develop 'smart' migration strategies. This chapter has shown the many ways in which ICTs are used by young migrants in places in-between, liminal, and transitional. In their everyday lives in transition, ICT technology is used to pass the time and as a source of information. ICT also plays an important role in maintaining contact with family and building new connections. It is used to reflect on the past and to plan future travel activities. In addition, it provides opportunities for the exercise of empowerment and self-assertion. As previously noted, Gough and Gough (2019) argue that Wi-Fi and smartphones bring comfort and a sense of familiarity that enables connections with family and friends during the transitional asylum phase, but also later ICTs and smartphones in particular, continue to play an important role in building a new life and maintaining transnational connections at the same time. The question, however, is whether the state of transition ever ends. According to Kanics (2015), even when unaccompanied minors reach their final destination, they often face multiple system restraints in securing a durable solution that would ensure young people transition into adulthood in a way that meets their needs.

Our research represents a small part of the broad research area that requires further active and participatory research, including topics such as the role of ICT in the integration of migrant children and the negative aspects and risks associated with ICT use.

References

Agier, M. 2016. *Borderlands: Towards an Anthropology of the Cosmopolitan Condition.* Chichester: John Wiley and Sons.

Appadurai, A. 1996. *Modernity at large: cultural dimensions of globalization.* Minneapolis: University of Minnesota Press.

Albanski, L. 2020. 'Shattered spaces of migrant childhood: Camps, borders and uncertain status'. *International Sociology Reviews,* Vol. 35(5), pp. 480–486.

Albanski, L. 2020. *Socjologia dzieciństwa: dyskusja nad pozycją dziecka w socjologii. Studia Edukacyjne.* 73-88. 10.14746/se.2017.46

Atalan, E. D., Akgül, G., Güney K. N. 2021. 'Ethnic-based cyberbullying: The role of adolescents' and their peers' attitudes towards immigrants'. *Turkish Journal of Education,* Vol. 10 (2), pp-139-156. Viewed 3.2.22 from https://dergipark.org.tr/en/download/article-file/1573950

Boyd, D. 2008. *Taken out of context. American teen sociality in networked publics.* Doctoral dissertation. Berkeley: University of California.

Boyd, D. 2014. *It's complicated: The social lives of networked teens.* New Haven: Yale University Press.

Caravita, S. *et al.* 2019. 'When the bullied peer is native-born vs. immigrant: A mixed-method study with a sample of native-born and immigrant adolescents'. *Scandinavian Journal of Psychology.* 61. 10.1111/sjop.12565

Collyer, M. 2010. 'Stranded Migrants and the Fragmented Journey'. *Journal of Refugee Studies* Vol. 23, No. 3, pp. 273-293.

Crawley, H. and Jones, K. 2020. 'Beyond here and there: (re)conceptualizing migrant journeys and the ´in-between´'. *Journal of Ethnic and Migration Studies.* 47. 1-17. 10.1080/1369183X.2020.1804190

Dale, K. and Burrell, G. 2008. *The Spaces of Organisation and the Organisation of Space: Power, Identity and Materiality at Work.* London: Palgrave Macmillan.

Dekker, R. *et al.* 2018. 'Smart refugees: how Syrian asylum migrants use social media information in migration decision-making'. *Social Media Soc.* pp. 1–11.

Denzin, N., K., Lincoln, Y. S. 2011. *The Sage Handbook of Qualitative Research.* London: Sage Publication.

Diminescu, D. 2008. 'The connected migrant: an epistemological manifesto'. *Migrants and clandestinity* 47/4, pp. 565-579.

European Political Strategy Centre. 2017. '10 trends shaping migration. European Union'. Viewed 3.2.22 from https://ec.europa.eu/home-affairs/sites/default/files/10_trends_shaping_migration.pdf

Fine, G. A., Sandstrom, K. L. 1999. *Knowing Children: Participant Observation with Minors.* Newbury Park, CA: SAGE.

Fortunati, L., Pertierra, R., and Vincent, J. 2012. 'Introduction: migrations and diasporas-making their world elsewhere'. In: Fortunati, L., Pertierra, R., & Vincent, J. (Eds.). *Migration, diaspora, and information technology in global societies* (p. 1-15). New York: Routledge.

Frouws, B. *et al.* 2016. 'Getting to Europe the WhatsApp way: the use of ICT in contemporary mixed migration flows to Europe'. *Regional mixed migration secretariat briefing paper.*

Genova, E., Zontini, E. 2020. *Liminal Lives: Navigating In-Betweenness in the Case of Bulgarian and Italian Migrants in Brexiting Britain.* Ośrodek Badań nad Migracjami: Uniwersytet Warszawski.

Goffman, E. 1959. *The presentation of self in everyday life.* New York: Anchor Books.

Gough, H. A., & Gough, K. V. 2019. *Disrupted becomings: The role of smartphones in Syrian refugees' physical and existential journeys.* Geoforum, 105, 89-98.

Ito, M. *et al.* 2010. *Hanging out, messing around and geeking out. Kids living and learning with new media.* Cambridge Massachussetts: The MIT Press.

Kanics, J. 2015. 'Ensuring Respect for the Best Interests of Children on the Move in Europe,' *Presentation at International Conference Children and Young People on the Move: Towards a More Precise Definition of their Best Interests,* 19 - 20th November 2015, Portorož, Slovenia.

Kohli, R. 2014. 'Protecting Asylum Seeking Children on the Move'. *Revue Européenne des Migrations Internationales* 30/1, 83–104.

Kutscher, N. and Kreß, L. 2018. 'The Ambivalent Potentials of Social Media Use by Unaccompanied Minor Refugees'. *Social Media + Society* January-March 2018: 1–10. Viewed 3.2.22 from https://reliefweb.int/sites/reliefweb.int/files/resources/SOWC_2017_ENG_WEB.pdf

Lenarčič, B. 2020. *Migracijski proces v omrežni družbi. Dve domovini: razprave o izseljenstvu,* No. 51, pp. 167-183.

Mancini, T *et al.* 2019. 'The opportunities and risks of mobile phones for refugees' experience': A scoping review. *PLoS ONE* 14(12).

Manjikian, L. 2010. 'Refugee "In-betweennes": A proactive existence'. *Refuge,* Vol 27. No. 1, pp. 50-58.

Mayeza, E. 2017. 'Doing child-Centreed ethnography: Unravelling the complexities of reducing the perceptions of adult male power during fieldwork' *International Journal of Qualitative Methods,* 16, 1–10.

Pérez, M., and Salgado, M. 2019. 'Mobility and the mobile: A study of adolescent migrants and their use of the mobile phone'. *Mobile Media & Communication* 1–20.

Mesec, B. 1998. 'Uvod v kvalitativno raziskovanje v socialnem delu'. *Introduction to the qualitative research in social work.* Ljubljana: Visoka šola za socialno delo.

Ministrstvo za notranje zadeve 2020. *Poročilo o delu direktorata za migracije za leto 2020.* Viewed 3.2.22 from https://www.gov.si/assets/ministrstva/MNZ/Dokumenti/DM/Maj-2021/Porocilo-o-delu-Direktorata-za-migracije-za-leto-2020.pdf

Mueller, C. 2019. 'Discussing Mobility in Liminal Spaces and Border Zones. An Analysis of Abbas Kidder's Der falsche Inder (2008) und Brief in die Auberginenrepublik (2013)'. Textpraxis. *Digitales Journal für Philologie # 17.*

Viewed 3.2.22 from https://www.textpraxis.net/carolin-mueller-discussing-mobility-in-liminal-spaces-andborder-Zones

Nabergoj, M. and Regvar, U. 20202. *Asylum Information Database: Country report Slovenia.* AIDA-SI_2020update.pdf (asylumineurope.org)

Nimo-Ilhan, A. 2016. *Going on Tahriib: The causes and consequences of Somali youth migration to Europe.* Published by the Rift Valley Institute, Viewed 3.2.22 from https://www.refworld.org/docid/57e92d114.html

Noussia, A., Lyons, M. 2009. 'Inhabiting Spaces of Liminality: Migrants in Omonia', Athens. *Journal of Ethnic and Migration Studies,* Vol. 35 (4), pp. 601-624.

Paynter, E. 2018. 'The Liminal Lives of Europe's Transit Migrants.'. *Contexts,* 17(2), 40–45. https://doi.org/10.1177/1536504218776959

Pottie, K., Ratnayake, A., Ahmed, R. *et al.* 2020. How refugee youth use social media: what does this mean for improving their health and welfare?;. *J Public Health Pol* 41, 268–278 (2020). https://doi.org/10.1057/s41271-020-00231-4

Rosenau, J. 2003. *Distant proximities: Dynamics beyond globalization.* Princeton, NJ: Princeton University Press.

Schapendonk, J. 2012. 'Migrants' Im/Mobilities on Their Way to the EU: Lost in Transit?' *Journal of Economics and Social Geography,* 103(5), 577–583.

UNICEF 2017. 'Children in a Digital World'. Published by *UNICEF Division of Communication,* New York. Viewed 3.2.22 from https://www.unicef.org/media/48601/file#:~:text=Youth%20(ages%2015%E2%80%9324),internet%20users%20around%20the%20world

Waardenburg, M. *et al.* 2018. 'Sport in liminal spaces: The meaning of sport activities for refugees living in a reception centre'. *International Review for the Sociology of Sport* 1–19.

Witteborn, S. 2015. 'Becoming (Im)Perceptible: Forced Migrants and Virtual Practice'. *Journal of Refugee Studies,* Volume 28, Issue 3, September 2015, pp. 350–367.

Zavratnik, S., & Krilić, S. C. 2018. *Digital Routes, »Digital Migrants«: From Empowerment to Control Over Refugees' Digital Footprints.* Družboslovne Razprave, 34(89), pp. 143-163.

Zhao, S. 2003. *Toward a taxonomy of copresence.* Presence 12/5, 445–455. Viewed 3.2.22 from http://astro.temple.edu/~bzhao001/Taxonomy_Copresence.pdf (12.9.2019)

Žakelj, Tjaša & Lenarčič, Blaž. 2017. Determination of the Best Interest of Unaccompanied Minors in Slovenia. Dve domovini / Two Homelands. 45. 79-95. 10.3986/dd.2017.1.06.

Chapter 5

Human Rights and the Reception of Unaccompanied Children: The Holistic Model of 'Homes for Hope' in Cyprus

Dialechti Chatzoudi

University of Cyprus, Cyprus

Abstract

Taking into account the vulnerability of unaccompanied children, the shelters 'Homes for Hope' in Cyprus were established and function through the scope of the UN Convention on the Rights of the Child. Specifically, the reception of unaccompanied children focuses on the CRC's basic concepts of provision, protection, and participation in children's rights. Thus, the shelters work through a holistic model and provide multidisciplinary services, combining the aspect of good practices and the country context. These services include rehabilitation, integration, and durable solutions strategies. The support provided goes beyond the basic needs of care (nutrition, clothing, medical care) and includes specialized services: a) educational opportunities, life skills training, and leisure activities; b) legal counselling and support on asylum procedures, challenging of negative decisions, family tracing and reunifications, return procedures, trafficking etc.; c) social orientation counselling, including social welfare, employment opportunities, vocational training, school records, etc.; and d) psychological assessment and individualized psychological support, psychoeducational prevention programmes, as well as crises interventions. This chapter focuses on the example of the psychological services provided to unaccompanied minors, relevant challenges, good practices, and recommendations.

Keywords: Human rights, reception, unaccompanied children, Cyprus

***

Introduction

According to the European Migration Network Glossary and the Art. 2(l) of Directive 2011/95/EU, an Unaccompanied Minor (UAM) is defined as a minor (usually considered as a person under 18 years old, unless a national law defines majority differently) who arrives on the territory of an EU Member unaccompanied by the adult responsible for them by law or by the practice of the EU Member State concerned, and for as long as they are not effectively taken into the care of such a person; or who is left unaccompanied after they have entered the territory of the EU Member State.

Unaccompanied minors are an especially vulnerable social group, as they are, by definition, away from their homeland and separated from their parents or guardians. The majority of them are usually forced to leave their countries having experienced extreme conditions of violence, such as war, exploitation, abductions, torture, and deprivation of access to basic needs and education (Menjívar and Perreira, 2019). Most of these children travel under difficult conditions and often endanger their lives. They are exposed to unhealthy and stressful conditions, rely on smugglers, and sometimes have to work in order to cover needed costs for travelling (Bolborici, 2018), and they often experience violence (UNICEF, 2017). Finally, even upon arrival in the host country, unaccompanied minors have to deal with adaptation to a new culture and community, adjustment to living without their family, stay in unsafe reception centres (Menjívar and Perreira, 2019), as well as with the consequences of traumatic migration experiences (UNICEF, 2017).

Taking into account the hardships unaccompanied minors go through at such a sensitive age, it can be recognized that they are a special category of children in terms of their needs for protection and care. This is in line with Article 22 of the UN Convention on the Rights of the Child (UNCRC, 1989), which considers children seeking asylum and refugee status (either accompanied or unaccompanied) in need to receive 'appropriate protection and humanitarian assistance' towards the assurance of enjoying their applicable rights as children. Especially in cases of unaccompanied children, the Convention raises the responsibility of member States to take action towards the protection of such a child and possible reunification with family members. Additionally, according to the Article 20 of the Convention, children who have been separated from or deprived of their family 'shall be entitled to special protection and assistance', and it is the State's responsibility to ensure alternative care for such children. Thus, migration is pointed out as a life experience calling for specialized care for children, in addition to the general rights that apply to all children without discrimination.

According to the above UNCRC recommendations, a special need arises to respect and promote unaccompanied minors' rights and focus on the provision of appropriate tailor-made services to this population. Taking into account this increased need, provision should include a combination of multifaceted services regarding basic survival needs (food, clothing, medical care, residence), education, recreational activities and play social inclusion, and mental health. Especially due to the vulnerability factors before, during, and after migration, as described above, mental health services turn out to be a core of the provisions required for unaccompanied minors. However, this consists of a complicated endeavour, as initial recent evidence shows that asylum seekers and refugees in the EU do not broadly use psychosocial support, although they tend to exhibit a higher need for these kind of services (Satinsky *et al.*, 2019).

History of the Issue/Problem

The unaccompanied minors' migration has been a recent years' history issue, mainly recognized during the last decade since 2011. Looking further at the longitudinal pathway of the issue, it is developing into an increasingly prevalent phenomenon both worldwide and at a European level. Ferrara *et al.* (2016) pointed out that during the first years of the phenomenon of unaccompanied children's lonely routes to migration, they were rendered as 'invisible children' to the authorities and the public, increasing the likelihood of abandoning the reception centres and even going missing. Only recently, after 2013, literature and research have started focusing on the issue of unaccompanied minors through social, legal, medical, and psychological perspectives (Migliorini, Rania, and Varani, 2019), showing the need for more specific investigation of their profile, and subsequent needs and required interventions. Finally, 2015 was a milestone in the history of unaccompanied minors' migration, as a peak in the number of unaccompanied children applying for asylum in Europe resulted in the public recognition of unaccompanied children as a 'crisis figure' (Lems, Oester and Strasser, 2020).

Statistical data from the European Commission Eurostat database indeed indicate such a huge increase in unaccompanied children seeking asylum in the EU, comparing 11690 unaccompanied minors in 2011 to 95205 unaccompanied minors in 2015. After 2015, a trend of decreased numbers can be observed, most probably reflecting more accurate or strict procedures in order to consider a minor as unaccompanied (e.g. age assessment examination) rather than a significant decrease in migration flows. Even during 2019 and 2020, the COVID-19 pandemic imposed obstacles in migration, as there is a high number of minors considered unaccompanied in the EU (a total of 14115 and 13550, respectively, according to the Eurostat database).

As far as the respective situation in Cyprus is concerned, an increasing pattern in the numbers of unaccompanied minors per year is recorded. According to the Eurostat database, Cyprus received only 15 unaccompanied minors back in 2011, while this number has increased on an annual basis, reaching 260 children in 2018 and more than double this number in 2019 (specifically 565 unaccompanied minors). There is also a stable pattern in the gender and age of unaccompanied minors in Cyprus, with the majority being boys (70-80% on average) and in the age range of 16-17 years old (80-85% on average of all UAM regardless of gender).

The statistical data depicting the flows of unaccompanied children in both the EU and Cyprus profoundly shed light on the need to accordingly design the reception conditions for this group of children. Although reception centres or camps are a common practice in many countries in Europe, vulnerable groups, such as unaccompanied minors, should stay in such settings only for very short periods of time, under the highest standards of living possible, and be transferred soon to appropriate settings (e.g. protected shelters or foster care) (Bolborici, 2018). Even more, when considering alternative solutions for the care of separated children, according to the Article 20 of the Convention on the Rights of the Child, 'due regard shall be paid to the desirability of continuity in a child's upbringing and to the child's ethnic, religious, cultural and linguistic background'. In order to design child-centred shelters suitable for unaccompanied children, states should also get guidance from the three general categories of children's rights, according to the UN Convention on the Rights of the Child, also known as the 'three Ps'. These categories refer to *Protection*: ensuring children's safety from dangers, abuse, and exploitation. *Provision*: covering children's needs, offering specialized services, and *Participation*: promoting active involvement of children in matters that are important in their lives (Flowers *et al*, 2009).

Although the increased flows of unaccompanied children in Cyprus are quite recent, there is a tendency to apply good practices according to the above children's rights approach. There is a First Reception Center, where all asylum seekers stay upon their arrival in Cyprus, and then vulnerable groups are identified and receive differential treatment. Especially unaccompanied minors are considered vulnerable by default, thus granting transfer to children's shelters. Only during 2020, due to COVID-19 restrictions, unaccompanied children had to stay in the First Reception Center for periods longer than 2-3 months (Asylum Information Database-AIDA report, 2021). In addition, UAM receives legal guardianship by the Social Welfare Services immediately and automatically upon their identification as unaccompanied children, ensuring their timely protection and care. Finally, the prohibition of detention of all asylum-seeking children according to the Refugee Law is respected in Cyprus since, in practice, overall, children are not detained. The only cases reported where unaccompanied children were arrested was in their attempt to leave the country with false/forged documents identifying them as over 18 years old (AIDA report, 2021).

Within this context of protection of unaccompanied minors as a vulnerable social group, the International, Humanitarian, Independent Organization 'Hope For Children' CRC Policy Center in Cyprus operates shelters for unaccompanied minors called 'Homes for Hope', in collaboration with the Social Welfare Services. This setting will be presented in this chapter, as an example of a children's rights-based centre, with an emphasis on its holistic model for the provision of specialized services to unaccompanied minors, in alignment with the CRC. Especially we will focus on the example of the psychological services offered to unaccompanied minors in this setting, as psychological needs emerge as a contemporary and challenging issue, especially for this vulnerable group of children.

Psychological Challenges Unaccompanied Youth Face

As the flow of unaccompanied children is a recent phenomenon, relevant studies examining their psychological difficulties and daily functionality are quite scarce and have been the focus of researchers mainly during the last decade. Some initial evidence for mental health difficulties came from studies engaging general samples of children with migrant or refugee backgrounds without separately taking into account the factor of being accompanied by a parent/guardian or not. A systematic review of relevant studies conducted between 2003 and 2008 (Bronstein and Montgomery, 2011) yielded some evidence that, generally refugee children are at high risk of exhibiting mental health difficulties, including post-traumatic stress, depressive symptoms, and emotional and behavioural issues. These difficulties were connected with high levels of distress stemming from demographic factors (e.g. country of origin), traumatic pre-migration experiences (e.g. separation from family members), and post-migration stressors (e.g. levels of support) (Bronstein and Montgomery, 2011).

After 2011, more and more studies have focused on the group of unaccompanied youth, emphasizing its vulnerability and associated difficulties. Jensen *et al.* (2015) highlighted the connection between severe life events and psychological symptoms exhibition in unaccompanied minors of a wide range of ages (10-16 years old). The most common stressful life events reported by unaccompanied youth were the death of a loved one (67.7%), witnessed physical violence (63.4%), war or armed military conflict (62.4%), drastic changes in the child's family (58.1%), and received physical violence (54.8%). These stressful life events were mostly associated with internalizing psychopathology -Post-Traumatic Stress Disorder (PTSD), depression, and anxiety- and significantly less with externalizing or oppositional behaviour. This is an important finding, indicating not only the basic symptomatology often found in unaccompanied youth but also the need for careful screening and assessments, as internalizing symptoms may stay undiscovered.

Apart from more focused research on the group of unaccompanied youth, a new wave of comparative studies shed light on possible differences in risk factors and subsequent psychological distress between accompanied and unaccompanied asylum-seeking children and the probability of enhanced needs for psychological services for the latter. Recent comparative studies tend to support that unaccompanied youth exhibit higher levels of psychological symptoms than their peers', mainly related to PTSD, depression, anxiety, somatoform disorders, and bereavement (Michelson and Sclare, 2009; Müller et al., 2019; Ramel et al., 2015; Seglem, Oppedal and Roysamb, 2014). There is also initial evidence that it is possible for unaccompanied youth to be hospitalized in inpatient psychiatric care because of self-harming and suicidal behaviours, than for accompanied refugee youth (Ramel et al., 2015).

These increased rates of psychological difficulties in unaccompanied youth seem to be connected to high incidences of traumatic events and daily hassles they experience compared to their peers. Unaccompanied minors are significantly more exposed to traumatic experiences than their accompanied counterparts are. Specifically, they are more likely to have experienced proximity to war, sudden or violent death of a loved one, serious accident or injury, attack, stab, or shot to oneself (Michelson and Sclare, 2009), as well as torture or rape, witnessed killing or serious injury, and a family member murdered or missing (Müller et al., 2019). Additionally, to accumulative traumatic experiences, unaccompanied youth are also more likely to have to deal with daily hassles, leading to increased stress and decreased life satisfaction (Seglem, Oppedal and Roysamb, 2014).

Taking into account all aspects of possible stressors accounting for the higher prevalence of psychological symptoms in unaccompanied youth, Müller et al. (2019) proposed an integrated model of risk factors in mental health difficulties. This holistic model supports a multifactorial approach, including pre-migration and migration risk factors -such as political violence, loss of family and loved ones, adversities while travelling-, post-migration factors - such as acculturative hassles, lack of social support, the experience of discrimination, uncertainty in the asylum process-, and factors not directly connected with migration –such as other types of abuse, and developmental challenges. Such an approach allows for a more precise understanding of how multiple factors can contribute to mental health difficulties, as well as how the combination of more risk factors may lead to increased difficulties.

Moreover, findings from recent research encompassing a longitudinal aspect are alarming as far as the mental health of unaccompanied minors and subsequent needs for psychological interventions are concerned. Not only are unaccompanied minors at high risk for exhibiting mental health difficulties but there is also a tendency to chronic pathways of these difficulties. Follow-up psychological assessments of unaccompanied youth after 18 months (Vervliet *et al.*, 2014), 2 years (Jensen et al., 2019; Jensen, Skårdalsmo, and Fjermestad, 2014), and 5 years (Jensen *et al.*, 2019) since arrival in the host country, have revealed that mental health difficulties, such as depressive symptoms, PTSD, suicidal ideation, somatization, and anxiety, remain at relatively high levels and do not seem to change substantially over time. Again, these studies showed that cumulative traumatic life events and daily stressors determine the persistence of mental health difficulties in the long run, especially in the absence of social support (Jensen *et al.*, 2019).

The above data indicate the need to provide intensive, long-term psychological interventions to unaccompanied minors due to their high risk for persistent mental health difficulties. Nevertheless, a tendency of under-utilisation of mental health services by unaccompanied minors is observed. Even in cases of increased psychological distress and severe post-traumatic stress symptoms, only a small proportion of unaccompanied minors might seek help; in a recent study, Sanchez-Cao, Kramer, and Hodes (2013) identified only 17% of a sample of 71 unaccompanied youth in high risk for PTSD and depression that received mental health services.

Thus, in order to be able to design tailor-made, suitable mental health services for the group of unaccompanied minors, it is necessary to identify possible obstacles to their engagement in therapeutic activities. Taking into account unaccompanied youth's own views on mental health and relevant services, as well as cultural elements of this understanding, may be enlightening. Majumder *et al.* (2015) interviewed 15 unaccompanied adolescents 15-18 years old having experienced the provision of mental health services in the host country, from which the attribution of psychological symptoms to physical causes and a negative view of mental health difficulties emerged. It seems that psychological difficulties still are a taboo topic connected with stigma in non-western cultures, often conceptualized as a dichotomy of either health or illness and connected with negative attitudes (e.g. being 'crazy') (Ellis *et al.*, 2011; Majumder *et al.*, 2015). As a result, there is also a different understanding of appropriate services; unaccompanied minors tend to find medication as a solution (connected with physical causes of mental illness), in contrast to psychotherapy or talking therapies, which they sometimes find difficult because of questions they have to answer or painful memories they have to recall (Majumder *et al.*, 2015).

In addition, there are some systemic and migration-related barriers for unaccompanied minors to engage with mental health services. There is a general mistrust towards authorities, systems, and service providers (Ellis *et al.*,

2011; Majumder *et al.*, 2015), often stemming from their past traumatic experiences with violent governments in the countries of origin and connections with smugglers during migration, jeopardizing their safety. Such mistrust is enhanced through the development of misconceptions of relations between mental health and other (e.g. legal) services (for example, believing that because of psychological difficulties, there is a risk of deportation) (Majumder *et al.*, 2015). Moreover, language barriers in communication and the existence of daily matters that unaccompanied youth have to deal with for their adaptation to the new social environment are important factors affecting access to or the prioritization of receiving mental health services (Ellis et al., 2011).

In view of the high resistance of unaccompanied youth to receive mental health services, professionals need to pay a lot of attention to the suitability of the settings where such services are provided. The provision of mental health services can be facilitated through the increase of some characteristics of services, such as availability, accessibility, child-friendliness, and cultural competence. These aspects of mental health services can reduce the associated stigma and make youth feel more comfortable. Fazel, Garcia and Alan Stein (2016) suggest that community-based mental health services, connected with other services, such as educational, social, and legal services, provide non-threatening and convenient locations for refugee adolescents to accept such services. From interviews they conducted with refugee adolescents, a preference for the school setting instead of a clinic or hospital setting emerged. Thus, professionals and carers working with unaccompanied youth have to deal with the responsibility and challenge of identifying their needs to encourage connection with mental health services in a way they will feel supported and not stigmatized.

The 'Homes for Hope' Example

'Hope For Children' CRC Policy Center is an International Humanitarian and Independent Institution based in Nicosia, Cyprus. It is established on the standards and principles of the UN Convention on the Rights of the Child and the European Union Law. It works on humanitarian and development policies relevant to the defence and promotion of children's rights. It does so through research, grassroots program design and implementation, and advisory services offered to governments and international organizations. The operation of the organization is founded on the principle of promoting and protecting the rights of children. This is achieved through the implementation of a variety of projects on a National, European and Global level.

The shelter 'Homes for Hope' falls under the Humanitarian Division of 'Hope For Children' CRC Policy Center and operate in close collaboration with the Social Welfare Services, the Director of which is the legal guardian of the unaccompanied children in Cyprus. The shelters are co-funded by the Asylum, Migration and Integration Fund (90%) and the Republic of Cyprus (10%).

'Homes for Hope's' intention is to provide unaccompanied children with more than just accommodation. They set up to provide multi-disciplinary and holistic services to children, which would cover all aspects of their daily lives and attend to their needs to the fullest extent possible, with a special focus on psycho-social support and legal guidance to unaccompanied children. This was designed in alignment with the CRC concepts of children's rights to protection, provision, and participation. More specifically, the goal of the shelters is to provide: (1) Effective protection and safety of the children, (2) Specialized legal services, (3) Ongoing psychosocial support and counselling, (4) Mechanisms of durable solutions for family tracing, assessment and reunification, (5) Smooth integration into the reception or host country, reintegration into the country of origin or a third country, (6) Provision of assistance in the transition period from adolescence to adulthood, (7) Coordinated and comprehensive assessment of the background of every child, and (8) an individualized approach to the services and support each minor needs. All these goals are planned in accordance with both professionals' assessments and the minors' points of view, promoting a collaborative and participatory model of services.

Interdisciplinary and Holistic Services

The 'Homes for Hope' shelters provide their services based on models that are considered good practice and are adjusted to Cyprus context and standards. The services model applied at the shelters draws from systemic views and holistic, integrated approaches and has gone through appropriate changes since the beginning of its operation based on evaluations of what works best. The referral of the children to the shelters is always done by the Director of the Social Welfare Services, who is the legal guardian of unaccompanied children in Cyprus, according to the National Law. Thus, the services to the children are provided through the close cooperation and monitoring of the Social Welfare Services. Additionally, external partners and volunteers support the educational and recreational activities provided at the shelters.

The services provided are grouped under three main pillars that form the operating mechanism of the shelters:

A) Rehabilitation Services

- Intake of social history / personal care plan
- Assisting in the procedure of age assessment

- Legal and social counselling services
- Psychological support/counselling and therapy (where deemed necessary, based on assessments)

B) Integration Services

- Legal and social counselling services
- Psychological support
- Language classes (Greek, English, etc.)
- Educational Activities (art, drama, dance, etc.)
- Educational Seminars (sexual education, human rights, anger management, hygiene, vaccinations, etc.)
- Supporting access to the public education system
- Assisting access to education
- Access to private schools through scholarships.

C) Durable Solution Services

- Family tracing and assessment, the possibility of family reunification with relatives in other EU member state (Dublin Regulation) and/or of voluntary return to the country of origin
- Exploring the possibility of placement in foster care
- Legal and social counselling services
- Psychological support/therapy
- Support during the procedures for integration into the community during the transition to adulthood.

'Homes for Hope' provide the services mentioned above by incorporating different roles and specializations in a multidisciplinary professional team. This approach is based on the notion that unaccompanied minors are a vulnerable social group in need of holistic, multifaceted services and special protection and care, as well as that all the needs and connected services are interrelated. For example, the asylum procedure is a factor contributing to the daily stress of the minors, thus, it leads not only to the need for legal guidance but at the same time to the need for psychological support.

The multidisciplinary team at 'Homes for Hope' consist of four main groups of professionals working together as an integral system: the Support Officers, the Child Protection Department, the Social Work Department, and the Psychology Department. The whole team is based at the shelters and works daily in close collaboration with the legal guardians assigned to the children by the Social Welfare Services (based on an external governmental setting). The

Support Officers are responsible for the 24/7 care of the minors residing at the shelter and monitoring the individualized needs of each minor so that they can proceed to the appropriate connections to the rest of the services. For the facilitation of this procedure, the role of the *Personal Officer* has been established; each minor is assigned a Personal Officer who functions as a focal point that is aware and in charge of them, so they will not be asked to repeat their wishes, wants and needs to multiple persons. The *Child Protection Department* provides legal counselling and support on asylum procedures, challenging negative decisions, family tracing and reunifications, return procedures, trafficking, etc. The *Social Work Department* offers social orientation counselling, including social welfare procedures, employment opportunities, vocational training, school records, etc. Finally, the *Psychology Department* is accountable for providing mental health services tailored to the individual needs of each child residing at the shelter. In addition to the professional team, there are also complimentary staff members supporting the cleaning, hygiene, and building maintenance of the shelters.

All the professional staff working at the shelters hold University degrees in social sciences, as well as extra specializations according to the specific Department they are assigned to. In addition to their academic background, they receive ongoing education and training in order to work according to up-to-date good practices. Moreover, all professionals working at 'Homes for Hope' are committed to following specific policies regarding the Protection of Children, the Protection of Personal Data and Confidentiality, the Code of Conduct, the Dress Code, as well as the Internal Procedures of the shelters. All these policies are designed to meet the criteria of best practices and services in order to serve in the best possible way the needs and the best interest of children and ensure the safety of the staff members and the smooth operation of the shelters. All professionals working at 'Homes for Hope' receive daily guidance and check-in one-to-one meetings by the respective Coordinator of their Department. They also participate in weekly Staff Meetings, where they can share their views on dealing with specific cases and/or challenges at the workplace. Finally, the Organization provides the shelters' staff with monthly group supervision with an external partner-psychologist, aiming at working through difficulties in the working environment and preventing burnout and secondary traumatization. The above-mentioned practices of staff management are in accordance with the trauma-informed principles of Safety, Trustworthiness, Choice, Collaboration, and Empowerment, suggested by The Institute on Trauma and Trauma-Informed Care (2020), as the challenges of working in a setting with a vulnerable population are recognized.

The Model of Psychological Services

The psychological services provided at the 'Homes for Hope' shelters consist of an integral part of the holistic model, always operating in conjunction with the rest of the services and activities offered to unaccompanied youth. The mental health services are designed and provided by the Psychology Department, and they are located in-house so that they are easily accessed and almost constantly available in a friendly and culturally sensitive environment, reducing the stigma of medical models of mental health services. Psychological services include not only direct, face-to-face interventions with the children but even more, they inform all practices applied at the shelters so that all actions contribute to the enhancement of mental health. This is in line with research findings suggesting that indirect interventions, such as engagement in daily activities and sports, socialization, and integration through language acquisition, affect the mental health condition of unaccompanied youth (Müller et al., 2019).

In addition, not all asylum-seeking children require personal therapy; thus, enhanced care and protection, as well as a focus on the development of their cognitive capacity, personal resources, coping and goal-setting skills, emotion regulation strategies, and acculturation processes, may play a significant role in children's adjustment and resilience (El-Awad *et al.*, 2017; Jensen *et al.*, 2015). Thus, the model of psychological services at 'Homes for Hope' simulates a primary support program, promoting mental health and adaptation for unaccompanied youth both with the need for individual therapy and with sub-clinical symptoms, not fulfilling criteria for a disorder diagnosis (El-Awad *et al.*, 2017).

Following a rights-based approach in implementing services for unaccompanied youth, we have addressed some barriers to receiving mental health services reported by Ellis *et al.* (2011) so that they are utilized to the maximum extent possible. Specifically, we have settled the psychological services inside the shelters, run by the independent Organization 'Hope For Children' CRC Policy Center, and separated from governmental authorities or public medical services, so that we reduce the effect of distrust of authority as well as the stigma of mental health services. In addition, the model of 'Homes for Hope' shows respect to the refugee view that resettlement factors have a primary priority, thus, it encompasses the integration of basic needs and care, social, psychological, and legal services altogether. Finally, linguistic and cultural barriers are taken into account in the provision of psychological (as well as all other connected services in the holistic model), and they are addressed through collaborations with interpreters and cultural mediators.

Within the psychological services, an integrative model of relevant services is used in accordance with the broader holistic model of 'Homes for Hope'. Psychological services are addressed to all residents at the shelters, focusing not only on individual therapy of severe cases but also even more on prevention and promotion of everyone's well-being.

Assessment: A psychological assessment is conducted for every new admission at the shelters as part of the individual care plan. Psychologists, along with Social Workers, are responsible for creating care plans for each resident. The care plan consists of two main parts: the social history of the minor and the psychological assessment, leading to specific individual goals to be achieved. This initial psychological assessment is the first step to evaluating the mental health condition of each minor, and then it is updated with new information and follow-up data during the whole period that the minor stays in the shelter. The psychological assessment is conducted mainly with clinical interviews, including the evaluation of the most common psychological difficulties identified in the literature and allowing for a more comfortable personal narration. Each psychologist is informed about the social history of the child (received by the social worker) before the psychological assessment so that they can identify associated risk and protective factors, as well as avoid repeated questions that could re-traumatize the child. Each case is assigned a specific Psychologist so that there is trust and consistency in the therapeutic relationship and care.

Multi-Disciplinary Meetings and Consultation: Apart from the services psychologists offer to the shelters' residents, they also provide their colleagues with a consultation so that all everyday practices conform to a trauma-informed psychosocial approach (in accordance with Papadopoulos, 2019, and The Institute on Trauma and Trauma-Informed Care, 2020 recommendations). In addition, these consultations contribute to handling difficult cases as well as to dealing with and modifying challenging behaviours. Psychologists also hold an integral role in the multi-disciplinary team of the shelters; along with social workers and the personal officer of each minor, they are responsible for conducting multidisciplinary meetings every three (3) months in collaboration with the child's legal guardian, as to set a holistic plan and check if the individual goals are met.

Individual Psychological Support: Psychologists engage in individual psychoeducational and psychotherapeutic meetings with minors. They design tailor-made therapeutic plans for each minor based on issues and needs identified in the psychological assessment, as well as on possible changes in circumstances, behaviour, daily functioning, or mood, as observed by the professional team working at the shelters. While the psychological interventions' priority is to be individualized, psychologists also focus on following evidence-based practices, although there is still only a limited number of effectiveness studies for psychotherapeutic approaches that work with the group of migrants, especially unaccompanied youth. Psychologists at 'Homes for Hope' mainly utilize systemic, cognitive behavioural and trauma-focused cognitive behavioural approaches, for which there is some initial evidence that they are appropriate (Alvarez and Alegría, 2016; Friedberg *et al.*, 2016; Unterhitzenberger *et al.*, 2015). Aspects of play, arts, and the use of unconventional spaces (i.e. outside the typical office of a psychologist) are often incorporated to create a child-friendly, non-stigmatizing environment. Special attention is paid to applying psychological interventions within a solid framework of high ethical standards and cultural sensitivity.

Rehabilitation Meetings: Psychologists of the shelters engage in so-called rehabilitation meetings with the minors during the last months before they reach adulthood (completing 18 years of age). These meetings are complimentary to the rehabilitation workshops conducted by social workers, which focus on social welfare procedures, housing, educational, and vocational opportunities. The aim of psychologists' rehabilitation meetings is to help the minor adapt to the transition to adulthood, to allow them to express their feelings and possible worries, and to learn how to deal with life changes.

System-Level Prevention: Apart from utilizing clinical interviews for psychological assessment purposes, the fact that psychologists are located inside the shelters gives the opportunity to use everyday behavioural observations as an effective preventative measure. Observation of everyday behaviour is of great importance to identify potential psychological risk factors (e.g. a minor's sudden isolated behaviour might be the result of bullying), social interactions among the children and the function of systemic dynamics. Based on observation, psychologists can also prevent harmful behaviours (e.g. eating disorders) and intervene early on before difficulties reach clinical levels. In addition to daily observations, psychologists use psychoeducational, experiential techniques; they prepare and execute workshops in the shelter and the community in order to prevent situations such as violence or drug abuse, and at the same time, empower minors to develop their skills (e.g. empathy, emotion regulation, communication). Prevention activities follow a holistic, system-level approach, as they also include and engage the rest of the team professionals, as well as external partners.

Crisis Intervention: The Psychology Department is responsible to guide and support the whole professional team of the 'Homes for Hope' on how to handle cases of crises, what approaches to use in the moment of crisis, follow-up discussions, and how to utilize self-care in order to stay resilient. Within this scope, the Psychology Department has created a manual with directions and good practices on crisis interventions inside the shelter, and the Coordinator of the Department offers relevant training to all team members working with unaccompanied minors. Psychologists are responsible for acting first in cases of crises and to engage colleagues at the same time.

Referrals: Although integrated psychological services are designed and offered in-house at the 'Homes for Hope', there is a provision for referrals to external services when deemed necessary for the protection and individualized care of a child. In such cases, the shelter's psychologist collaborates with the minor's legal guardian, who then acts as a liaison with community-based services. For example, in unexpected serious incidents (e.g., a manic episode), very severe psychopathology (e.g., psychotic symptoms), or cases of imminent danger for a minor or for others (e.g., self-destructive or uncontrollable aggressive behaviour), a referral may be needed for psychiatric assessment and additive interventions, such as pharmacotherapy or hospitalization. The shelter's psychologist supports the relevant procedures by providing other mental health professionals with available reports and history of the minor's mental health condition, as well as contributing to informing the minor about these procedures in a child-friendly manner.

Mapping the Future of Services Provided to UAM

In light of the principles of the UN Convention on the Rights of the Child, especially the main concepts of protection, provision, and participation, as well as the vulnerability of unaccompanied minors, the holistic model of 'Homes for Hope' in Cyprus proposes a good practice, applicable and transferable to other protective settings for unaccompanied youth. Its multidisciplinary nature and the central role of the provision of professional services in-house contribute to multifaceted, easily accessible, high-quality care. The way the psychological services are designed and offered within this holistic model serves as a good example of a rights-centred, child-friendly, culturally sensitive approach that is very promising in overcoming usual barriers that keep unaccompanied minors away from these services, despite their increased need for mental health interventions.

Since the issue of unaccompanied minors' flows and reception in host countries is recent, and relevant research regarding their needs for mental health services are still limited. It is expected that within the next years, more good practices will be tried, enriched, and lend support for their effectiveness. Taking into account the existing literature on psychological difficulties unaccompanied youth face and challenges in implementing appropriate mental health services for this population, as well as our professional experience from the 'Homes for Hope', we anticipate that future endeavours in services provision may incorporate an increased focus on resilience, trauma-informed practices, and cultural awareness.

   Although post-traumatic stress is very common and persistent in unaccompanied youth, and there is a need to provide relevant interventions, it is crucial, at the same time, to identify the strengths these minors exhibit. Despite the cumulative stressors they have been experiencing from their country of origin through the migration route until the adaptation to the host country, it seems that they are still able to gain a sense of contentment and well-being, maybe by realizing that they managed to survive (Seglem, Oppedal, and Roysamb, 2014). Thus, instead of focusing only on traumatic experiences, professionals and researchers should also seek protective factors predicting unaccompanied minors' adaptation longitudinally (Jensen *et al.*, 2015). This allows for a shift from dealing with difficulties to developing psychological resilience, which refers to keeping and/or gaining some positive characteristics or outcomes in the face of adversity. This is a very promising approach, as resilience is not an inherent trait, but it can emerge with support and take the form of adversity-activated development (Papadopoulos, 2019).

   Taking into account both difficulties and strengths, trauma-informed practices in protection settings for unaccompanied minors may enhance their daily functioning and adaptation. Thus, professionals and systems working with unaccompanied youth should aim at incorporating five basic principles in their practice: 1) *safety-* inspiring both physical and emotional security and reducing triggers for trauma-related reactions; 2) *trustworthiness-* establishing appropriate professional and consistent boundaries, as well as giving explanations in a simple language; 3) *choice-* promoting the child's participation in decision making and providing options when possible; 4) *collaboration-* including children's views on their care plan and therapeutic activities; and 5) *empowerment-* recognizing the minor's abilities and enhancing skills development (The Institute on Trauma and Trauma-Informed Care, 2020). This model is consistent with the resilience perspective and the rights-based approach of protection-provision-participation.

   Finally, future services provision to unaccompanied minors could include more cultural awareness elements, leading to increased acceptance and utilization, especially of mental health services. Since unaccompanied youth tend to report difficulties in answering many questions or responding to talking therapies (Majumder *et al.*, 2015), alternative strategies need to be added. Standardization of brief psychometric tools in samples of unaccompanied minors with different cultural and linguistic backgrounds could assist in the psychological assessments' effectiveness and validity. In the psychological interventions, engaging non-verbal techniques, such as play and art therapy, could minimize minors' sense of being threatened or exposed and reduce psychological symptoms simultaneously (Ugurlu, Akca and Acarturk, 2016).

Overall, combining findings from recent research and case studies, such as the example of 'Homes for Hope' in Cyprus, there are several promising additions to improve the existing situation of services offered to unaccompanied youth and overcome any barriers in the utilization of multifaceted services.

References

Alvarez, K. and Alegría, M. 2016. 'Understanding and addressing the needs of unaccompanied immigrant minors0. Washington, DC: *American Psychological Association.* Viewed 5.13.22 from https://www.apa.org/pi/families/resources/newsletter/2016/06/immigrant-minors

Bolborici, A. M. 2018. 'The migrant children and unaccompanied minors in the EU. Perspectives on the action plan'. *Bulletin of the Transilvania University of Braşov, Series VII: Social Sciences and Law, 11*(2-Suppl), 19-24.

Bronstein, I. and Montgomery, P. 2011. 'Psychological distress in refugee children: a systematic review'. *Clinical Child and Family Psychology Review, 14*(1), 44-56.

Cyprus Refugee Council. 2021. 'Country Report: Cyprus'. *Asylum Information Database* (AIDA). Viewed 5.13.22 from https://asylumineurope.org/reports/country/cyprus/

El-Awad, U. *et al.* 2017. 'Promoting mental health in unaccompanied refugee minors: Recommendations for primary support programmes'. *Brain Sciences, 7*(11), 146.

Ellis, B. H. *et al.* 2011. 'New directions in refugee youth mental health services: Overcoming barriers to engagement.' *Journal of Child & Adolescent Trauma, 4*(1), 69-85.

European Commission Eurostat Database 2021. 'Asylum applicants considered to be unaccompanied minors by citizenship, age and sex - annual data'. Viewed 4.19.22 from https://ec.europa.eu/eurostat/databrowser/view/MIGR_ASYUNAA__custom_985242/default/table?lang=en. Accessed 23 May 2021

European Migration Network Glossary. (2021). What we do. Viewed 5.13.22 from https://ec.europa.eu/home-affairs/what-we-do/networks/european_migration_network/glossary_search/unaccompanied-minor_en

Fazel, M., Garcia, J., & Stein, A. 2016. 'The right location? Experiences of refugee adolescents seen by school-based mental health services'. *Clinical Child Psychology and Psychiatry, 21*(3), 368-380.

Ferrara, P. *et al.* 2016. The 'invisible children': uncertain future of unaccompanied minor migrants in Europe. *The Journal of pediatrics, 169*, 332-333.

Flowers, N. et al., 2009. *Compasito: Manual on human rights education for children (2nd ed).* Hungary: Council of Europe.

Friedberg, R. D. *et al.*, 2016. 'Cognitive-Behavioral Therapy for Immigrant Youth: The Essentials'. In S. Patel and D. Reicherter (Eds.), *Psychotherapy for Immigrant Youth* (pp. 27–47). Switzerland: Springer International Publishing.

Jensen, T. K. *et al.*, 2015. 'Stressful life experiences and mental health problems among unaccompanied asylum-seeking children'. *Clinical Child Psychology and Psychiatry, 20*(1), 106-116.

Jensen, T. K. *et al.*, 2019. 'Long-term mental health in unaccompanied refugee minors: pre-and post-flight predictors'. *European Child & Adolescent Psychiatry, 28*(12), 1671-1682.

Jensen, T. K., Skårdalsmo, E. M. B., and Fjermestad, K. W., 2014. 'Development of mental health problems-a follow-up study of unaccompanied refugee minors'. *Child and Adolescent Psychiatry and Mental Health, 8*(1), 1-10.

Lems, A., Oester, K., and Strasser, S., 2020. 'Children of the crisis: ethnographic perspectives on unaccompanied refugee youth in and en route to Europe'. *Journal of Ethnic and Migration Studies, 46*(2), 315-335.

Majumder, P. *et al.*, 2015. 'This doctor, I not trust him, I'm not safe': The perceptions of mental health and services by unaccompanied refugee adolescents. *International Journal of Social Psychiatry, 61*(2), 129-136.

Menjívar, C. and Perreira, K. M., 2019. 'Undocumented and unaccompanied: children of migration in the European Union and the United States', *Journal of Ethnic and Migration Studies, 45*(2), 197-217.

Michelson, D., and Sclare, I., 2009. 'Psychological needs, service utilization and provision of care in a specialist mental health clinic for young refugees: a comparative study'. *Clinical Child Psychology and Psychiatry, 14*(2), 273-296.

Migliori, L, Rania, N., and Varani, N., 2019. 'Unaccompanied Migrant Minors: Trends, Challenges, and Well-Being'. In L. Descoteaux (Ed.), *Immigration and Migration: Trends, Management, and Challenges* (pp. 99–121). New York: Nova Science Publishers.

Müller, L. R. F. *et al.*, 2019. 'Mental health and associated stress factors in accompanied and unaccompanied refugee minors resettled in Germany: a cross-sectional study'. *Child and Adolescent Psychiatry and Mental Health, 13*(1), 1-13.

Papadopoulos, R. K. (Ed.) 2019. *Psychosocial aspects of the refugee situation - Synergic approach*. Athens: Publication of the Day Center Babel and the Centre for Trauma, Asylum and Refugees (University of Essex). Αθήνα, 2019.

Sanchez-Cao, E., Kramer, T., and Hodes, M., 2013. 'Psychological distress and mental health service contact of unaccompanied asylum-seeking children'. *Child: Care, Health and Development, 39*(5), 651-659.

Satinsky, E. *et al.*, 2019. 'Mental health care utilisation and access among refugees and asylum seekers in Europe: A systematic review'. *Health Policy, 123*(9), 851-863.

Seglem, K. B., Oppedal, B., and Roysamb, E. 2014. 'Daily hassles and coping dispositions as predictors of psychological adjustment: A comparative study of young unaccompanied refugees and youth in the resettlement country'. *International Journal of Behavioral Development, 38*(3), 293-303.

The Institute on Trauma and Trauma-Informed Care. 2020. *Using the 5 Trauma-Informed Guiding Values/Principles (Adapted from Harris & Fallot, 2001)*. Accessed through the Conference 'Links to Identifying, Preventing and Addressing Trauma Symposium', organized by the Center for Childhood & Youth Studies, Salem State University, April 2021.

Ugurlu, N., Akca, L., and Acarturk, C., 2016. 'An art therapy intervention for symptoms of post-traumatic stress, depression and anxiety among Syrian refugee children'. *Vulnerable Children and Youth Studies*, 11(2), 89-102.

UNICEF. 2017. *A Deadly Journey for Children: The Central Mediterranean Migration Route.* New York: UNICEF.

United Nations. 1989. *Convention on the Rights of the Child.* New York. Viewed 5.13.22 from https://www.ohchr.org/en/professionalinterest/pages/crc.aspx

Unterhitzenberger, J. *et al.*, .2015.. 'Trauma-focused cognitive behavioral therapy with unaccompanied refugee minors: a case series'. *BMC Psychiatry*, 15(1), 1-9.

Vervliet, M. *et al.*, .2014. 'Longitudinal follow-up of the mental health of unaccompanied refugee minors'. *European Child & Adolescent Psychiatry*, 23(5), 337-346.

Chapter 6

The Right to Education of Children and Adult Refugees in Portugal

Graça Santos

Escola Superior de Educação of the Polytechnic Institute of Bragança, Portugal; CEAD - Center for Research in Adult Education and Community Intervention

Sofia Bergano

Escola Superior de Educação of the Polytechnic Institute of Bragança, Portugal; CEAD - Center for Research in Adult Education and Community Intervention

Abstract

In Portugal, access to education is a right consecrated in the legislation in the area of immigration and integration of refugees. Through education, children and adults access and consolidate knowledge and instrumental skills, which are essential for their development in different dimensions of their lives. The social inclusion of children and adults can be promoted through community processes to provide access to education, health, housing and employment. The search for better living conditions, safety and well-being is a challenge, which can be successful if adequate situations are found in the destination context to respond to the educational and social needs of immigrant populations, specifically refugees. Policies and support measures have attempted to favour the reception and integration of refugee immigrants in Portugal. The problem of the inclusion of refugee immigrants must be seen in terms of achieving individual benefits for these people, but also the positive consequences for the country of destination. In this chapter, we seek to analyse how Portugal has developed the work of integrating refugee immigrants through the mobilisation of specific services and resources. We start by analysing data provided by national and international organisations collected from official documents.

Keywords: Education, social inclusion, policies and measures to support immigrants and refugees, Portugal

***

From Education to Social Inclusion

Through education, we favour inclusion on a daily basis, developing a critical spirit, favouring knowledge, questioning prejudices, mobilising action and civic participation in the community. It is recommended in article 26 of the Universal Declaration of Human Rights (1948), that everyone has the right to education, reinforced by the United Nations Convention on the Rights of the Child (1989) and the UNESCO Salamanca Statement (1994). It is necessary to create conditions for inclusion, respecting and valuing each and every person. It is important to say that exclusion is not acceptable and that if we all work towards this, we will assume indignation and awareness of situations of injustice in the fight against discrimination in different contexts. In this context, we need to mention migrant people, in particular, children and adult refugees.

Migration is marked by the search for a better life, where the needs in terms of security, employment, and well-being can be met. The arrival at a new destination or host country is motivated by the expectation of change. The initial conditions often justify the assumption of associated uncertainties and risks, especially challenging in the case of adult refugees and, in particular, children.

In this domain, it is important to clarify some concepts. According to EC [European Commission] (2018),

> the term 'people with a migrant background' refers to: - third-country nationals; - applicants for and beneficiaries of international protection; - stateless people; - people with undetermined nationality; - EU [European Union] citizens with a migrant background. It should be noted that mobile EU citizens are not included in this category (p. 8).

It is important to distinguish in general terms what is meant by refugee, migrant and asylum seeker. According to the European Youth Portal (2020), refugees flee armed conflict or persecution, asylum seekers claim to be refugees but have not yet been recognised as such, and migrants decide to leave their country to pursue better living conditions (life, work, education, meeting family members). The reasons why people decide to leave their country of origin and become refugees are many and can be related to race, religion, nationality, gender, sexual orientation, political opinions or belonging to a particular social group. Not all asylum seekers are able to obtain refugee status.

In legal terms, refugees are recognised by international law, specifically by the 1951 Convention relating to their status. On the other hand, migrants are covered by immigration laws and procedures adopted by different countries. To obtain refugee status, an asylum seeker must apply for protection in the first European Union country he or she is able to enter but may simultaneously apply for another form of international protection and await decisions by the national authorities.

In this perspective, the great diversity of situations that characterise the different migratory movements requires the need to conceive and implement strategies that promote support and accompaniment for people in these circumstances.

For successful integration, culminating in the real inclusion of migrants, it is essential that the process be accompanied by services with specific functions in this field. For example, in Portugal, the *Centros Nacionais de Apoio à Integração de Migrantes (CNAIM)* [National Support Centres for the Integration of Migrants] were created in 2004 to respond to the different difficulties experienced and to support migrants in their integration process. These people are confronted with various situations arising from cultural, organisational and legislative differences, often having to resort to different, dispersed services, leading the *Alto Comissariado para as Migrações, I.P. (ACM, I.P.)* [High Commission for Migrations] to create a place that would bring together, in the same space, different services, institutions and support offices for migrants. A space designed especially for migrants (ACM, 2021). The creation of this public entity aims to intervene in the implementation of public policies on migration, considering all the diversity that characterises current migratory movements and the challenges they pose.

Public measures to support emigrants at a central level are included in the Strategic Plan for Migration and are operationalised through the Municipal Plans for the Integration of Migrants. These Municipal Plans define strategies based on a previous diagnosis, which take into account local realities and the identified needs. The areas of intervention defined in these plans are quite diverse: reception and integration services, urbanism and housing, labour market and entrepreneurship, training, education and language, culture, health, solidarity and social response, citizenship and civic participation, fighting racism and discrimination, international relations, religion, media and public awareness, among others that are considered relevant, according to the context. As can be seen, an intervention that extends to different spheres of life is advocated and requires a multi-sectoral and integrated intervention. However, despite the existence of these legal instruments, there are still difficulties experienced by refugees in Portugal, particularly with regard to learning the Portuguese language and access to the labour market in line with the qualifications obtained by refugees in their countries of origin (Barbosa *et al.*, 2021). In these highly complex processes, attention has been given to the particular situation of migrant and refugee children and young people, considering the various challenges to their integration in relation to education, employment and access to basic services (health and housing). This concern finds international visibility, namely in the European Youth Portal, which states that

> Students with a migrant background often face difficulties in adapting to a new learning environment. The social inclusion of all young people, including those with a migrant background, is one of the priorities of the EU Youth Strategy (2019-2027).

In order to promote inclusion, it is important to consider the right to education. Education can be a key element for social inclusion. As referred by Anderson *et al.* (2004),

> With the world on the move in a way it has never been before, refugee children are becoming an identifiable and increasing group in today's schools. Refugee children share common refugee experiences of traumatic separation from their homeland and multiple experiences of loss, which contribute to a complex psychological, emotional, and social resettlement process (p. 1).

Education is a fundamental human right for everyone, which has to be guaranteed in a concrete way. In that regard, it is necessary to give legal and practical guidance to those who are working toward the achievement of Sustainable Development Goal 4 – Quality education (SDG4) (UNESCO, 2019). Educating implies the development of the individual and of society, and that is why it is important to consider the education of each and every person. It is here that it is important to highlight the role that has been developed: i) in the education of children and young people (in the creation of conditions in the schools to be welcomed - in terms of learning and reinforcing the knowledge of the Portuguese language and school learning and also because in the course of migrants that may have remained for a long time without access to school; ii) in adults – in the reinforcement of the Portuguese language, with the support of public schools. When highlighting education, it is also important to take into account the role of teachers, especially in classrooms, as mentioned by April *et al.* (2018),

> In addition, culturally responsive pedagogical approaches allow teachers to achieve greater inclusion and to offer full and equitable access to education for students from all cultures.

> Thus, teachers are prepared to include - and empower - migrants and refugee students with diverse needs in the classroom (so they can

welcome them in age-appropriate and regular classes). They use cultural references to impart knowledge, skills and attitudes (p. 13).

As referred to by EC (2018), regarding education - Ensuring access to inclusive and non-segregated education,

> Children with a migrant background face more disadvantages with regard to the type of school, duration of school attendance, indicators of achievement, drop-out rates, and types and level of school diploma attained. It is particularly striking that, as early as the end of primary school education, children with a migrant background achieve substantially lower scores than other children. Furthermore, children with a migrant background are over-represented in schools for special education. Education and training are among the most powerful tools for integration and access to them should be ensured and promoted as early as possible (p. 18).

There are several challenges, namely in terms of spatial isolation; school segregation; selection of students; language ability; school performance; school capacity; special educational facilities for students with learning difficulties; organisation, resources and needs of different stakeholders; attendance in early childhood education and care (ECEC). Faced with these challenges, it is important to know some measures: reforms in educational policy, subscription mechanisms; measures to improve access to non-segregated, regular and inclusive education; community building; participation in early childhood education services. There is also an indication of good practices and challenges, specifically targeting young refugees (FRA, 2019) and aiming at their integration into the EU.

There is a need to rethink refugee education to promote inclusion, as Pastoor (2016) defends, proposing a holistic and whole-school approach to refugee education. Cerna (2019) also proposed a holistic model, meeting the educational, social and emotional needs of refugee students. In this sense,

> Policies for refugee students often focus on providing access to education or meeting their mental health needs. However, it is important that policies address their educational, social and emotional needs through a holistic model. Some components of the model may have more weight than others, depending on their specific needs in different classrooms, schools and education systems. A holistic methodology also works in conjunction with other relevant institutions, such as social work, labour market agencies, health organisations and community associations, to address multiple and complex needs. (p. 65).

From this proposal, the following recommendations stand out: provide refugee access to all levels of education and allow flexible trajectories; introduce early assessment and develop individualised development and learning plans; provide flexible learning options, trajectories and transitions for older students; promote linguistic support specifically targeted at refugee students and to facilitate mother tongue language development; provide specific teacher training and professional development to support the needs of refugee students; provide a supportive learning environment for refugee students; create opportunities for social interactions between refugees and other students; adopt comprehensive school and community strategies to welcome and include refugee students and their families; support refugees welfare needs, including mental health; improve data collection and monitoring of student refugee outcomes; promote inclusive education that responds to the needs of all students.

We must understand what constitutes inclusive education (Taylor and Sidhu, 2012). The need to promote inclusion is recognised at the European, national and local levels. As Taylor and Sidhu (2012) question, 'what constitutes inclusive education?'. This recognition presupposes a willingness to take concerted measures at the European level in order to promote inclusion, in a concerted manner, by the different organisations and institutions on the field. Thus, the EU-Council of Europe (2021) states that:

> There is an ongoing reflection on how to promote a more coordinated and efficient integration of young migrants and refugees. Themes such as integration into the school system, access to labour market, inclusion and participation in public life, are amongst the key issues that need to be addressed together by different stakeholders to contribute to a long-term integration of these young people.
>
> Youth work providers have a key role in this context as they have the capacity to read and adapt quickly to new realities, a longstanding experience of working towards inclusion and diversity in societies and the capacity to put forward innovative ideas that link knowledge, policy and practice.

It is essential that inclusion is ensured by meeting individual and social needs. Access to employment, especially qualified ones, can be improved by investing in education and certification of skills. Issues with access to housing and good health conditions should also be addressed when mobilising means and strategies to promote inclusion. Immersion in the closest social environment, where daily challenges are placed through interaction between community members, can be facilitated by community processes of social intervention, where the participation of each and every person is guaranteed. It is important to support host entities, namely municipalities (these people are often welcome in large cities because they concentrate most of the resources), but also in others that can guarantee access to affordable housing, health (sometimes already associated with the outset) and education (children, young people and adults).

Policies and Measures to Support Immigrants and Refugees in Portugal

Support policies are of great relevance, with effects on demographic, economic and social levels. Portugal has adopted policies to support immigrants and refugees, being considered one of the first countries to approve the *Plano Nacional de Implementação do Pacto Global para as Migrações* [National Plan for the Implementation of the Global Pact for Migration], according to the Council of Ministers No. 141/2019, of 20 August. This plan is developed around five axes:

> i) promoting safe, orderly and regular migrations, as the most effective way of framing human mobility movements, managing demographic dynamics and valuing their contribution to the development of countries of origin, transit and destination (p 45); ii) improving the processes of organisation of migratory flows and integrated border management, particularly with regard to visa applications and authorizations essential for regular immigration and with regard to border security, through the fight against human trafficking, the containment of irregular migration and the promotion of document security (p. 45); iii) promoting the reception and integration of immigrants, ensuring their regular situation, promoting family reunion, favouring the mastery of the Portuguese language, the schooling of children and young people and the education and professional training of adults, improving conditions of access to housing, health and social protection, and encouraging their integration and civic participation (p. 46); iv) support for the connection of migrants to their country of origin and their return projects (p. 46); v) increased partnerships for development with countries of origin and transit, thus addressing the root causes of migration and reducing the weight of factors linked to material deprivation, inequalities and discrimination, the absence of work opportunities or the lack of minimum conditions of well-being (p. 46).

In general terms, Portugal takes inclusive education as a challenge to be implemented in the current reality (Decree-Law n.º 54/2018, of 6 July). In particular, Portugal has made a commitment to support migrants in their integration efforts over the years and, in particular, in the face of current demands. The *Alto Comissariado para as Migrações (ACM)* [The High Commissioner for Migration] discloses the *Plano Estratégico para as Migrações*

2015-2020 (PEM) [the Strategic Plan for Migration], which is based on five priority political axes: i) immigrant integration policies; ii) policies to promote the inclusion of new nationals; iii) policies for coordinating migration flows; iv) policies to strengthen migratory legality and the quality of migration services; v) policies to strengthen the connection, monitoring and support for the return of national emigrant citizens. For each of these axes, their own objectives are defined.

For the first axis, the objectives point to 'the consolidation of the work of integration, training and combatting discrimination against immigrants and ethnic groups in the Portuguese society'. The aim is to better mobilise the talent and skills of these people, as well as the 'appreciation of cultural and religious diversity, the reinforcement of social mobility, the decentralisation of integration policies and a better articulation with the policy of employment and of access to a common citizenship'. With the second axis, the intention is to 'reinforce the measures to promote the integration and inclusion of new nationals', including the descendants of immigrants and also all those who 'accede to Portuguese nationality, through actions in the areas of education, professional training, transition to the labour market, civic and political participation, digital inclusion, entrepreneurship and training'. As for the third axis, the objectives are oriented towards the 'international valorisation and promotion of Portugal as a migratory destination, through national and international actions of identification, attraction and settlement of migrants' and in this way, it is intended to contribute 'to a more adequate and intelligent management of migratory flows and to reinforce the attraction and circulation of talents and human capital'. Regarding the fourth axis, they refer to 'the reinforcement of the transversal intervention capacity in the execution of the migration policy, through the deepening of the partnerships network with public and private entities' also 'in the framework and monitoring of potential migrants, in the use of electronic tools, in the flexibility of entry procedures and in the affirmation of a reinforced culture of quality and good practices in the provision of migration services'. For the fifth axis, the objectives are oriented towards 'actions and programmes, in close articulation with the *Ministério dos Negócios Estrangeiros*' [The Ministry of Foreign Affairs], in order to promote, accompany and support 'the return of national citizens who emigrated abroad or the strengthening of their ties with Portugal, thus contributing to the reversal of the migratory movement of Portuguese citizens abroad' (ACM, 2015).

The legislation in the area of immigration and refugees, updated on November 2, 2020, refers to international and European legal instruments and national implementation. According to the *Alto Comissariado para as Migrações (ACM*, 2021) [The High Commissioner for Migration], the country has evolved in policies and practices for the reception and integration of immigrants at national and local levels. This effort implies the involvement of community partners and agents in promoting development and truly personal and social inclusion. The challenges are multiple; namely, the particular situation caused by COVID had repercussions at the international level in the lives of migrants and refugees. As reported by the UN (2021), the

> border restriction measures during the pandemic led to a drop of around 35% of the total number of refugees worldwide. The amount dropped from 64,000 in 2019 to 22,800 last year. The situation remains marked by difficulties in resettling vulnerable people, according to a new report by the UN Refugee Agency, ACNUR, and the World Bank.

At the level of asylum systems, there were very negative effects in some cases (because of the total or partial suspension of their operation), but there were also opportunities and positive situations, as is the case in Portugal, in the measures adopted regarding identity documents for asylum seekers or the granting of residence. According to UNHCR (2021),

> Other measures taken to adapt to the situation were made possible through positive political will. This included the automatic extension by law of identity documents for asylum seekers in several European Union Member States, as well as in Brazil, Ghana and the Russian Federation, and the granting of residence rights to asylum seekers in Portugal. Other States have adopted group-based approaches to ensure protection in large-scale movements. Examples include Brazil's application of the broader refugee criteria under the Cartagena Declaration to Venezuelans, among other nationalities; Sudan's declaration of prima facie recognition for Ethiopian refugees; and the granting or extension of temporary protection status to persons of various nationalities in the United States of America in 2021 (p. 6).

In 2021, the International Organisation for Migration (OIM) in Portugal reported to UN Portugal some projects that are in operation: Apoio ao Retorno Voluntário e à Reintegração (Projeto ARVoRe) [Support for Voluntary Return and Reintegration]; support to British citizens (after the UK exited the European Union, in order to guarantee their rights); relocation and resettlement of asylum seekers and refugees. In quantitative terms, in 2020, IOM's role translates into 340 migrants supported in their voluntary return to their countries of origin; 222 refugees resettled; 809 participants in 46 information sessions organised by IOM; 72 unaccompanied foreign children and young people relocated in Portugal; 104 migrants referenced by partners in Brazil; 614 UK citizens supported by the organisation; 9 languages used in materials produced by IOM on COVID-19; 24 asylum seekers from Greece, Italy and Malta who were relocated; 17 people who benefited from psychosocial support (UNRIC, 2021).

Legislation in the area of Immigration and Refugees (*Assembleia da República*, 2020) [Assembly of the Republic] is diverse but we highlight the one which refers to the right to education: i) basic and secondary education - Decree-Law No. 227/2005, of 28 December - Consolidated text (defines the new regime for granting equivalence of foreign qualifications in primary and secondary education, partially revoking Decree-Law No. 219/97, of 20 August); ii) higher education - Decree-Law No. 66/2018, of 16 August (approves the legal regime for the recognition of academic degrees and diplomas of higher education granted by foreign higher education institutions); iii) recognition of higher education qualifications in the European region - *Resolução da Assembleia da República* n.º 25/2000 [Resolution of the Assembly of the Republic], of 30 March (approves, for ratification, the *Convenção sobre o Reconhecimento das Qualificações Relativas ao Ensino Superior na Região Europa* [the Convention on the recognition of Qualifications concerning Higher Education in the European Region], open for signature by the member states of the *Conselho da Europa* [Council of Europe] in Lisbon, on April 11, 1997).

The effects of the inclusion of refugee immigrants must be equated on the basis of the individual benefits for themselves, but also the positive effects for the countries of destination. This multifaceted reality must be seen from the effects on community structures and processes, which can play a relevant role. Complex issues of a cultural and religious nature are raised, with an impact on demographic changes, learning, employment, and the very assumption of rights, as well as on the duties of citizenship, from a global perspective.

International Protection in Portugal, An Analysis of Trends

Based on the analysis of data provided by national and international organisations, accessible in official documents, the aim is to analyse the way in which Portugal has developed the work of integrating refugee immigrants, seeking to resort to the mobilisation of specific services and resources.

The data presented in the *Relatório Estatístico Anual: Indicadores de Integração de Imigrantes* (2020) [Annual Statistical Report: Indicators of Immigrant Integration], of the *Observatório das Migrações* [Migration Observatory]. This report highlights information on requests for international protection and the granting of refugee and subsidiary protection status.

Regarding requests for international protection in Portugal, it can be seen that these have generally increased since 2014, according to data from the SEF (Serviços de Estrangeiros e Fronteiras [Foreigners and Borders Services], cited by Oliveira, 2020).

It turns out there was a sharp increase in the number of requests in 2015, and since then, the high number of requests has remained, although, in 2018, there was a certain decrease corrected in the following year, resuming the growth trend.

Another relevant indicator in this analysis is the one related to the granting of refugee status and subsidiary protection; 2015 is also the year in which the granting of refugee status and subsidiary protection increased substantially. A fact that seems relevant to us when analysing the data is the observation that the decrease in requests for international protection that occurred in 2018 does not correspond to a decrease in the granting of refugee status and subsidiary protection, as it is, precisely the year in which the highest numbers of Residence Permits for subsidiary protection and refugee status are granted. It should be noted that the data presented refers only to situations in which people who apply in Portugal, not considering all people who arrive in Portugal already with refugee status under the resettlement mechanisms in place.

The increase in requests for international protection, as well as the granting of refugee status and subsidiary protection in Portugal, corresponds to an international dynamic, which reflects the increase of migratory routes associated with situations in which the search for security may constitute the first migratory objective. Another aspect that should prompt reflection is the relationship between requests for international protection and the granting of refugee status and subsidiary protection. From this analysis, we can consider the importance of analysing this difference. Unaccompanied children and young people are targeted for special protection, as their status as minors overlaps with their status as migrants, and for this reason, the State has the responsibility to provide their protection and well-being. The exact numbers for unaccompanied migrant minors are difficult to determine, as only those flagged by administrative services in host or destination countries are counted. However, despite this difficulty, it seems to be relatively consensual that this number has been increasing (Oliveira, 2020b; Roberto and Moleiro, 2021). The data allow us to observe an overrepresentation of male children, according to a trend registered in Europe (Oliveira, 2020b), although the author also mentions the existence of some variability of this effect, depending on the country of origin. Issues related to the care of unaccompanied children require awareness of their specific needs, which require integrated measures different from those existing in the regular national child protection system.

Final considerations

Education has an important role in promoting inclusion. Many are those who leave in search of better living conditions, seeking to satisfy their needs and ensure a better future for themselves and, eventually, for their family. Migration is motivated by the need to find security, employment and welfare needs, including financial, educational and cultural factors. Risks and challenges are assumed, particularly in the case of adult and child refugees.

For true inclusion of migrants, it is essential to ensure the right to education as a crucial condition for personal development and successful social inclusion. To this end, the process must be accompanied by entities with specific functions that support migrants in dealing with different situations arising from cultural, organisational and legislative differences. In particular, in integrating young migrants and refugees, major challenges arise in relation to education, employment and access to basic services, namely in terms of access to health and housing. Promoting the integration of refugees and migrants in Europe has triggered different responses. There are common problems that require secure and coherent positions that create conditions to fight discrimination, prejudice, racism and xenophobia. Faced with these challenges, it is important to value issues related to education, of each and every person, from a global and emancipatory perspective.

Guaranteeing the right to education through appropriate legislation is a fundamental element of social inclusion, which implies the development of the individual and of society in order to promote access to inclusive and non-segregated education. Faced with the challenges, it is necessary to adopt concrete measures that combine educational policy determinations with decisions that have an impact on good practices in everyday reality. By proposing a holistic model, Cerna (2019) alerts to the educational, social and emotional needs of refugee students, pointing out recommendations that must be met.

When promoting inclusion, it is important to take concerted measures, at a European level, which should motivate good practices, for example, of teachers in schools, in classrooms, but also from different organisations and institutions in the field. It is in this sense that the creation of conditions allowing access to employment, especially qualified employment, housing and good health conditions, can be improved, namely through community processes of social intervention, where civic participation should be promoted.

Portugal has adopted policies to support immigrants and refugees, with repercussions at demographic, economic and social levels. The impacts of migration are visible in the countries of origin and destination. In host countries, in particular, it is important to create active networks of partners and community agents who organise themselves to, in a social work of proximity, promote real personal and social inclusion. In exceptional situations such as those we are experiencing with the pandemic, Portugal stood out in the adoption of necessary measures, for example, for identity documents for asylum seekers or for granting of residence. Also, in 2021, Portugal presented some projects of reference.

We start from the analysis of data provided by national and international entities contained in official documents in order to analyse how Portugal has developed the work of integrating refugee immigrants. Given its real impact on the lives of migrants, we select applications for international protection and for the granting of refugee status and subsidiary protection. We see that requests for international protection in Portugal have been increasing, generally since 2014. In particular, there was an increase in the number of requests in 2015, and since then, the high number of requests has been maintained, with only a slight decrease in 2018, resuming the growth trend of the following year. As for the granting of refugee status and subsidiary protection, there was a substantial increase in 2015. It is worth noting that the decrease in requests for international protection in 2018 did not correspond to a decrease in the granting of refugee and subsidiary protection status. It should be noted that the data presented refers only to situations where people apply in Portugal. It is also worth mentioning the Portuguese Council for Refugees as an entity that provides various services (information and legal support, reception, legal and social assistance and in the context of integration, training and awareness and support for children).

The analysis of these trends corresponds to an international dynamic that reflects the increase in migratory movements associated with situations of the search for security, which may constitute the first migratory objective. In this context, it is essential to reflect on the difference between requests for international protection and the granting of refugee status and subsidiary protection. Issues related to unaccompanied children and young people are crucial, as they are the target of special protection, with the State being responsible for ensuring their protection and well-being. Meeting their individual needs becomes a requirement in promoting integrated measures appropriate to their specificity.

In summary, we believe that the inclusion of refugee immigrants and its effects are decisive, posing challenges of a cultural, religious, and demographic nature, with implications for education, learning, employment, and the assumption of rights and duties of citizenship. It is important to create and consolidate guidelines which support recommendations for intervention in the social and educational spheres, with a special impact on local and community development and which may have expression at national and international levels.

References

ACM - Alto Comissariado para as Migrações. 2015. *Plano Estratégico para as Migrações 2015-2020 (PEM)*. Retrieved from: https://www.acm.gov.pt/documents/10181/222357/PEM_net.pdf/3a515909-7e66-41e8-8179-e3aa5e0c7195

ACM - Alto Comissariado para as Migrações. 2021. *Centro Nacional de Apoio à Integração de Migrantes (CNAIM)*. Retrieved from: https://www.acm.gov.pt/pt/-/cnai-centro-nacional-de-apoio-ao-imigrante

Anderson, A. et al., 2004. 'Education of refugee children: Theoretical perspectives and best practice'. In R. Hamilton and D. Moore (eds.). *Schools, teachers and education of refugee children, Routledge Falmer.* New York.

April, D. *et al.*, 2018. 'Issues of Cultural Diversity, Migration, and Displacement in Teacher Education Programmes'. Paper commissioned for the *2019 Global Education Monitoring Report, Migration, displacement and education: Building bridges, not walls.*

Assembleia da República – Portugal. 2018. *Decree-Law n.º 54/2018, of 6 July.* Retrieved from: https://data.dre.pt/eli/dec-lei/54/2018/07/06/p/dre/pt/html

Assembleia da República – Portugal. 2020. *Legislação na área da imigração e refugiados*. Retrieved from: https://www.parlamento.pt/Legislacao/Paginas/Leis_area_Imigracao.aspx

Barbosa, M. *et al.*, 2021. 'Welcoming refugees in Portugal: preliminary assessment through the voices of refugee families'. *International Journal of Inclusive Education*, 25:1, 66-80, DOI: 10.1080/13603116.2019.1678752

Cerna, L. 2019. *Educação para os refugiados: modelos e práticas de integração nos países da OCDE.* Documento de trabalho. Retrieved from: https://www.oecd.org/centrodemexico/medios/Portugues_22may20_web_low3.pdf

CPR - Conselho Português para os Refugiados. 2020. Infografia Proteção Internacional em Portugal em 2019. Retrieved from: https://cpr.pt/wp-content/uploads/2020/07/Infografia-CPR-Protec%C3%A7%C3%A3o-Internacional-em-Portugal-2019-1.pdf

CPR - Conselho Português para os Refugiados 2021. ComUnidade. Retrieved from: https://cpr.pt/realizado-o-primeiro-encontro-das-ongds-sobre-o-patrocinio-comunitario-em-portugal/

EC - European Commission. 2018. *Toolkit on the use of EU funds for the integration of people with a migrant background (2018).* Retrieved from: https://ec.europa.eu/regional_policy/sources/policy/themes/social-inclusion/integration-of-migrants/toolkit-integration-of-migrants.pdf

EU - European Union-Council of Europe 2021. *Rights, inclusion and participation of young refugees.* Retrieved from: https://pjp-eu.coe.int/en/web/youth-partnership/rights-inclusion-and-participation-of-young-refugees

FRA - European Union Agency for Fundamental Rights 2019. *Integration of young refugees in the EU: good practices and challenges.* Retrieved from: https://fra.europa.eu/sites/default/files/fra_uploads/fra-2019-integration-young-refugees_en.pdf

Oliveira, C. (Coord.). 2020a. *Relatório Estatístico Anual: Indicadores de Integração de Imigrantes (2020) do Observatório das Migrações.* Alto Comissariado para as Migrações.

Oliveira, C. 2020b. *Entrada, Acolhimento e Integração de Requerentes e Beneficiários de Proteção Internacional em Portugal Relatório Estatístico do Asilo 2020.* Alto Comissariado para as Migrações/Observatório das Migrações.

Pastoor, L. 2016. 'Rethinking refugee education: principles, policies and practice from a European perspective'. *Annual Review of Comparative and International Education*, Vol. 30, pp. 107-116.

Portal Europeu da Juventude. 2020. *A situação dos migrantes e dos refugiados na Europa.* Retrieved from: https://europa.eu/youth/get-involved/your%20 rights%20and%20inclusion/situation-migrants-and-refugees-europe_pt

Roberto, S., and Moleiro, C. 2021. *De menor a maior: acolhimento e autonomia de vida em menores não acompanhados.* Observatório das Migrações.

Taylor, S. and Sidhu, R. 2012. 'Supporting refugee students in schools: what constitutes inclusive education?'. *International Journal of Inclusive Education*, Vol. 16/1, pp. 39-56, http://dx.doi.org/10.1080/13603110903560085

UN – United Nations. 2021. *Migrantes e Refugiados.* Retrieved from: https:// news.un.org/pt/news/topic/migrants-and-refugees

UNESCO - United Nations Educational, Scientific and Cultural Organization. 2019. *The Right to Education Handbook.* Right to Education Initiative. Retrieved from https://inee.org/resources/right-education-handbook

UNHCR - United Nations High Commissioner for Refugees. 2021. *Standing Committee. 81st meeting. EC/72/SC/CRP.10.* Executive Committee of the High Commissioner's Programme. Retrieved from: https://www.unhcr.org/60e449 bf4.pdf

UNRIC - Centro Regional de Informação para a Europa Ocidental. 2021. *OIM Portugal: Migrações seguras em pandemia e prioridades para a reabertura de fronteiras.* Retrieved from: https://unric.org/pt/oim-portugal-migracoes-seguras-em-pandemia-e-prioridades-para-a-reabertura-de-fronteiras/

Chapter 7

Services for Refugee, Asylee, and Victim of Human Trafficking Youth in South Florida

Regina Bernadin

International Rescue Committee, USA

Cristobal Pérez

Independent Scholar

Raúl Fernández-Calienes

St. Thomas University, USA

Abstract

For the past few years, the United States (U.S.) has seen an increase in unaccompanied minors coming across the southern border of the country; in contrast, the number of refugees (including unaccompanied refugee minors) has decreased significantly. A common ground most of the youth have is that no matter their nationality, each arrives with a different history of trauma. Carrying emotional and physical scars, they are drawn to the U.S. because it offers a safe haven and opportunities for a different life. Based on these lived experiences, some might qualify for one of the various immigration remedies as refugees, asylees, victims of trafficking, or combinations of these. Once in the U.S., each community might have a different approach or programming to assist these youth in the integration process.

In Miami, Florida, three different types of federally funded programmes offer support through a combination of services, including education, social services, and social integration, with the hope of supporting these youth in fully engaging and feeling part of South Florida. These three programmes highlighted are the following: (1) Post Release Services for Unaccompanied Children, (2) the Unaccompanied Refugee Minors Program and (3) Services for Survivors of Human Trafficking. The goal of this chapter is to introduce this programming and explain why they are necessary in assisting unaccompanied refugee, asylee, and trafficked youth.

Keywords: Immigration, unaccompanied refugee minors, unaccompanied children, borders, human trafficking

***

Introduction

For the past few years, the United States (U.S.) has seen an increase of unaccompanied minors coming across the southern border of the country; in contrast, the number of refugees (including unaccompanied refugee minors) has decreased significantly. A common ground most of the youth have is that no matter their nationality, each arrives with a different history of trauma. Carrying emotional and physical scars, they are drawn to the U.S. because it offers a safe haven and opportunities for a different life. Based on these lived experiences, some might qualify for one of the various immigration remedies as refugees, asylees, victims of trafficking, or combinations of these. Once in the U.S., each community might have a different approach or programming to assist these youth in the integration process.

In Miami, Florida, three different types of federally funded programmes offer support through a combination of services, including education, social services, and social integration, with the hope of supporting these youth in fully engaging and feeling part of South Florida. These three programmes highlighted are the following: (1) Post Release Services for Unaccompanied Children, (2) the Unaccompanied Refugee Minors Program and (3) Services for Survivors of Human Trafficking. The goal of this chapter is to introduce this programming and explain why they are necessary for assisting unaccompanied refugee, asylee, and trafficked youth.

Immigrant and Refugee Population and History in the United States

General Background

The population of the U.S., being made up of large numbers of immigrants, is well documented. For years, sources from federal, state, and local governments, as well as academia and news media, have recorded details of generations of immigrants reaching the U.S., transitioning into an area, and contributing to the work and social life of communities all across the nation. The main groups of immigrants that will be discussed in this chapter are the following:

Refugee - The Office of Refugee Resettlement (ORR), a department of the Administration for Children & Families within the United States Department of Health and Human Services, defines a refugee as an individual who is outside his/her country of nationality or habitual residence, and is unable or unwilling to return to or seek the protection of that country due to a well-founded fear of persecution based on race, religion, nationality, membership in a particular social group, or political opinion (cf., USDHHS-ACF-ORR, October 2, 2012b).

Asylee - ORR defines an asylee as someone who, on his/her own, travels to the U.S. and then applies for/receives a grant of asylum. Asylees do not enter the United States as refugees. Once in the U.S., or at a land border or port of entry, they apply to the U.S. Department of Homeland Security for asylum.

Victim of trafficking - The U.S. federal government defines 'severe forms of trafficking in persons' as; a) sex trafficking: the recruitment, harbouring, transportation, provision, obtaining, patronizing, or soliciting of a person for the purpose of a commercial sex act, in which a commercial sex act is induced by force, fraud, or coercion, or in which the person forced to perform such an act is under the age of 18 years; or b) labour trafficking: the recruitment, harbouring, transportation, provision, or obtaining of a person for labour or services, through the use of force, fraud or coercion for the purpose of subjection to involuntary servitude, peonage, debt bondage or slavery (cf., USDHHS-ACF-ORR, n.d.).

Unaccompanied Alien Child or UAC - Defined as someone who enters the United States and is (a) under the age of 18 years of age, (b) has no lawful immigration status in the United States, and c) Has no parent or legal guardian in the United States (or no parent or legal guardian in the United States is available to provide care and physical custody). UAC is a legal term; however, Unaccompanied Child is the preferred term used by the U.S. federal government agencies and programmes and will be utilized throughout this chapter (cf., USDHHS-ACF-ORR, May 19, 2021).

Understanding more about the scope and the numbers related to population and migration is essential to this topic, so global, national, and local figures are essential to help fill in the picture.

Recent Numbers for Population

The United States Census Bureau (April 26, 2021) records the 2020 resident population of the U.S. at 331.4 million persons and of Florida at 21.5 million persons. This is an increase of 14.6% over the 2010 figures at 308.7 million for the U.S. and 18.8 million for Florida.

Table 7.1: Resident Population of the U.S. and Florida

Place	2020	2010
U.S.	331,449,281	308,745,538
Florida	21,538,187	18,801,310

Source: USCB, April 26, 2021.

Recent Migration Numbers for Refugees

ORR records the total number of arrivals to the U.S. in Fiscal Year (FY) 2018 at 92,889; of that number, 22,491 (or 24%) were refugees (USDHHS-ACF-ORR, March 1, 2021, p. 8). The process of determining the number of refugees allowed into the country is dictated by federal law, in which at the beginning of each Federal Fiscal Year (FFY), October 1, the President of the United States, along with Congress sign a Presidential Determination (PD). This PD sets a goal for refugee admissions for the upcoming FFY. The United States Conference of Catholic Bishops (2021) explains that the past

> four PDs have been successively all-time low refugee admission goals: 45,000 (2018), 30,000 (2019), 18,000 (2020), and now 15,000. Prior to this… the average annual PD over the four decades of the refugee program has been 95,000' (n.p.). In FY 2018, the entire U.S. received 22,491 refugees (100%), while Florida only received 591 refugees (2.63%) of the total number of refugees (USDHHS-ACF-ORR, March 1, 2021).

Historically, unaccompanied refugee children have come to the U.S. from the African and Asian continents. These minors are identified and screened overseas. It has been noted that generally, the range of age of these youth has been 15-17 at the time of referral (USCCB, 2013). As noted, the past four years have impacted the number of refugee arrivals to the U.S. and included the number of arrivals of unaccompanied refugee minors. There has been a consistent decrease in youth coming to the country, displayed by numbers USSCB and Lutheran Immigration and Refugee Services resettled in FFY2015 (294) and FFY2019 (147) (USCCB, 2021). In 2020, these numbers were further impacted by the COVID-19 pandemic, as various components of the refugee resettlement process were delayed and impacted these youth. Those that have been able to come to the United States in the past years are from countries like the Democratic Republic of Congo, Burma, and Eritrea. More recently, the war in Afghanistan affected these numbers. Reports indicate that in August 2021, more than 1,400 minors were evacuated from Afghanistan to the United States without their parents (CNN, 2021).

Recent Immigration Surge of Unaccompanied Children in the United States

A large part of the recent immigration to the U.S. is from Central America. A very significant proportion of the figures from that region is from the Northern Triangle countries of Guatemala, El Salvador, and Honduras (USDHHS-ACF-ORR, 01 March 2021, p. 1). Specifically, people from those nations comprise of '92% of UACs in ORR custody' (p. 47). In the early 2000s, it was determined that ORR would be legally responsible for unaccompanied children in the U.S.

On March 1, 2003, the Homeland Security Act of 2002, Section 462, transferred responsibilities for the care and placement of unaccompanied children from the Commissioner of the Immigration and Naturalization Service to the Director of the Office of Refugee Resettlement (ORR). Since then, ORR has cared for over 409,550 children, incorporating child welfare values as well as the principles and provisions established by the Flores Agreement in 1997, the Trafficking Victims Protection Act of 2000, and its subsequent reauthorization acts, including the William Wilberforce Trafficking Victims Protection Reauthorization Act (TVPRA) of 2005 and 2008.

Unaccompanied children apprehended by the Department of Homeland Security (DHS) immigration officials are transferred to the care and custody of ORR. ORR promptly places an unaccompanied child in the least restrictive setting that is in the best interests of the child, taking into consideration danger to self, danger to the community, and risk of flight. ORR takes into consideration the unique nature of each child's situation and incorporates child welfare principles when making placement, clinical, case management, and release decisions that are in the best interest of the child. (USDHHS-ACF-ORR, 01 March 2021, p. 1)

ORR's most recently published data on this topic is from its *Annual Report to Congress: Office of Refugee Resettlement Fiscal Year 2018*. Table 4 (below) summarizes important information from that report.

Table 7.2: Unaccompanied Children by the Numbers (all in Fiscal Year 2018)

Refugee Resettlement (RR) Program

$537.9+ million	ORR funding level for the RR Program
22,491	Number of refugee arrivals served by ORR (=24% of total arrivals)
73	Numbers for 'country of birth' of refugee arrivals
48	Number of states in which refugees arrived

Unaccompanied Children (UC) Program

$1.3+ million	ORR funding level for the UC Program
49,100	Number of UC served by ORR in FY 2018
16.9	Percent increase over previous year (FY 2017) of UAC served by ORR
7,211	Number of UC housed by ORR in FY 2008
680.9	Percent increase over previous 10 years (FY 2008) of AC served by ORR
49	Number of states to which ORR released UC to sponsors
3	'Country of birth' of majority of UC placed in ORR custody (Guatemala, El Salvador, Honduras)
89	Percent of UC initially placed in a shelter (approximately)
10	Percent of UC initially placed in foster care (approximately)
71 and 29	Percent for males and females (respectively) of children in ORR custody

Unaccompanied Refugee Minors (URM) Program

1,966	Number of youth served by URM Program
1,158	Number of refugee youth served by URM Program
199	Number of victims of trafficking served by URM Program
52	Numbers for 'country of birth' of participants in URM Program
24	Number of participants in URM Program in Florida

Funding for Various Programmes in Florida

$35.2+ million	Refugee Support Services Grantees
$21 million	Cash and Medical Assistance Grantees
$1 million	Refugee School Impact Grantees (Florida Department of Children and Families)
$450,000	Survivors of Torture Grantees (Gulf Coast Jewish Family and Community Service)
$250,000	Refugee Career Pathways Grantees (Broward College)
$150,000	Ethnic Community Self-Help Program Grantees (Coptic Orthodox Charities)
$108,000	Refugee Health Promotion Grantees (Florida Department of Health)
$ 0	Individual Development Account Grantees
$ 0	Microenterprise Development Grantees
$ 0	Refugee Agricultural Partnership Program Grantees
$ 0	Wilson/Fish Grantees
$ 0	Youth Mentoring Grantees

Sources: USDHHS-ACF-ORR, April 20, 2011; USDHHS-ACF-ORR, March 1, 2021.

While the total number of unaccompanied trafficked youth is unknown, youth who entered the [Unaccompanied Refugee Minors] Program as victims of human trafficking increased in both the number and percentage of youth entering the Program since 2014 and made up nearly a third of youth entering the Program in 2018 (Foley, Rodler, Elkin, & Williams, 2021, p. v)]. Programmes are not mandated to track the status of guardianship. Thus the only figures available are those captured by other programmes such as the Unaccompanied

Refugee Minors and the Post Release Services for Unaccompanied Children initiatives, two of the community-based programmes highlighted below.

Summary

Immigrants come from all over the world to the United States for a better life. Many of the refugees who arrive are young persons from Central America. Each unaccompanied child comes to the U.S. with a different lived experience. In many cases, they begin to find a 'better life' with the help of special government and community initiatives that address their specific needs. Some of these programmes will be presented in the next sections.

Post-Release Services (PRS)

Background of the Program

As stated in the introduction, unaccompanied minors are placed in the custody of ORR. Once minors are placed in ORR care, the minors are placed in shelters throughout the country. It then is determined whether a child has a potential guardian with whom they can live while awaiting their immigration proceedings. If a guardian or sponsor is identified, the minor is released to him or her after the screening process. In this case, a sponsor is an adult, such as a biological parent, sibling, extended family member, or one who is authorized by the minor's legal guardian to serve as their representative while in the United States. The minor will then be released into their custody, and they will help them navigate through the court process as the minor will need to seek immigration relief to remain in the United States.

Once youth are released from the shelter, community programmes have been created to assist the youth with this transition. In particular, ORR provides post-release services (PRS) to minors who might benefit from further assistance from a social service provider. The three priority groups are if the child 'received a home study, was released to a non-relative sponsor, or was determined to be safe and appropriate, but the unaccompanied alien child and sponsor would benefit from ongoing [support]' (USDHHS-ACF-ORR, June 15, 2016).

Post-release services generally can range from 90 days to years and are to be terminated when the youth turns 18 years of age. The length of services also depends on the complexity and status of a case and may include connecting the minors and sponsors to community resources and other needs the youth may have. Two levels of assistance are available, with Level 2 cases receiving additional and more frequent care.

Once a case worker or advocate is assigned to the case, they work with the minor, their sponsor, and family to ensure that the youth is safe and enrolled in school, that they have identified a legal provider to assist their petition for immigration relief, and overall that integration is in process. The case worker also will address the topics of placement, family stabilization, and guardianship, as well as medical and mental health, substance use, and gang prevention.

PRS in Florida

According to a report from the Migration Policy Institute (2022), between 2014 and October 2021, more than 419,900 minors were released to sponsors in the United States. Of these youth, the report states that Miami-Dade County has received 9,760, the third largest number of cases in all counties of the United States, after Harris County in Texas and Los Angeles County in California.

In addition to the provision of services under the PRS model, agencies in South Florida have developed unique ideas to assist the youth. This includes the development of a Task Force, which includes social service providers, immigration attorneys, school representatives, consulate or embassy representatives, and human trafficking case managers, among others. The concept was to create a space to provide peer-to-peer learning, learn from each other's experiences, and include community members needed to make sure the integration of these youth is being accomplished.

The task force also is responsive to local trends. With increased incidences of trauma reported among stakeholders, one of the community-based agencies requested and was awarded federal funds to implement a program providing free evidence-based therapy. They also include support groups for unaccompanied minors ages 15 and up. The intention of these groups is to help in promoting the importance of mental health care and self-care, healthy peer relationships, and learning how to navigate challenges UC's might face in their new host community – most commonly related to immigration, education, and public health (IRC, 2020).

Trafficking by Sponsors

Another trend that was first brought to light by PRS workers was the trafficking of youth after reunification with a sponsor in the United States. The Centre for Migration Studies (2022) supported the anecdotal information in its report that found these minors are exposed to experiencing human trafficking not only in their home country or migration but also during reunification when they are released from ORR custody to sponsors or family members. They describe scenarios, including in 2016, when 13 children were identified by the Permanent Subcommittee of Investigations of the United States Senate Homeland Security Committee as a youth being released to sponsors that posed as sponsors but were human traffickers. There were an additional 15 cases suspected to be linked to human trafficking. There are also instances in which disruption exists in the home, forcing the youth to find a new placement, further exposing them to potential re-exploitation. This reinforces the need for PRS and for these youth, as PRS workers might be the only individuals who are able to see the interaction between the minor and their new living arrangement.

Observations and a Look Ahead

The PRS Program continues to be a source of support to recently arrived or reunified youth. In many communities where there are not enough legal providers, or there's a lack of access to public benefits, it continues to be the primary coordinating provider for many. Advocates argue that PRS should be an option for all minors released from ORR custody and that the time allotted for services should be extended. This is something that will require additional funding allocations at the federal level.

Most recently, '…Afghan children evacuated from Afghanistan are being granted humanitarian parole if they are not admitted as refugees or on special immigrant visas' (USDHHS-ACF-ORR, 9 November 2021, p. 1).

Additionally, exceptions in their placement with non-parental caregivers were made, showing that ORR seems open to adjusting its policies. This is important because these situations are likely to occur again. Learning from trends and existing programming helps to improve programming that will keep youth safe and to be successful in their integration into the United States.

Services for Survivors of Human Trafficking Funded by the U.S. Department of Justice and the U.S. Department of Health and Human Services

Background of the Program

In the year 2000, U.S. Congress passed a comprehensive law to address human trafficking, the Trafficking Victims Protection Act of 2000, to date, having reauthorized it six times (2003, 2005, 2008, 2013, 2015, 2018-19) since its inception. This law offered a framework to respond to this crime that involved a '3 P' paradigm: protection, prosecution, and prevention (a fourth 'P,' partnership, was added later through one of its reauthorizations). Among the various mechanisms the TVPA offered to victims of trafficking, it created an array of victim assistance programmes and an inter-disciplinary response.

Different types of grants within various government agencies have been created. For example, the U.S. Department of Justice, Office for Victims of Crime (OVC), offers grants to non-governmental service providers to offer direct assistance to victims of all forms of human trafficking. These services include but are not limited to assistance with case management, applying for public benefit, safety planning, mental health counselling, education, mentorship and referrals to others offering legal assistance and medical care. It also has created special categories that focus on more specific needs, such as ones that are housing and population-specific, like those that serve minor victims of labour trafficking.

More recently, the Bureau of Justice Assistance (BJA) developed an anti-trafficking task force initiative, funding working groups and coalitions throughout the country that have mobilized partners in communities around the country. These local law enforcement agencies generally collaborate and work with service providers, academia, and different levels of government to offer victims of trafficking a holistic approach to their cases. The exemplify the idea that collaboration and capacity building are key to successful protection-based aid.

Unaccompanied Minors and Human Trafficking

In the twenty-first century, there has been an inclusion of new and dedicated programming to assist unaccompanied minors who have been forced to work against their will. That includes those who have been trafficked in their country of origin and arrived in the United States to escape persecution, as well as those who might have been exploited in the U.S. because of their vulnerability as a youth. Further elaborating on what was described earlier by The Centre for Migration Studies, according to the OVC, Training and Technical Assistance Centre, foreign national minors are at risk at several points during migration (in their home country, in transit, and within the United States). OVC details each point in the following way (USDOJ-OJP-OVC-TTAC, 2021):

In the home country: Due to poverty, gang violence, and civil and political unrest, minors may grow up in environments that make them vulnerable to trafficking exploitation. They may experience child abuse, gender-based violence, lack of educational opportunities or be forced into drug trafficking or labour trafficking, such as domestic servitude. Many minors are also trafficked for sex prior to entry into the United States, especially by gangs.

In transit: On route to the United States, many minors pass through other countries and dangerous territories, sometimes alone. Some immigrant minors are used for forced labour and sex trafficking by drug cartels and organized crime, particularly in the areas surrounding U.S. border states. Some minors are kidnapped or fraudulently coerced into becoming drug mules or forced to work for the drug industry in other ways. Some, who have had their money stolen along the way, are forced to work in dangerous conditions to earn money to continue their journey. Other minors have reported being coerced to work on fishing boats as they tried to make their way into this country.

In the United States: Like adult migrants, minors are charged heavy fees by the people who smuggle them into the United States and are expected to earn the money to pay back the fees or pay additional expenses for their housing and food. This can lead to peonage, debt bondage, or both. Minors also may be victimized by family members upon their arrival. Instead of providing care and better opportunities, minors may be treated like domestic servants and forced to work long hours with no time off or be pressured to work in commercial sex to pay their debts.

Unaccompanied minors have been eligible for services since the passage of the federal law; however, 2014 marked the beginning of the largest influx of UC's entering the U.S. when many programmes began seeing trafficked youth in their caseloads for the first time. Since then, UC's have been assisted throughout the country.

In 2020, the U.S. Department of Justice provided $270 million dollars in funding to serve survivors in 46 states; Washington, D.C.; and the Northern Mariana Islands. 22% (2,254) of the victims served were identified as minors (this is both accompanied and unaccompanied as well as U.S born and foreign-national) (USDOJ-OJP-OVC-TTAC, 2021). Federally funded programmes, like the ones described earlier, support this population with a myriad of services. Many, however, do not distinguish between an accompanied and unaccompanied minor or one that is supported by a system-based structure like foster care. As a response to advocates in the field learning more about the specific needs of this population, the U.S. government has designated youth-specific funding to pilot initiatives that will focus on this population.

Unaccompanied Trafficked Minors in Florida

Since 2003, providers in the South Florida region have been recipients of multiple federal grants that have allowed the community to build the local capacity and create a framework to aid youth who have been forced to engage in commercial sex or to work against their will. Through formal and informal relationships, the passing of child-specific state laws, and the universal support of immigrant rights, a multi-disciplinary approach was created to serve this population in a manner that is trauma-informed, comprehensive, and culturally appropriate. PRS and URM providers are just two of the stakeholders that partner with mainstream anti-trafficking providers and law enforcement to avoid duplication of services and instead create a safety net around the care of the minor who has experienced exploitation and abuse.

Observations and a Look Ahead

Unaccompanied trafficked minors face unique challenges in being identified and in being able to obtain the services they need once out of the trafficking situation. Furthermore, unaccompanied minors might feel pressure to continue working once out of the situation and have no intention of studying, which is an expectation that many in the United States might have. This can create tension when serving them, even have some go back to the trafficking situation or simply run away because they want (or feel pressure) to continue working. Since this might be the case, agencies in South Florida must be proactive and strengthen their approach, focusing on engagement in a trauma-informed manner. This is also important because this phenomenon is not unique to South Florida. With global push and pull factors exacerbating conditions, more and more youth are vulnerable to exploitation.

The Unaccompanied Refugee Minors (URM) Program

Background of the Program

As authorized by provisions of the Refugee Act of 1980, as well as in compliance with Subpart H, 'Child Welfare Services' of 45 CFR Part 400, ORR, establishes and supervises program goals and guidelines for the State-administered Unaccompanied Refugee Minor Programmes (URMP). These programmes were developed in the 1980s by the United States government to assist minors from Southeast Asia who did not have a guardian or parents to raise them. Since its inception, ORR states that more than 13,000 minors from different countries around the world have become eligible to enrol into this program (Foley *et al.*, 2021, p. 2). As of 2021, ORR stated that youth who are refugees, entrants, asylees, victims of trafficking, certain minors with Special Immigrant Juvenile (SIJ) Status, and U Nonimmigrant Status (U-Visa) holders qualify to enrol.[1] It

---

[1] ORR defines Cuban and Haitian entrants as (a) 'Any individual granted parole status (by DHS) as a Cuban/Haitian Entrant (Status Pending) or granted any other special status subsequently established under the immigration laws for nationals of Cuba or Haiti, regardless of the status of the individual at the time assistance or services are provided and (b) Any other national of Cuba or Haiti (1) Who: (i) was paroled into the United States and has not acquired any other status under the INA; (ii) is the subject of exclusion or deportation proceedings under the INA; or (iii) has an application for asylum pending with (DHS); and (2) With respect to whom a final, non-appealable, and legally enforceable order of deportation or exclusion has not been entered. 45 CFR § 401.2. Cuban and Haitian Entrants, along with Cubans in certain other categories, are after one year in the U.S. eligible to apply for adjustment of status, at which time when a full medical exam would be required by USCIS' (USDHHS-ACF-ORR, October 2, 2012a, n.p.).

should also be clarified that most youths in the URMP are documented – having been granted status prior to their enrolment in the program – and may receive services as eligible populations listed above. However, an important caveat is that victims of trafficking are the only category that may be undocumented while receiving these services, as they might be eligible to receive these services only by having an 'eligibility letter.' This letter follows an assessment in the shelter and a determination that the minor experienced trafficking in their country of origin or during migration to the United States. It does not give the minor status in the United States; it is a document given by the U.S. Department of Health and Human Services, Office Trafficking in Persons, to identify foreign-born child victims of human trafficking, enabling them to receive federally funded benefits and services to the same extent as a refugee. While some victims of trafficking might have obtained a T-Visa, which is immigration relief specifically for trafficked individuals, it is important to note that youth who might be undocumented can receive these URMP services (USCIS, May 10, 2018).

The eligible minors described above may enrol into the URM Program through multiple pathways. The U.S. Department of State identifies unaccompanied refugee cases from abroad who are under 18 years of age. Other youths are identified by ORR after arrival in the United States. Most of these minors often are first identified as unaccompanied minors from Central America and are referred to the URM Program after an eligibility determination. Most unaccompanied minors who qualify for the URMP qualify as youth with SIJ Status, victims of trafficking, or asylees. A 2021 ORR publication stated that youth with SIJ status were the second largest group of youth receiving these services and that more than half of the youth who enrolled between Federal Fiscal Year (FFY) 2014 and FFY 2018 were age 17 (United States Citizenship and Immigration Services, n.d.).

The URMP currently is offered in 25 different cities in 14 different states plus Washington, D.C. (USDHHS-ACF-ORR, July 15, 2021, n.p.). Each of the 15 locations offering these services either does it through direct services (considered public custody) or subcontracts this assistance to local providers (considered a private custody State). ORR coordinates these placement

---

USCIS states that SIJ status is a protection offered to minors who have been abused, abandoned, or neglected by a parent (USCIS, May 10, 2018).

The U nonimmigrant status (U visa) is for victims of certain crimes (including but not limited to domestic violence, sexual assault, human trafficking) who have suffered mental or physical abuse and are helpful to law enforcement or government officials in the investigation or prosecution of criminal activity.

services nationally with the United States Conference of Catholic Bishops, Lutheran Immigration and Refugee Services, or both.

Any program, whether it is considered a 'public' or a 'private' petition state must follow or mimic the State government's child welfare services that are offered to any youth in that system in order for the minor to receive services that are the same or as close as possible. As stated in the federal statute § 400.116, which describes service for unaccompanied refugee minors:

> A State must provide unaccompanied minors with the same range of child welfare benefits and services available in foster care cases to other children in the State. Allowable benefits and services may include foster care maintenance (room, board, and clothing) payments; medical assistance; support services; services identified in the State's plans under titles IV-B and IV-E of the Social Security Act; services permissible under title XX of the Social Security Act; and expenditures incurred in establishing legal responsibility (United States Government Publishing Office, 2017, n.p.).

Furthermore, the services and goals in the URMP are similar in all of the states providing these services, as they follow general federal guidelines. Reunification of the children with the minor's parents or adult relatives (conducted through family tracing avenues) is generally the goal; however, when that is not possible, other permanency options are considered for the youth being served. In addition to permanency planning, URMs follow state regulations that include a written case plan for the services and care for the minor. According to federal regulations, these case plans must address the following:

Social adjustment

English language training

Career planning

Education/training

Health needs

Least restrictive mode of care setting

Development of socialization skills

Family reunification

Preservation of ethnic and religious heritage

Mental health needs (if necessary)

In addition, it is important to note that ORR's goal is to have these youth in the least restrictive care settings as soon as possible, establish legal responsibility, and ultimately assist them in obtaining the needed skills to become economically and socially self-sufficient. This is achieved through child welfare services delivered in a culturally sensitive manner. This culturally sensitive manner is an important focus this program offers not only through the social service employees that work with the youth but also with the licensed placement options with which the programmes work.

URMP in Florida

Florida is considered a 'private custody' State, as it offers its URM services through contracted services with a social service provider agency located in Miami-Dade County. Following ORR's mission and goals, this agency states that its 'program places children in licensed Foster Care homes and offers supportive Case Management services that address the legal, educational, medical and psychological needs of the minors in care' (Catholic Charities of the Archdiocese of Miami, 2022, p. 1).

In addition to all of the federal guidelines and services that ORR requires the programmes to assist the youth with, The Florida Department of Children and Families, Florida's Centre for Child Welfare (2022) describes that all minors in the State foster care system receive a case plan detailing the needs of each child. This case plan is submitted and in supervision with the dependency system in Florida. This also would apply to URMs, as they mimic these protocols.

In terms of placement options, they also play a role, as they do in the regular foster care system. URMs are placed in licensed placement options, mainly foster homes. The provider states that 'we are looking for families and individuals who would like to become foster parents. These individuals would mentor, assist and resettle the refugee minor with dignity, love and compassion' (Florida Department of Children and Families, Florida's Centre for Child Welfare, 2021). The program trains and guides foster parents through this process, making sure they obtain the needed support. The URMP focuses on finding individuals or families that are not only interested in becoming foster parents but also fostering foreign-born youth who enrol into this program.

Observations and a Look Ahead

Due to its cultural demographic and make up, the URM Program in South Florida is set up uniquely to assist minors from Central America. While this might be the case, it is essential to build and offer additional placement options to youth from all over the world. It is vital for URMP to not only understand the needs of youth coming into the program and helping them as needed but also know the services that are locally available to them. For youth to be successful in the community, they need to establish lasting relationships and find people, agencies, or both that can offer them guidance and help. It will always be important for URMP staff to be alert of new services available to youth and establish connections. Obtaining resources for the youth might allow them to establish roots in the community and feel part of something.

Summary

While not all unaccompanied minors qualify for the URMP, there are clear benefits to youth who are eligible to receive these services. Having programmes that can not only mimic what the foster care system can do but also can do it in a culturally sensitive way, understanding their trauma, challenges, and general backgrounds can provide assistance to them in their acculturation process.

Conclusion

It is important to continue learning about the evolving needs and trends that these youth face. Understanding and offering tailored programmes that address their specific needs and challenges should always be at the forefront of all of those serving these minors and the communities that host them. The three programmes highlighted not only provide direct assistance but also advocate to policymakers, who, at a macro level, can learn, adapt, and create the appropriate programming.

The influence of these decision-makers has longstanding impacts at a micro level, particularly in the lives of youth whose lives have already been filled with disruption and trauma. The programming examples highlighted in this chapter are worthy of showcasing and replicating as they focus on aiding and supporting this vulnerable group – that has endured so much at such an early stage in their lives – in a person-Centred and holistic manner.

References

Catholic Charities of the Archdiocese of Miami. 2022. 'Unaccompanied Refugee Minors Program.' Miami, FL. Accessed April 21, 2022. https://www.ccadm.org/sh_projects/unaccompanied-refugee-minors-program/

Centre for Migration Studies. 2022. 'Unaccompanied Minors from Central America: Keeping Them Safe in the United States.' New York, N.Y. Accessed April 21, 2022. https://cmsny.org/keeping-uacs-safe/

CNN. 2021. '1,450 Afghan kids were evacuated to the US without their parents. Some are still in limbo.' Accessed May 16, 2022. https://www.cnn.com/2021/12/27/us/afghan-children-evacuated-without-parents-cec/index.html

Florida Department of Children and Families, Florida's Centre for Child Welfare. 2022. 'Administrative Rule 65C: 65C-30.006 Case Pending.' Tallahassee, FL. Accessed April 21, 2022. http://Centreforchildwelfare.org/DCF%20Family%20Safety/65C%20-%20Rules.htm#C30006

Foley, K., *et al.*, 2021. 'Final Report from the Descriptive Study of the Unaccompanied Refugee Minors Program. Service Provision, Trends, and Evaluation Recommendations'. OPRE Report #2021-81, May 2021. Washington, D.C.: Office of Planning, Research, and Evaluation, Administration for Children and Families, U.S. Department of Health and Human Services. Accessed May 16, 2022. https://www.acf.hhs.gov/sites/default/files/documents/opre/descriptive-study-unaccompanied-refugee-minors-may-2021.pdf

International Rescue Committee [IRC]. 2020, June 16. 'The IRC in Miami: Unaccompanied Children in South Florida.' Miami, FL. Accessed April 21, 2022. https://www.rescue.org/announcement/irc-miami-unaccompanied-children-south-florida

Migration Policy Institute. 2022. 'Unaccompanied Children Released to Sponsors by State and County, FY 2014-Present.' Washington, D.C. Accessed April 21, 2022. https://www.migrationpolicy.org/programmes/data-hub/charts/unaccompanied-children-released-sponsors-state-and-county

United Nations. 2022. 'Figures at a Glance.' Geneva, Switzerland. Accessed April 22, 2022. https://www.unhcr.org/figures-at-a-glance.html

United States Census Bureau [USCB]. 2021, April 26. 'Historical Population Change Data (1910-2020).' Washington, D.C. Accessed April 21, 2022. https://www.census.gov/data/tables/time-series/dec/popchange-data-text.html

United States Citizenship and Immigration Services [USCIS]. n.d. 'Special Immigrant Juvenile Status: Information for Juvenile Courts.' Washington, D.C. Accessed April 22, 2022. https://immigrantjustice.org/sites/immigrant justice.org/files/BestPracticesManual_17.%20USCIS%20SIJS%20Information %20for%20Juvenile%20Courts.pdf

United States Citizenship and Immigration Services [USCIS]. 2018, May 10. 'Victims of Human Trafficking: T Nonimmigrant Status.' Washington, D.C. Accessed April 22, 2022. https://www.uscis.gov/humanitarian/victims-of-human-trafficking-and-other-crimes/victims-of-human-trafficking-t-nonimmigrant-status

United States Conference of Catholic Bishops [USCCB]. 2021. 'FAQ: Presidential Determination on Refugee Admissions for Fiscal Year 2021.' Washington, D.C. Accessed April 21, 2022. https://justiceforimmigrants.org/what-we-are-working-on/refugees/faq-presidential-determination-on-refugee-admissions-for-fiscal-year-2021/

United States Department of Health and Human Services, Administration for Children and Families, Office of Refugee Resettlement [USDHHS-ACF-ORR]. n.d. 'Fact Sheet: Victims of Human Trafficking.' Washington, D.C. Accessed April 22, 2022. https://www.acf.hhs.gov/sites/default/files/documents/orr/orr_fact_sheet_victim_of_trafficking.pdf

United States Department of Health and Human Services, Administration for Children and Families, Office of Refugee Resettlement [USDHHS-ACF-ORR]. 2011, April 20. 'Office of Refugee Resettlement Annual Report to Congress 2011.' Washington, D.C. Accessed April 22, 2022. https://www.acf.hhs.gov/orr/report/office-refugee-resettlement-annual-report-congress-2011

United States Department of Health and Human Services, Administration for Children and Families, Office of Refugee Resettlement [USDHHS-ACF-ORR]. 2012a, October 2. 'Who We Serve – Cuban/Haitian Entrants.' Washington,

D.C. Accessed April 22, 2022. https://www.acf.hhs.gov/orr/policy-guidance/who-we-serve-cuban/haitian-entrants

United States Department of Health and Human Services, Administration for Children and Families, Office of Refugee Resettlement [USDHHS-ACF-ORR]. 2012b, October 2. 'Who We Serve – Refugees.' Washington, D.C. Accessed April 22, 2022. https://www.acf.hhs.gov/orr/policy-guidance/who-we-serve-refugees

United States Department of Health and Human Services, Administration for Children and Families, Office of Refugee Resettlement [USDHHS-ACF-ORR]. 2016, June 15. 'Children Entering the United States Unaccompanied: Section 6.' Washington, D.C. Accessed April 22, 2022. https://www.acf.hhs.gov/orr/policy-guidance/children-entering-united-states-unaccompanied-section-6

United States Department of Health and Human Services, Administration for Children and Families, Office of Refugee Resettlement [USDHHS-ACF-ORR]. 2021, March 1. 'Annual report to Congress: Office of Refugee Resettlement Fiscal Year 2018.' Washington, D.C. Accessed April 22, 2022. https://www.acf.hhs.gov/sites/default/files/documents/orr/ARC_FY2018_508_2_28_2021.pdf

United States Department of Health and Human Services, Administration for Children and Families, Office of Refugee Resettlement [USDHHS-ACF-ORR]. 2021, March 11. 'Facts and Data.' Washington, D.C. Accessed April 22, 2022. https://www.acf.hhs.gov/orr/about/ucs/facts-and-data

United States Department of Health and Human Services, Administration for Children and Families, Office of Refugee Resettlement [USDHHS-ACF-ORR]. 2021, May 19. "Key Documents for the Unaccompanied Children Program." Washington, D.C. Accessed April 22, 2022. https://www.acf.hhs.gov/orr/policy-guidance/unaccompanied-children-program

United States Department of Health and Human Services, Administration for Children and Families, Office of Refugee Resettlement [USDHHS-ACF-ORR]. (2021, June 7). 'Children Entering the United States Unaccompanied.' Washington, D.C. Accessed April 21, 2022. https://www.acf.hhs.gov/orr/policy-guidance/children-entering-united-states-unaccompanied

United States Department of Health and Human Services, Administration for Children and Families, Office of Refugee Resettlement [USDHHS-ACF-ORR]. 2021, July 15. 'About Unaccompanied Refugee Minors Program.' Washington, D.C. Accessed April 22, 2022. https://www.acf.hhs.gov/orr/programmes/urm/about

United States Department of Health and Human Services, Administration for Children and Families, Office of Refugee Resettlement [USDHHS-ACF-ORR]. 2021, November 9. 'Field Guidance – Revised November 9, 2021 (First Issued September 4, 2021). Re: Field Guidance #19 – Unaccompanied Afghan Minor Processing.' Washington, D.C. Accessed May 16, 2022. https://www.acf.hhs.gov/sites/default/files/documents/orr/fg-19-uam-processing-rev-11-9-21.pdf

United States Department of Justice, Office of Justice Programmes, Office for Victims of Crime [USDOJ-OJP-OVC]. January 10, 2019. 'Announcements: Twenty Years of Progress in the Anti-Trafficking Movement.' Washington, D.C. Accessed April 22, 2022. https://ovc.ojp.gov/microsite-subpage/announcements#102820b

United States Department of Justice, Office of Justice Programmes, Office for Victims of Crime, Training and Technical Assistance Centre [USDOJ-OJP-

OVC-TTAC]. 2021. 'Foreign National Minors.' Washington, D.C. Accessed April 22, 2022. https://www.ovcttac.gov/taskforceguide/eguide/4-supporting-victims/45-victim-populations/minors-adolescents/foreign-national-minors/

United States Government Publishing Office. 2017. 'Electronic Code of Federal Regulations, Title 45, Subtitle B, Chapter IV, Part 400, Subpart H, Section 400.116.' Washington, D.C. Accessed April 22, 2022. https://web.archive.org/web/20170528143251/https://www.ecfr.gov/cgi-bin/text-idx?SID=d52ed117734d057986e1bd1b8db1912f&mc=true&node=se45.2.400_1116&rgn=div8

Appendix – Acronyms

BJA - Bureau of Justice Assistance

DHS - United States Department of Health and Human Services

FFY - Federal Fiscal Year

IRC - International Rescue Committee

ORR - Office of Refugee Resettlement

OVC - United States Department of Justice, Office for Victims of Crime

PD - Presidential Determination

PRS - Post-Release Services

RR - Refugee Resettlement

SIJ - Special Immigrant Juvenile Status

U-Visa - U Nonimmigrant Status

UAC - Unaccompanied Alien Child

UC - Unaccompanied Children

URM - Unaccompanied Refugee Minors

URMP - Unaccompanied Refugee Minors Program

U.S. - United States

USCB - United States Census Bureau

USCCB - United States Conference of Catholic Bishops

USCIS - United States Citizenship and Immigration Services

USDHHS-ACF-ORR - United States Department of Health and Human Services, Administration for Children and Families, Office of Refugee Resettlement

USDOJ-OJP-OVC - United States Department of Justice, Office of Justice Programmes, Office for Victims of Crime

USDOJ-OJP-OVC-TTAC - United States Department of Justice, Office of Justice Programmes, Office for Victims of Crime, Training and Technical Assistance Centre

Chapter 8

Resilience in Liberia: An Initial Study

Greg Carroll

Salem State University

Allan Shwedel

Salem State University

George Weagba

United Methodist University, Liberia

Joe Buttner

Salem State University

David Mercer

Salem State University

Abstract

This chapter reports on the findings of a study conducted at the United Methodist University (UMU) in Liberia, West Africa, that developed out of a Fulbright award to the first author. The initial purpose of the study was for UMU to gain a better understanding of who their students are in terms of needs and aspirations. What is reported here is a study of student *Resilience*. While the data here only represent the initial phase of our research, a number of characteristics emerged that have warranted further investigation given the recent history of Liberia, having suffered through two civil wars and two pandemics, one of which is ongoing (Ebola and COVID-19).

We found that even given the multiple negative events that many students experienced (loss of family members, dislocation both internally displaced and refugee), there was a level of optimism for the future. As a result, we utilized the concepts of ACEs and HOPEs (Adverse Childhood Experiences and Healthy Outcomes from Positive Experiences) as a way of framing students' self-reports and utilized this to propose some general guidelines for practice, not only for UMU but also for the Government of Liberia.

Keywords: Resilience, Post Conflict, Adverse Childhood Experiences (ACEs), Helthy Outcomes from Positive Experiences (HOPEs)

***

Introduction

Liberia the oldest African Democracy, one of only two African countries that was arguably never colonized[1], and one of only a minority of countries in the world that has elected a female head of state. It is also undeniable that the period from April 12th, 1980, when Master Sergeant Doe summarily executed President William Tolbert and 13 of his ministers, to August 11, 2003 when the then President Charles Taylor flew into exile in Nigeria, the country was wracked by gross human rights violations. As stated by Brehun (1991) with regards to the first civil war:

> In all frankness, the Liberian civil and guerrilla war topped and surpassed [all other wars] in form and character, in intensity, in depravity, in savagery, in barbarism and in horror (p.113).

It is also worth noting that the second civil war (April 1999 – August 2003) was a similarly brutal affair, with all sides continuing the use of child soldiers (Podder, 2011). Though there are long antecedents to the conflict and aggression in Liberia (Ellis, 1995, 2006; Sawyer, 1992, 2005), the conflict, which can be said to cover the years 1980 -2003 more accurately, can be described in two phases; the first from 1980 to the signing of and the enacting of a peace agreement with the subsequent election of Charles Taylor in July 1997. The second phase began in 1999 and ended with Taylor flying into exile in Nigeria on August 11th 2003, ahead of the signing of the Accra Comprehensive Peace Agreement.

While the events above 'book-end' the conflicts, anybody who possesses more than a passing knowledge of this time period would be aware of the name Joshua Milton Blahyi, or at least his *nom de guerre*, General Butt Naked (Tabor,

---

[1] Another reading, however, is that freed and free-born African Americans colonized the country and functioned as the ruling elite from 1822 till 1980, when Master Sergeant Samuel Kanyon Doe installed himself as President. Indeed, in the history of Liberia only two Presidents have not claimed Americo-Liberian status: Samuel Doe and the current president George Weah.

2016). Though our undergraduate students here in the States smirk at the first mention of his name, for Liberians during the first Liberian Civil War, the mention of his name struck fear. It was he, along with his Naked Commandos, who carried out ritual sacrifice and cannibalism. It is Blahyi's Naked Commandos that provide a classic example of Adverse Childhood Experiences, given that one of the initiation rites to become one of Blahyi's child soldiers was to get drunk or high and kill their parents. The impact of these adverse childhood experiences, as documented in the film 'The Redemption of General Butt Naked' (Anastasion and Strauss, 2011), highlights the former child soldiers' rejection by their community and consequent dependence on drugs and crime. These former Butt Naked Commandos were a pretty sorry lot until they were re-acquainted with Blahyi at the war's end. Blahyi inserted himself back into their lives and provided them with structure and a belief in religion. Unfortunately for most of these former combatants, Blahyi's subsequent abrupt disappearance left them with no external structure to rely on, and they fell back into destructive old ways of drugs and crime (ibid.). In this anecdote, we can see that counter to the negative experiences of the Naked Commandos were the positive/protective factors of Relationships, Community and Shared Brotherhood. This, as well as the negative consequences of the removal of these positive factors.

Researchers in the medical field have noted the relationship between violent experiences during childhood and subsequent poor health issues (Felitti *et al.*, 1998). Subsequently, other researchers have noted that:

> Given linkages between exposure to violence in childhood and future violence perpetration, there is a need to identify protective factors that buffer the impact of exposure to ACEs [Adverse Childhood Experiences] (Davis *et al.*, 2019, p.2345).

Acknowledging the extent of adverse experiences that Liberians lived through, following Davis *et al.* (2019), our chapter seeks to explore the ways Liberians have buffered these negative experiences with positive ones.

It is in this context we examine the ongoing impact of conflict and identify *protective factors* that can lead to and support the resilience of the Liberian people, particularly their youth, many of whom were observers if not victims or active participants. In this context, we identify the protective factors of Relationships, Family, and Community (largely following Bronfenbrenner (1977), but see also Assanga (2009). For the purpose of this chapter, we assess the impact of the conflict on a segment of the community as represented by a subset of sophomore students enrolled at the United Methodist University in Monrovia (data were collected during the Fall semester of 2017). In doing this, we are utilizing the framework of Adverse Childhood Experiences (ACEs), as outlined in the seminal study by Felitti *et al.* (1998). While Felitti *et al.*'s study was carried out in Southern California, the efficacy of the model has been validated within the United States (Aguilar, 2019; Davis *et al.*, 2019; Dube *et al.*, 2003; Finkelhor *et al.*, 2013; McEwen and Gregerson, 2019), in Africa (Cluver *et al.*, 2015; Kabiru *et al.*, 2010; Kazeem, 2015; Kiburi *et al.*, 2018; Kobayashi *et al.*, 2020; Naicker *et al.*, 2017; Oladeji *et al.*, 2010), and Liberia specifically (Levey *et al.*, 2017; Manyema and Richter, 2019; Kim *et al.*, 2021).

In many respects, it is to be marvelled that today's Liberia is the stable and largely peaceful place it is. Since Taylor's exile, the country has gone through three election cycles, all of which have been declared largely free and fair, and one transition of power. Though Liberians have continued to face challenging odds, they remain largely optimistic about the future despite the horrendous Ebola outbreak from March 2014 to June 2016 resulted in 'more than 10,600 cases and 4,800 deaths in Liberia' (Soucheray, 2018) and the more recent COVID-19 pandemic (5,824 reported cases and 287 reported deaths as of December 1st, 2021) (Johns Hopkins Coronavirus Resource Centre, 2021). Though for both these pandemics, these figures should be regarded as minimums rather than the actual counts.

For Liberians, Ebola and COVID-19 are just the latest adverse experiences coming on top of a seventeen-year period of civil and guerrilla war. As we outline from our study (n=361), 43% of all respondents stated that they lost family during the conflicts and 21% identified as Refugee or Internally Displaced Person (IDP) for at least some time during the conflicts. Given such context, it is to be marvelled at the overall resilience of the Liberian people. While the data and analyses presented here are not exhaustive, we do hold that it is illustrative and highlights avenues for further study.

Figure 8.1: Negative Life Status // Increased Risk Taking

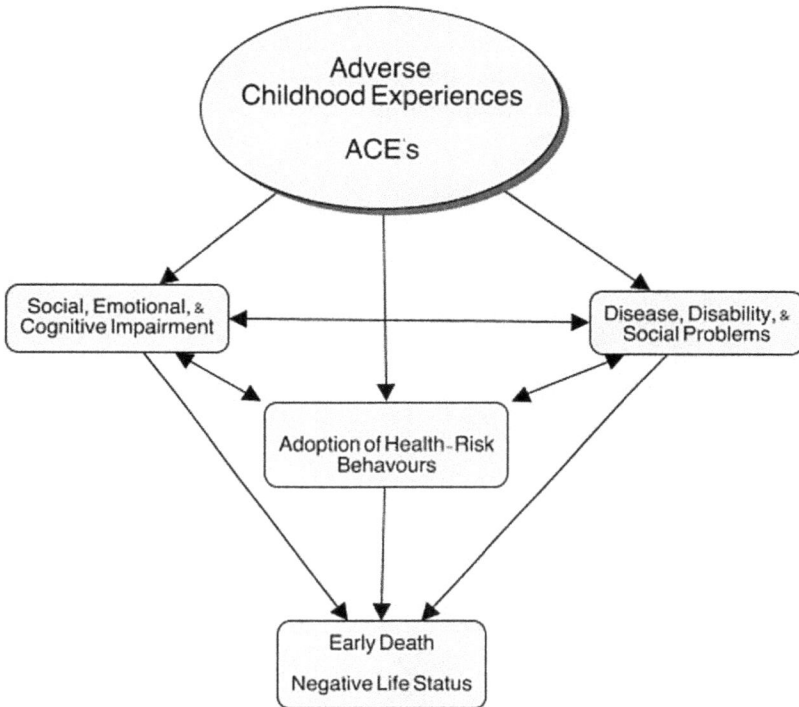

Note: Adapted from Felitti *et al.*, (1998)

The above diagram (Figure 8.1) provides a generalized path from Adverse Childhood Experiences to potentially an earlier death as the result of increased social, emotional and cognitive impairment and the adoption of greater health risk behaviours (such as drug and alcohol usage and/or transactional sexual activity), such behaviours lead to and reinforce the increased likelihood of disease, disability and social problems; all of which can add to a negative life status. Given all that has transpired in Liberia, it would be entirely rational to believe that as a country, with its recent past, Liberians would largely be suffering from an overwhelming negative life status. While the current life expectancy in Liberia (64.1 years) has slowly been improving, it is lower than the current global average (72.5 years) or the US (78.78 years) (data.worldbank.org).

While the picture above looks somewhat bleak, there is, however, a growing body of research that highlights the importance of positive childhood experiences and relationships that can mitigate and build resilience against negative experiences (Burstein *et al.*, 2021; Sege and Linkenbach, 2014; Sege *et al.*, 2017). Figure 8.2 presents the logical flow as to how resilience can emerge among individuals who have had adverse childhood experiences.

While our research in Liberia is only at the early stage, we do see evidence that is suggestive of an interplay between Adverse Childhood Experiences (ACEs), what is known as Healthy Outcomes from Positive Experiences (HOPEs) that are indicative of directions that institutions and public policy can take to mitigate if not fully ameliorate the negative experiences many Liberians have faced over the past 40 years.

Figure 8.2: Positive Quality of Life // Resilience

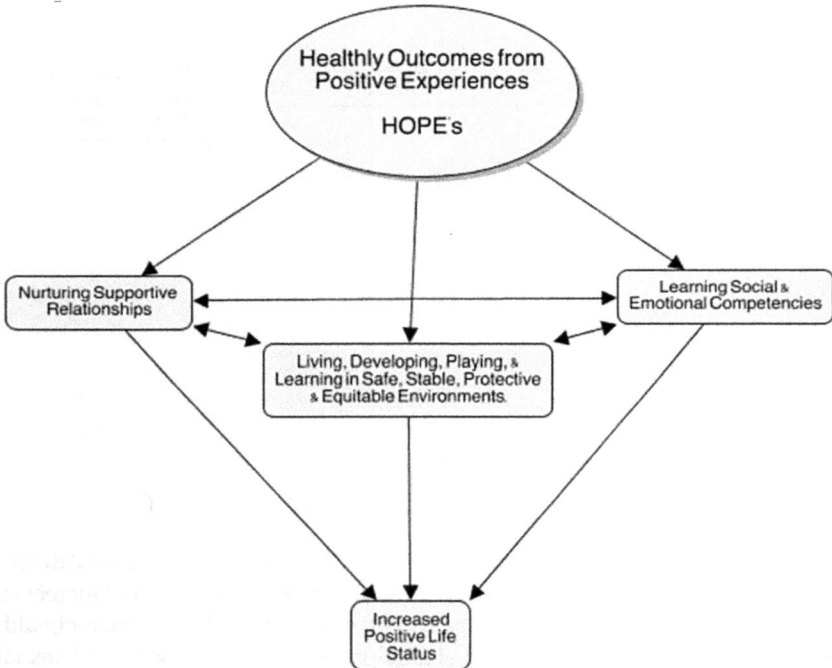

Note: Adapted from Sege & Harper Browne, 2017.

The approach presented above speaks to the complex Liberian situation at the national level. The authors of this chapter are not politicians but rather academics. Thus, from our perspective, we want to understand the situation at the level of individuals. What are the prior/current conditions that Liberian youth experience and thus bring into their daily lives, and what might be the possibilities for mitigating potential negative experiences?

Research Design

In the Fall of 2017, we had the opportunity to conduct a survey with undergraduates at the Monrovia campus of the United Methodist University of

Liberia. The paper and pencil survey was designed to provide the university's administration with information about their students in areas related to their basic demographic information, living situation, current health, and services they wanted the university to provide. There were also additional questions on the survey that sought to paint a picture of the student's experiences during the conflict.[2] A total of 361 undergraduate students completed at least part of the survey. For the various analyses presented below, the number of valid responses will vary due to missing data on one or more of the topics being examined.

Our core research question examines the potential interplay between ACEs and HOPEs in terms of the students' quality of life and risk-taking behaviour. We have operationalized quality of life in three distinct domains, i.e., health, social well-being, and economic security. Based on our survey items, health is represented by asking about students' current health. Societal well-being is represented by asking if the respondents had ever been a victim of a crime, and economic security was represented by a survey item regarding the ownership of a means of transportation. Going beyond the narrow conception of quality of life, we also wanted to examine students' sense of future possibilities for their country. To operationalize this, we asked about their hopes for Liberia's future.

While there are many definitions of risk-taking behaviour, for our purposes, we use the definition from Ben-Zur and Zeidner (2009):

> *risk taking* refers to one's purposive participation in some form of behavior that involves potential negative consequences or losses (social, monetary, interpersonal) as well as perceived positive consequences or gains. Indeed, many of life's decisions involve a balance between anticipated rewards and losses. A broad conception of risk taking encompasses an array of behaviors that can lead to not only grave losses to self and significant others but also unintentional harm to innocent others (p. 110).

For the purpose of this study, the negative risk-taking behaviours were operationalized via survey questions related to alcohol use, sexual activity and gang participation. The key questions we examine here relate to the impact of two ACEs and two HOPEs. The ACEs are (1) loss of one or more relatives during the conflict and (2) did your family move during the conflict? The HOPEs are (1) residing with at least one other person when the university is not in session and (2) someone in the family attends the same church the respondent attends.

---

[2] Please contact the first author for a copy of the pilot survey used in this study.

It should be noted at the outset that all of the students who participated in our survey should be classified as at least somewhat resilient since each of them would have had at least some experience of the civil war, lived through the Ebola epidemic, and have managed to be enrolled in a Christian-based university.

Basic Demographic Characteristics

As can be seen in Table 8.1, the overall sample is relatively evenly split in terms of gender and age group. Females represent 51.7% of the sample, and 48.3% are males. There is a very similar split in terms of age group, with 48.3% of the sample being 26 and younger and 51.7% being older than 26 at the time they completed the survey. There is a slightly different pattern when we look within subgroups. For example, a greater percentage of the female respondents are in the younger age group, while the opposite is true for males, where a greater percentage are 26 or older. A chi-square test indicates that these differences in frequencies cross gender by age are statistically significant ($\chi^2 = 7.22$, df = 1, $p = .0072$). As to be expected in a Post-conflict society, the age profile of students attending university is older than a 'Western' university age profile. This in itself does give an indication of resilience in that we can assume many had paused their education during the conflict and have subsequently returned. Highlighting their resilience and the perceived importance of obtaining an education.

Table 8.1: Age Group by Gender

Age Group	Female		Male			
	% of Total	#	% of Total	#	Total %	Total #
26 and younger	28.9	86	19.5	58	48.3	144
26+	22.8	68	28.9	86	51.7	154
Total	51.7	154	48.3	144	100.0	298

Religious affiliation data from our sample do not quite match the country-wide profile of religious affiliation as reported by the US State Department[3], these being '85.6% Christian, 12.2% Muslim, 1.4% persons who claim no religion, 0.6% adherents of indigenous religious beliefs'. Such discrepancy, however, is to be expected given we are sampling from a Christian University.

While our sample on religious affiliation is somewhat skewed from reported statistics of the general population, we did find that in terms of ethnic makeup, our sample broadly reflected that of the general population (CIA, 2022) and therefore, we have reasonable confidence that we have been able to capture a representative cross sample.

---

[3] www.state.gov, 2008

Table 8.2: Religious Affiliation

Religion	%	#
Catholic	1.4	4
Christian/Protestant	91.0	263
Muslim	7.3	21
Other	0.3	1
Total	100.0	289

Note: Excludes respondents with missing data for age and/or gender.

The sample represents participants from all 17 of Liberia's officially recognized ethnic/cultural groups plus three Americo-Liberians (Liberia Institute of Statistics and Geo-Information Services, 2011), and the sample largely mirrors the ethnic composition of Liberia. (See Table 8.3). Twenty students indicated that they belonged to more than one ethnic/cultural group. They have been included multiple times within the relevant groups listed in this table.

Table 8.3: Ethnic Group Affiliation

	#	%	World Fact Book %
Kpelle	55	16.92	20.30
Kru	41	12.62	6.00
Grebo	34	10.46	10.00
Bassa	30	9.23	13.40
Mano	24	7.38	7.90
Gio	20	6.15	8.00
Kissi	19	5.85	4.80
Loma	17	5.23	5.10
Krahn	14	4.31	4.00
Mandingo	14	4.31	3.20
Gola	13	4.00	4.40
Val	9	2.77	4.00
Belle	8	2.46	----
Mende	7	2.15	1.30
Gbandi	6	1.85	3.00
Americo-Liberian	3	0.92	----
Deys	2	0.62	----
Sapo	1	0.31	1.30
Unknown	8	2.46	----

Note: Students could belong to more than one ethnic group, thus, the total number is greater than the number of students in our analysis pool.
Note: World Fact Book (CIA, 2022)

Negative Life Indicators

In the design of the survey, we wanted to determine the impact of the conflict on the students' current lives. As such, there were two key questions on the survey. One was 'Did you lose family members during the conflict?' and the other was 'Where did you live during the conflict (1989 – 2003)?' Thus, for our sample, 43% of the students indicated that they lost one or more family members during the conflict, and 21% said that their family moved during the conflict. (See Table 8.4). About 11% of the sample reported both losing family members and moving during the conflict. We feel that data for having moved during the conflict is a significant underestimate. While the response options to the question about loss were 'yes' and 'no', the question about location was open-ended. Thus, for the living location during the conflict, it was often impossible to determine if the student's family actually moved. For example, many students wrote 'Liberia' or a specific village or area. Thus, we coded many items as 'unknown' when in fact, the student's family may have actually moved during the conflict. Given this underestimate of having moved during the conflict, for all subsequent analyses, respondents who reported just one ACE (42.6%) are with respondents who reported two ACEs (10.7%).

Table 8.4: ACEs: Lost Family Members During the Conflict by Moved During the Conflict

Lost 1 or More Family Members	Moved During the Conflict					
	Yes		Unknown			
	% of Total	#	% of Total	#	Total %	Total #
Yes	10.7	32	32.2	96	43.0	128
No	9.7	29	35.2	105	45.0	134
Unknown	0.7	2	11.4	34	12.1	36
Total	21.1	63	78.2	235	100.0	298

Positive Life Indicators

In terms of HOPEs, nearly two-thirds of the students (66.1%) live with someone else when the university is not in session. (See Table 8.5). And over one-third of the sample (36.2%) have a family member who attends the same church that they attend. Finally, about one-quarter of the group (25.8%) reported both HOPEs. There was a small group of students who left the item blank for one or the other HOPE. For purposes of the subsequent analyses, these 'unknowns' were included in their respective 'No HOPE' groups.

Table 8.5: HOPEs: Live with Someone Else by Family Member Attends the Same Church

Lives with Someone Else when the University is not in Session	Family Member Attends the Same Church							
	Yes		No		Unknown		Row Total	
	% of Total	#	% of Total	#	% of Total	#	%	#
Yes	25.8	77	31.9	95	8.4	25	66.1	197
No	7.0	21	17.4	52	4.0	12	28.5	85
Unknown	3.4	10	2.0	6	0.0	0	5.4	16
Total	36.2	108	51.3	153	12.4	37	100.0	298

Comparison of Positive Life Indicators and Negative Life Indicators

The relationships between the frequency of reported ACEs and HOPEs are displayed in Tables 8.6a and 8.6b. Among those who reported HOPEs, they were about equally likely to report either No ACEs (N = 115) or Yes ACEs (N = 112). Interestingly among those who did not report any HOPEs, they were less likely to report No ACEs (N = 24) than Yes ACEs (N = 47).

Table 8.6a: Number of HOPEs by Number of ACEs

# of HOPEs Reported	# of ACES Reported							
	0		1		2		Total	
	% of Total	#	% of Total	#	% of Total	#	% of Total	#
2	11.7	35	10.4	31	3.7	11	25.8	77
1	26.8	80	19.5	58	4.0	12	50.3	150
0	8.1	24	12.8	38	3.0	9	23.8	71
Grand Total	46.6	139	42.6	127	10.7	32	100.0	298

$\chi^2 = 8.80$, df = 2, $p = .067$

Table 8.6b: Reported HOPEs and No HOPEs by Reported ACEs and No ACEs

HOPEs	ACEs					
	No ACEs Reported		Yes ACEs Reported		Overall Total	
	% of Total	#	% of Total	#	%	#
Yes, HOPEs Reported	38.6	115	37.6	112	76.2	227
No HOPEs Reported	8.1	24	15.8	47	23.8	71
Total	46.6	139	53.4	159	100.0	298

$\chi^2 = 6.18$, df = 1, $p = .013$

Results

Quality of Life Indicators

Health:

From Table 8.7, we see that students who assessed their health as either very good or good current health were more likely to have no ACEs reported, 84.3%, versus students who did report ACEs, only 77%. The overall chi-square was statistically significant (χ^2 (1) = 7.29, p = .007). While the impact of HOPEs is minimal for students who reported one or two ACEs, the relationship is far more pronounced for students who did not report any ACEs. Among this group, nearly 87% of students with reported HOPE's indicated that their health was very good or good, while among those who did not report any HOPE's the figure dropped to approximately 73% as reporting very good or good health.

Table 8.7: Current Health by ACEs and HOPEs

	Health is Very Good or Good	
	%	N
ACEs Reported	77.2	122
Yes, HOPEs Reported	77.7	87
No HOPEs Reported	76.1	35
No ACEs Reported	84.3	113
Yes, HOPEs Reported	86.6	97
No HOPEs Reported	72.7	16
Total	80.5	235

$\chi^2 = 7.29$, df = 1, $p = .007$

About 10% of the respondents indicated that they had been a victim of a crime (Table 11). Having adverse childhood experiences is associated with having been a victim of a crime, 14.0% versus 5.2% for those respondents who did not report any adverse childhood experiences. Although being a victim of a crime is somewhat uncommon among this sample, and the chi-square test was non-significant, once again, we see the apparent positive impact of HOPEs. For both the ACEs and No ACEs groups, we observe lower rates of victimhood among those who reported one or two HOPEs. Interestingly, this relationship is most apparent among the No ACEs reported group, where 13.3% of those with No HOPEs and only 3.7% with HOPEs were victims of a crime.

Table 8.8: Social Wellbeing - Have You Ever Been a Victim of a Crime by ACEs and HOPEs

	Yes, Victim of a Crime	
	%	#
ACEs Reported	14.0	19
Yes, HOPEs Reported	12.4	12
No HOPEs Reported	17.9	7
No ACEs Reported	5.2	5
Yes, HOPEs Reported	3.7	3
No HOPEs Reported	13.3	2
Total	10.3	24

$\chi^2 = 0.193$, df = 1, $p = .66$ (with Yates correction)

Economic Security:

Most students in our sample did not own their own means of transportation, which could include a bicycle, motorbike, kekeh (three-wheeled motorcycle), or automobile. However, Table 8.9 once again shows the impact of ACEs on students' status in terms of transportation ownership, even though the chi-square test was statistically non-significant. Students who reported ACEs' were less likely to be a transportation owner, 15.6%, compared to students who did not report any ACEs, 19.5%. Looking at the potential impact of HOPEs, we see in Table 12 that HOPEs are associated with better outcomes for both those who did and those who did not report any ACEs. Here the association between HOPEs and being a transportation owner were stronger for those who reported ACEs.

Table 8.9: Economic Security - Do You Own a Means of Transportation by ACEs and HOPEs

	Yes, I Own a Form of Transportation	
	%	#
ACEs Reported	15.6	24
Yes, HOPEs Reported	17.3	19
No HOPEs Reported	11.4	5
No ACEs Reported	19.5	26
Yes, HOPEs Reported	20.0	22
No HOPEs Reported	17.4	4
Total	17.4	50

$\chi^2 = 0.018$, df = 1, $p = .89$ (with Yates correction)

Hopes for Liberia's Future:

In terms of the respondents' hopes for Liberia's future, economic development, education, peace, and political stability were the most cited specific hopes. (See Table 8.10). For this open-ended item, respondents could and often did list multiple hopes. There is no obvious pattern across groups or subgroups. For the ACEs versus No ACEs Reported groups, the category with the largest difference was Economic Development, but here, the prevalent frequencies flipped across groups, with Economic Development being cited more frequently by those respondents who did not report ACEs. In terms of HOPEs versus No HOPEs reported, the category with the largest difference was Peace with this category being cited most frequently among the HOPEs reported group.

Table 8.10: Hopes for Liberia's Future

	Areas of Hope				
	Better in General	Economic Development	Education	Peace	Political
ACEs Reported	38.4	13.8	18.9	12.6	11.3
Yes, HOPEs Reported	43.8	10.7	15.2	13.4	9.8
No HOPEs Reported	25.5	21.3	27.7	10.6	14.9
No ACEs Reported	36.7	19.4	12.2	13.7	10.1
Yes, HOPEs Reported	34.8	20.9	13.0	15.7	10.4
No HOPEs Reported	45.8	12.5	8.3	4.2	8.3
Total	37.6	16.4	15.8	13.1	10.7

Note: Only categories with more than 10% of the total sample responding are listed.
Note: Percentages represent the percentage of respondents within each of the four subgroups. Thus, the total percentage across rows does not equal 100%.

Risk-Taking Behaviors

Alcohol Use:

Turning out attention to risk-taking behaviours and experiences, Table 8.11 presents data related to students' use of alcohol. Keeping in mind that the students were attending a university that is affiliated with a church that does not condone alcohol consumption, about one-quarter of the respondents reported that they did consume alcohol. Once again, while the chi-square test was statistically non-significant, here, we see the negative impact of ACEs where slightly more ACEs students said that they drank alcohol, 27.7% versus non-ACEs students, 23.9%. Once again, we see the apparent positive impact of HOPEs on alcohol consumption. For both ACEs and non-ACEs students, those who reported HOPEs were less likely to drink alcohol. As can be seen in Table 8.11, this positive association was more pronounced among ACEs students than non-ACEs students.

While alcohol consumption was low, cigarette smoking was rare; only one student reported smoking cigarettes.

Table 8.11: Do You Drink Alcohol by ACEs and HOPEs

	Yes	
	%	#
ACEs Reported	27.7	43
Yes, HOPEs Reported	22.9	25
No HOPEs Reported	39.1	18
No ACEs Reported	23.9	28
Yes, HOPEs Reported	22.4	22
No HOPEs Reported	31.6	6
Total	26.1	71

$\chi^2 = 2.316$, df = 1, $p = .13$ (with Yates correction)

Sexual Activity:

From Table 8.12, we see that sexual activity is quite common among this group of respondents. Unfortunately, this version of our survey did not give participants the opportunity to indicate if they were sexually active with a regular partner or had multiple partners. Being sexually active was more frequently indicated among the ACEs reported group, 69.1%, than among the No ACEs group, 49.2%. Once again, the chi-square test was statistically non-significant, but as with previous outcome indicators, we observe the apparent impact of HOPEs where those who reported HOPEs within each ACEs group were less likely to be sexually active. The apparent positive impact of HOPEs is most evident among those who did not report any ACEs. It should be noted that this data related to sexual activity may be highly influenced by marriage patterns that are, in turn, related to age. Our survey did not include any questions regarding marital status. The ACEs group has more older respondents than the No ACEs group.

Another potential interpretation of these results is that, as seen in other post-conflict settings, transactional sex is a strong driver in communities recovering from conflict (Atwood, 2011). While the context of our survey was not specifically about transactional sex and given that the age of respondents is higher than in a number of reported studies, we find that the pattern is females report slightly less sexual activity (53.0%) than males (68.3%). While this does appear to go against the literature (Okigbo et al., 2014; Hutchinson et al., 2016; Beber et al., 2017; Stoebenau et al., 2016; Muhwezi et al., 2011), it is worth noting (again) that in individuals (both male and female) sexual activity was much higher amongst individuals who have experienced ACEs than those who had experienced no ACEs.

Table 8.12: Are You Sexually Active by ACEs and HOPEs

	Yes	
	%	#
ACEs Reported	69.1	103
Yes, HOPEs Reported	67.6	71
No HOPEs Reported	72.7	32
No ACEs Reported	49.2	58
Yes, HOPEs Reported	46.4	45
No HOPEs Reported	61.9	13
Total	60.3	161

$\chi^2 = 0.984$, df = 1, $p = .32$ (with Yates correction)

Note: The survey **did not include** an option to indicate if one was sexually active with a regular partner.

Gang Participation:

Turning our attention to gang membership, another risk-taking behaviour, we see a somewhat different pattern in terms of ACEs and HOPEs in Table 8.13. While overall gang membership is low, only 2.8% in this sample, respondents with no ACEs are more likely to report participating in a gang, 4.8% versus 1.4% among the ACEs reported group. Perhaps students who have experienced ACEs related to the conflict are more wary or more sensitive to the potential negative consequences of gang membership. In contrast to the ACEs pattern, the same apparent positive impact of HOPEs is seen for both the ACEs Reported and the No ACEs Reported groups. Respondents with HOPEs are less likely to participate in a gang. It should be noted that, as with the other risk-taking behaviours, the overall difference is statistically non-significant.

Table 8.13: Do You Currently or Have You Ever Belonged to a Gang by ACEs

	Yes	
	%	#
ACEs Reported	1.4	2
Yes, HOPEs Reported	1.0	1
No HOPEs Reported	2.3	1
No ACEs Reported	4.8	5
Yes, HOPEs Reported	4.7	4
No HOPEs Reported	5.3	1
Total	2.8	7

(with Yates correction: $\chi^2 = 0.018$, df = 1, $p = .43$)

Discussion

The students' reports about their quality of life and risk-taking behaviours present a very consistent picture of both the negative impact of ACEs related to the long-lasting internal conflict and the positive impact of HOPEs for both those who were negatively affected by the conflict and those who did not report any conflict related ACEs. While the chi-square tests were statistically non-significant for all indicators except Health, Table 8.14 displays this generally small but consistent pattern of impacts. Living with someone else when university is not in session and/or attending the same church as a member of one's own family is associated with at least a small positive impact across all of our indicators. It must be kept in mind that we cannot make causal attributions from this survey data. Nonetheless, the data do suggest that even for students who are resilient, as evidenced by their attendance at the university, there are factors that can provide support to them. Resilience should not be viewed as a 'once and done' shield. Rather resilience should be viewed as a characteristic akin to the human body's immune system that both fluctuates over time and responds to a myriad of changing external pressures. As such, the effectiveness of resiliency at any one point in time is reflected in one's concurrent quality of life and risk-taking behaviour.

Table 8.14: Summary of Apparent Impacts of ACEs and HOPEs

	Apparent Impact of ACEs	Apparent Impact of HOPEs	Table #
Quality of Life Indicators			
Health (Very Good or Good)	Negative	Minimal for ACEs group Positive for No ACEs group	#7
Victim of a Crime (Yes)	Negative	Positive for both ACES and No ACEs groups	#8
Transportation Ownership (Yes)	Negative	Positive for both ACES and No ACEs groups	#9
Hopes for Liberia's Future (specific comments)	Education most often cited	Economic Development, Peace and Education most cited	#10
Risk Taking Indicators			
Consumes Alcohol (Yes)	Minimally Negative	Positive for both ACES and No ACEs groups	#11
Active Sexually (Yes)	Negative	Positive for both ACES and No ACEs groups	#12
Belongs to a Gang (Yes)	Negative	Positive for both ACES and No ACEs groups	#13

Implications and Conclusions

These data are from a group of young adults who have been affected by multiple adverse experiences during their youth. The adjectives we choose to label these 'adverse experiences' vary, ranging from difficult, challenging, scaring, to devastating and unbearable. With respect to this group of students, we are not able to assign specific adjectives to their experiences, but the data clearly show that adverse experiences are associated with a greater frequency of risk-taking behaviours and a somewhat diminished quality of life. Yet, importantly, the data also show that experiencing HOPEs is associated with positive or mitigating impacts on these adverse indicators. Furthermore, these positive associations from HOPEs apply to both those who experienced specific adverse experiences related to conflict and those who did not. It is worth noting that we do see that Positive Outcomes for students who report HOPEs are more pronounced when there is also a report of ACEs.

The results from this study point to two areas for future research. First and foremost, it is important to determine if the findings related to the apparent impact of HOPEs are an artefact of our pilot sample or if they reflect a more substantive effect. Thus, data should be collected from a much broader sample of Liberian youth both geographically and socioeconomically, including those at other institutions of higher education, those who are employed, and those who are not in the labour force. Somewhat inadvertently, our study has broadened the notion of ACEs and HOPEs-related areas of impact. As noted above, initial research on ACEs and HOPEs focused on the potential impact of various childhood experiences on health-related outcomes, Burstein *et al.*, (2021). In our study, the antecedent indicators of potential ACEs and HOPEs were in keeping with previous research. However, in terms of outcomes, our quality-of-life indicators moved beyond the crucial but narrow focus on health to include indicators related to economic stability and social well-being. Future research in Liberia and other countries should follow up to see if ACEs and HOPEs are indeed precursors to a wide range of quality-of-life indicators. These research studies should be based on both cross-sectional and longitudinal methodologies.

Given the findings of our research, we find that: paying attention to the creation and support of HOPEs is not only good institutionally, but it is also good public policy. This takes on a vital component with respect to post-conflict societies and communities that have experienced trauma, something Liberia has experienced all too frequently and recently.

While this survey was done within the context of a faith-based higher education institution, building community and the provision of services should not just be left to religious institutions, even though they play an important role, particularly in Liberia. It is important for structures to be established across religious and ethnic lines, as these will have positive impacts not only for youth but also for longer-term benefits. Along with religious institutions, organizations like sporting, artistic and cultural clubs can and should be developed and utilized to build resilience. We often see such organizations as a sign of a thriving community, but this research on HOPEs suggests a more fundamental and important role. Rather than being viewed merely 'icing on the cake', these organizations can serve as a fundamental component with respect to rebuilding and maintaining societies. All too often, when times are hard and money is tight, one of the first places that institutions and governments seek to trim budgets is in the artistic, cultural and sporting areas. In contrast, as noted above, our results would indicate that it is precisely in these situations that the promotion of HOPEs is called for. Similarly, alas we recognize that when the discussion turns to efforts to promote longer-term benefits, political will often tend to be remarkably short-sighted. While national economies studiously measure profit and loss, perhaps there is something to be learned from the tiny kingdom of Bhutan, which has since 1972 concerned itself with the promotion and measuring of Gross National Happiness (Ura *et al.*, 2012; Burns, 2011). As we have seen through this research, it is precisely these things that can bring people together and give them HOPE that are the things that are most responsible for overcoming negative experiences, providing possibilities for a positive way forward.

References

Aguilar, A. 2019. *Childhood and trauma: The effects of adverse childhood experiences on the brain, behavior, and learning in the elementary school classroom* [Master's Thesis]. Humboldt State University. Viewed 2.20.23 from https://digitalcommons.humboldt.edu/etd/242/

Anastasion, D., and Strauss, E. (Directors) 2011. *The Redemption of General Butt Naked* [Documentary Film]. Sundance Institute and Film Festival.

Atwood, K. A. *et al.*, 2011. 'Transactional Sex among Youths in Post-conflict Liberia'. *Journal of Health, Population and Nutrition, 29*(2), 113-122.

Beber, B. *et al.*, 2017. 'Peacekeeping, compliance with international norms, and transactional sex in Monrovia, Liberia'. *International Organization, 71*(1), 1–30.

Ben-Zur H, and Zeidner M., 2009. 'Threat to Life and Risk-Taking Behaviors: A Review of Empirical Findings and Explanatory Models'. *Personality and Social Psychology Review, 13*(2):109-128. doi:10.1177/1088868308330104

Brehun, L. 1991. *Liberia War of Horror.* Accra, Ghana: Adwinsa Publications.

Bronfenbrenner, U. 1977. 'Toward an experimental ecology of human development'. *American Psychologist, 32*(7), 513.

Burns, G. W. 2011. Gross National Happiness: A gift from Bhutan to the world. In R. Biswas-Diener (Ed.), *Positive psychology as social change* (pp. 73–87). Springer.

Burstein, D. *et al.* 2021. 'Transforming practice with HOPE (Healthy Outcomes from Positive Experiences)'. *Maternal and Child Health Journal, 25*(7), 1019–1024.

Cluver, L. *et al.* 2015. 'Child and adolescent suicide attempts, suicidal behavior, and adverse childhood experiences in South Africa: A prospective study'. *Journal of Adolescent Health, 57*(1), 52–59.

Davis, J. P. *et al.*, 2019. 'Understanding the buffering effects of protective factors on the relationship between adverse childhood experiences and teen dating violence perpetration'. *Journal of Youth and Adolescence, 48*, 2343-2359.

Dube, S. R. *et al.*, 2003. 'Childhood abuse, neglect, and household dysfunction and the risk of illicit drug use: The adverse childhood experiences study'. *Pediatrics, 111*(3), 564–572.

Ellis, S. 1995. 'Liberia 1989-1994: A study of ethnic and spiritual violence'. *African Affairs, 94*(375), 165–197.

Ellis, S. 2006. *The Mask of Anarchy Updated Edition: The Destruction of Liberia and the Religious Dimension of an African Civil War* (2nd Revised & Updated ed. edition). NYU Press.

Felitti, V. *et al.*, 1998, 'Relationship of Childhood Abuse and Household Dysfunction to Many of the Leading Causes of Death in Adults: The Adverse Childhood Experiences (ACE) Study.' *American Journal of Preventive Medicine 14*(4) (1998): 245–258.

Finkelhor, D. *et al.*, 2013. 'Improving the adverse childhood experiences study scale'. *JAMA Pediatrics, 167*(1), 70–75.

Hutchinson, A. *et al.*, 2016. 'Understanding early marriage and transactional sex in the context of armed conflict: protection at a price'. *International Perspectives on Sexual and Reproductive Health, 42*(1), 45–49.

Johns Hopkins Coronavirus Resource Centre. 2021. December 1. *Liberia—COVID-19 Overview—Johns Hopkins.*. Viewed December 1, 2021, from https://coronavirus.jhu.edu/region/liberia

Kabiru, C. W. *et al.*, 2010. 'Self-reported drunkenness among adolescents in four sub-Saharan African countries: Associations with adverse childhood experiences'. *Child and Adolescent Psychiatry and Mental Health, 4*(1), 1–13.

Kazeem, O. T. 2015. 'A validation of the adverse childhood experiences scale in Nigeria'. *Research on Humanities and Social Sciences, 5*(11), 18–23.

Kiburi, S. K. *et al.*, 2018. 'Adverse childhood experiences among patients with substance use disorders at a referral psychiatric hospital in Kenya'. *BMC Psychiatry, 18*(1), 1–12.

Kim, A. *et al.*, 2021. 'Adverse Childhood Experiences and Adult Cardiometabolic Risk Factors and Disease Outcomes: Cross-Sectional, Population-Based Study of Adults in Rural Uganda.' *Journal of Global Health 11*(04035), 1-10. https://doi.org/10.7189/jogh.11.04035.

Kobayashi, L. C. et al., 2020. 'Adverse childhood experiences and domain-specific cognitive function in a population-based study of older adults in rural South Africa'. *Psychology and Aging, 35*(6), 818.

Levey, E. et al., 2017. 'A Qualitative Analysis of Parental Loss and Family Separation among Youth in Post-Conflict Liberia'. *Vulnerable Children and Youth Studies, 12*(1), 1–16. https://doi.org/10.1080/17450128.2016.1262978.

Liberia Institute of Statistics and Geo-Information Services. 2011. *2008 Population and Housing Census. Monrovia, Liberia: LISGIS*. Retrieved 12-29-21 from http://lisgis.net/pg_img/Population%20size%20210512.pdf

Manyema, M., and Richter, L. M. 2019. 'Adverse childhood experiences: Prevalence and associated factors among South African young adults'. *Heliyon, 5*(12), 1-10.

McEwen, C. A., and Gregerson, S. F. 2019. 'A critical assessment of the adverse childhood experiences study at 20 years'. *American Journal of Preventive Medicine, 56*(6), 790–794.

Muhwezi, W. W. *et al.*, 2011. 'Vulnerability to high risk sexual behaviour (HRSB) following exposure to war trauma as seen in post-conflict communities in eastern Uganda: A qualitative study'. *Conflict and Health, 5*(1), 1–15.

Naicker, S. N. *et al.*, 2017. 'An analysis of retrospective and repeat prospective reports of adverse childhood experiences from the South African Birth to Twenty Plus cohort'. *PloS One, 12*(7), e0181522.

Okigbo, C. C. *et al.*, 2014. 'Risk factors for transactional sex among young females in post-conflict Liberia'. *African Journal of Reproductive Health, 18*(3), 133–141.

Oladeji, B. D., Makanjuola, V. A., and Gureje, O. 2010. 'Family-related adverse childhood experiences as risk factors for psychiatric disorders in Nigeria'. *The British Journal of Psychiatry, 196*(3), 186–191.

Podder, S. 2011. 'Child soldier recruitment in the Liberian Civil Wars: Individual motivations and rebel group tactics'. In *Child soldiers: From recruitment to reintegration* (pp. 50–75). Springer.

Sawyer, A. 1992. *The emergence of autocracy in Liberia: Tragedy and challenge.* San Francisco: ICS Press.

Sawyer, A. 2005. *Beyond plunder: Toward democratic governance in Liberia.* Boulder, CO: Lynne Rienner Publishers.

Sege, R., *et al.*, 2017. 'Balancing adverse childhood experiences (ACES) with HOPE: New insights into the role of positive experience on child and family development'. *Boston, MA: The Medical Foundation.*

Sege, R., and Linkenbach, J. 2014. 'Essentials for childhood: promoting healthy outcomes from positive experiences'. *Pediatrics, 133*(6), e1489–e1491.

Soucheray, S., 2018. *Flare-up of Ebola in Liberian family highlights virus persistence.* CIDRAP. Retrieved January 13, 2022, from https://www.cidrap.umn.edu/news-perspective/2018/07/flare-ebola-liberian-family-highlights-virus-persistence

Stoebenau, K. *et al.*, 2016. 'Revisiting the understanding of 'transactional sex' in sub-Saharan Africa: A review and synthesis of the literature'. *Social Science & Medicine, 168*, 186–197.

Tabor, D. 2016, March 7. 'The Greater the Sinner: A Liberian warlord's unlikely path to forgiveness'. *The New Yorker.* https://www.newyorker.com/magazine/2016/03/14/general-butt-naked-the-repentant-warlord

Ura, K. *et al.*, 2012. *An Extensive Analysis of GNH Index.* The Centre for Bhutan Studies. https://doi.org/10.35648/20.500.12413/11781/ii036

Chapter 9

Safe and Empowered Communities: Ending FGM Investing in Migrant Women's Lifelong Learning

Sofia Leitão

Rinova Ltd

Amanda Francis

Rinova Ltd

Sami Atif

Rinova Ltd

Abstract

The chapter addresses lifelong learning as a catalyst for the sustained promotion of safe communities in the context of migration by raising awareness, informing and building competencies that allow migrant women to take a central role in counteracting sexual abuse. The chapter focuses on female genital mutilation (FGM), providing an overview of the phenomenon and presenting a case study resulting from the pilot implementation, in the UK, of the project *BASE: Migrant and refugee child-friendly support services in cases of sexual and gender-based violence*. BASE is aimed at counteracting gender-based violence (GBV) against refugee/migrant girls through the development and sustainability of strategies to nurture inclusive communication and a culture of trust between support service professionals (social workers; health professionals; NGO support officers; psychologists; school staff; law enforcement) victims, families and communities, thus preventing victim re-traumatisation and encouraging reporting of GBV. FGM is a violation of Human Rights, a practice deeply rooted in social, cultural, and traditional aspects inflicting long-term physical, psychological and sexual harm on its survivors. The authors advocate for the pressing need for continuous educational programmes that affect change in attitudes and behaviours from within the community.

Keywords: Gender based violence, Female genital mutilation, Lifelong learning, child-friendly support

***

Gender-Based Violence in the UK

The term Gender-Based Violence, abbreviated as GBV, is defined in the UN Declaration on the Elimination of Violence against Women at a basic level as any violence resulting in 'physical, sexual or psychological harm or suffering to women' (UN General Assembly, 1993). From this, there are many derivations as to the specifics of what this entails, many of which are addressed further in the UN declaration. The international charity Women for Women defines gender-based violence as including 'physical, sexual, verbal, emotional, and psychological abuse, threats, coercion, and economic or educational deprivation.' (Ott, 2017). This very closely resembles the UN definition and suggests a broader definition of violence when in the context of GBV than what is often considered an act of violence, usually limited to the use or threat of 'physical force or power' (Krug *et al.*, 2002), further suggesting that GBV can, in fact, be interpreted as a term for general gender-based abuse. This notion is purported by another UK-based charity, Against Violence & Abuse:

> Gender based violence and abuse has become an umbrella term for any harm that is perpetrated against a person's will, and that results from power inequalities that are based on gender roles. The 'gender based' aspect highlights the fact that violence against women is an expression of power inequalities between women and men. (Against Violence & Abuse, n.d.)

Furthermore, this definition also touches on another important point; the concept that gender-based violence is, in many ways, a manifestation of gender inequality as a whole, particularly in terms of power held by each gender. This is also a concept which inherently relates to issues of violence against children, with age being the denominator of power inequality rather than gender.

In addition to this, it is important to note that UK legislation does not specifically address gender-based violence as a distinct term but instead addresses gender issues in the context of equality. In the Equality Act of 2010, Section 11 defines sex as a protected characteristic, which is referenced to as such throughout the rest of the act, such as in section 26, which defines harassment in relation to these characteristics. Within this section, paragraph 26(1)(b) lists specific examples of what constitutes harassment, which includes 'creating an intimidating, hostile, degrading, humiliating or offensive environment', which covers part of what the UN (UN General Assembly, 1993), Against

Violence & Abuse (Against Violence & Abuse, n.d.) and Women for Women (Ott, 2017) define as GBV.

In late 2018 the House of Commons Library published a briefing paper on the subject, which addressed: definitions, the scale of the issue, legal solutions, current government action and proposed legislation (Strickland and Allen, 2018). An important point in this paper is that it highlights the lack of a statutory definition of domestic violence, noting that there is, in fact, a statutory definition in the upcoming Domestic Violence and Abuse Bill (Home Office & Ministry of Justice, 2019), but presenting a non-statutory definition to be referenced in the time being. This definition, originally published by the Home Office in 2012 (Home Office, 2012), very much resembles the definitions of GBV which have already been discussed in this section, in the sense that it also includes psychological and emotional forms of abuse, as well as physical, under the umbrella term of violence, although not specifically relating them to gender.

Best Interest of the Child

Another key concept is the 'best interest of the child.' The concept itself is notably used in the UN Convention on the Rights of the Child (UN General Assembly, 1989), frequently occurs in writing on child protection and is referenced in various legislation and government publications on the subject, both in the UK and internationally (Department for Children Schools and Families, 2003).

In her lecture on the subject, Emily Logan (Logan, 2008) explains that prior to the 1989 convention, the phrase had also been used in the Declaration of Rights on the Child (UN General Assembly, 1959) and in the Convention on the Elimination of All forms of Discrimination Against Women (UN General Assembly, 1979). She goes on to explain later in her lecture that the 1989 convention "does not specifically define 'best interests'" and states that this was done with the purpose of allowing adaptation to fit into already existing frameworks (Logan, 2008).

The concept is first referenced in UK legislation in the Children Act 1989 and has since been further included in subsequent legislation such as the Children Act 2004. In the former, one of the ways in which the term is used is as a guideline for judgment calls in procedures for child protection being defined within the act. For example, in paragraph 46(10)(b), which defines the procedures for protective police custody over a child in emergency situations, it is the officer's judgment on whether it is in the best interests of the child that has ultimate authority over whether the child's guardians may have contact. This relates to Logan's explanation for the lack of any specific definition by the

United Nations (Logan, 2008), as here we see an example of the term being adapted as a guideline for police decision-making in a very specific situation. It could be argued that its primary purpose in this context is to ensure that judgments made in situations such as these always prioritise the child's well-being and safety above all other factors, giving protection services the legal authority to determine this.

A recent need for further definition in the UK was brought about due high profile cases around the time of the second act, wherein government services had failed to identify and prevent abuse on multiple occasions, resulting in an inquiry (Laming *et al.* 2003), and subsequent green paper within which this is reported (Department for Children School and Families, 2003). The child protection legislative framework in the UK is spread across a multitude of different laws and regulations, which are periodically amended or added to and improved as new or different sociological circumstances and needs come to light over time, as well as different government strategies which have arguably prioritised different aspects of child protection and used different approaches. A particularly useful document that serves as an effective starting point for understanding this framework is the NSPCC factsheet on the issue, published in 2012 (NSPCC, 2012). Near the beginning of this document, it is emphasised that it does not provide full extensive coverage of the UK's legislative framework on the issue, especially when considering the individual laws of each nation within the UK (ibid) but does provide a summary of each major piece of country-level legislation.

GBV and Migrant Communities

One of the major focuses addressed by research and discussion on GBV in the UK has, in the past few decades, become Female Genital Mutilation (FGM). One 2016 study includes an analysis of the shift in attitudes and asserts, based on data gathered for the study, that between 2010 and 2016 in particular, 'strong progress has been made in raising awareness' (Brown and Porter, 2016), continuing to later attribute this to a number of factors, including legal and policy changes, as well as a 'renewed focus on FGM by the media'. This is regarded by the study as an important aspect of progress on the issue, somewhat easier to combat through exposure, some of the stigma surrounding it has dissipated, and victims are more likely to speak out. The study also addresses in considerable detail specifics on certain communities affected and how they compare in terms of progress. The study explains some responses indicated that women from larger migrant communities, such as Somalis, have found it easier to speak out due to support from community organisations, whereas less progress in this regard has been made within smaller migrant communities, such as Gambians or Libyans (ibid).

Another interesting piece addressing violence specifically against migrant women is a journal article for the European Journal of Homelessness, which investigates how GBV contributes to putting migrant women in situations which lead to homelessness (Mayock *et al.*, 2012). The article begins by establishing that it is internationally recognised that domestic violence is one of the leading causes of homelessness among women, continuing to demonstrate that research done in the UK on the subject confirms that this is the case in the UK. An interesting point, which is made on this, is that despite this being such a widely recognised cause, not enough study has been done on why this is such a prevailing cause of female homelessness. Relating this specifically to migrant women, the authors argue that this issue is particularly prevalent with migrant women, as they are generally less likely to disclose GBV experiences in abusive homes to friends or family, which often limits the amount of support they receive.

Somewhat surprisingly, there seems to be a lack of readily available literature on the subject of GBV against children in the UK. A large number of NGOs in the UK seem to focus their studies and analysis on other countries rather than the domestic situation. However, there are a selection of studies that do provide extensive insight into GBV and children, such as the NSPCC study from 2011 (Radford *et al.*, 2011). Although this study, as the title would suggest, broadly looks at 'Child Abuse and Neglect in the UK', it has dedicated chapters focusing specifically on the role of gender within this, as well as breaking down most of the statistics it uses by gender. In one section, specifically looking at 'Gender and Maltreatment', the study compares different viewpoints on how much of an effect gender has on rates and severity of abuse, stating that there is a 'history of heated debate' on the subject. The study establishes that despite this debate, there is a clear statistical gender asymmetry when looking specifically at sexual abuse in terms of victim and perpetrator. It explains that most perpetrators of sexual abuse were male and 'known to the child or young person' and that girls between the ages of 15 and 17 reported the highest rates of past sexual abuse. This last part, in particular, demonstrates one of the difficulties in fully understanding the issue, as the age at which reporting occurs is more than often long after the abuse has happened. The study also adds that it has been argued that more severe abuse is likely to be more gender asymmetrical. It addresses this again later on, explaining that young girls below the age of 10 tended to have higher overall trauma scores in relation to family abuse and violence. Interestingly, the study did find that, in the context of delinquency as an indicator. Teenage girls seemed to be more severely impacted by abuse from a female parent or guardian (ibid). In reference to severe maltreatment, it also argues that being a victim of childhood abuse increases the likelihood of re-victimisation, extending into adulthood. This suggests a potential link between childhood abuse and higher rates of victimisation of women.

The Victoria Climbie Inquiry report (Laming *et al.*, 2003) and subsequent Every Child Matters study (Department for Children Schools and Families, 2003) are also useful but limited pieces of literature on the topic. The former has a limited scope on the subject as a whole, addressing only the single case of Victoria Climbie, but it is nonetheless useful as a case study. The latter is a general study and uses diversified statistical data. However, it scarcely addresses gender specifically, and where it does, it fails to provide substantial analysis based on its findings.

Largely due to general national statistical services such as the Office of National Statistics and the Crime Survey for England and Wales, there is a plethora of statistical and demographic data in the UK, which can be used to inform analysis of the specifics of GBV nationally. The House of Commons Library briefing paper uses the Crime Survey for England and Wales as its primary data source, explaining that as a household survey, it 'picks up more crime than official police figures', including those that remain unreported and unrecorded (Stickland and Allen, 2018). The briefing paper focuses on domestic violence as a whole but uses these statistics to breakdown the frequency at which it affects each gender, illustrating that according to data from 2016/17, 26% of women and 15% of men between 16 and 59 years old in the UK had experienced domestic violence at some point throughout their adult lives, equating to 4.3 and 2.4 million victims respectively.

The discussion surrounding the Domestic Violence Bill (Home Office & Ministry of Justice, 2019) has been partly focused on its ability to protect migrant women, in particular, from domestic violence, which is particularly damaging to this group, often leading to homelessness (Mayock *et al.*, 2012). In reference to the bill in particular, a briefing note produced by multiple universities in collaboration (Bates *et al.* 2018) referred that 10% of the victims interviewed who were not EU or UK nationals ended up being homeless, with 30% in refugees. The summary also highlights that this is significantly larger than the 3% for each category for respondents who were EU or UK nationals, strongly suggesting that non-UK or EU nationals are much less likely to benefit from support after experiencing domestic or sexual violence. Additionally, the briefing note presents two other data sets comparing the experiences of victims with and without EU or UK nationality.

The first of these compares types of abuse experienced, demonstrating that in all instances other than severe sexual violence, victims without EU or UK nationality were more likely to be affected. This was most prevalent in the categories of 'Multiple DA perpetrators' and 'Honour based violence', which were both at 14% for those who were nationals and 41% and 38% for those who weren't. It is also noted that 'there may be more taboo or shame for migrant women in recognising and disclosing sexual violence' (ibid, p.3), which may explain why that is the only outlier in this data set.

The last data set that the briefing note provides is on police response to reported violence by victims, assessing the extent to which these reports were taken in terms of the justice system. This data shows that in every category, victims who were nationals received a more thorough response, with the percentage being approximately double in all categories other than 'Arrest made'. The analysis towards the end of the briefing note explains in reference to this that the statistics suggest that although an initial police response is relatively common, further action and justice seldom occur for migrant women. In this same analysis, another study is also referenced, which conducted qualitative research for the HM Inspectorate of Constabulary through the form of interviews and found evidence that supported this, with many migrant women reporting that they were quickly temporarily removed from the household after contacting the police, but that often they were not asked if they would like to press charges. Furthermore, it was reported in a number of cases that the perpetrator or their family offered the solution to the police of sending the migrant woman back to the country she was originally from (Hester et al., 2015).

Female Genital Mutilation

In terms of statistics on GBV specifically affecting migrant women, one of the major focuses remains FGM, with there being numerous reports on the subject available. One notable and quite in-depth example of this is a report using experimental statistics published by an information branch of the UK's National Health Service called NHS Digital (Clinical Audit and Registries Management Service, 2017). This report is useful because of the ways in which it breaks down the data, giving detailed numbers on a large variety of variables in conjunction with each other, such as country of birth and age at which it occurred, which is particularly useful in understanding demographic trends. In terms of age of occurrence, the report presents the chart below, providing a percentage breakdown of when FGM occurs based on 4 age groups. A clear majority affects girls under the age of 10, making it very evident that this is without a doubt an issue that affects younger girls in particular, with the study even noting that the age 'was under 10 in over four-fifths of the newly recorded cases.'. One additional aspect which should be noted about the data is that it is not completely reflective of all recorded cases of FGM and is only based on what the victims have been able to provide. For example, in the chart pictured above, only 31% of victims were able to provide the age at which FGM was undertaken. This could be indicative of a variety of things, including, but not limited to, a higher occurrence at younger ages, as this would explain a lack of memory surrounding the circumstances. Another important data set, which the NHS report provides, is the country of birth of the victims. The chart pictured below, among numerous others, is presented in relation to this, which is broken down into Eastern, Northern and Western Africa, the United Kingdom, and the Rest of the World. For this data set, this information was known for 46% of those recorded. This problem almost solely affects migrant women, with only 4% of the women affected being born in the UK. Looking at the country where FGM occurred, there is a correlation between the two, where the percentage of occurrences in the UK matches at 4%. It is, however, worth noting, that this data set does have a particularly low rate of disclosure, at only 26%. Additional data further on in the report also shows that the majority of those reported to have taken place in the UK occurred after the victim had turned 18, but again, only with a 26% disclosure rate.

The Female Genital Mutilation Act of 2003 was primarily an update on already existing legislation to do with the issue, filling gaps by adding new legal specifications and clarifying already existing ones. The act updated its terminology from its predecessor, named the Prohibition of Female Circumcision Act 1985, dropping the term circumcision and using mutilation instead. A guidance document on the issue by multiple government departments from 2016 explains that using the term circumcision is 'anatomically incorrect and misleading in terms of the harm FGM can cause' (Department for Education and Department for Health and Social Care, 2016), which makes the reasoning for this change clear. Aside from clarifying and updating already existing laws from its predecessor, the act also notably made it illegal to perform or assist someone in performing FGM abroad on a UK national. This was an important addition, especially when considering what the statistics on FGM referenced in the previous section demonstrated. The government's strategy from 2016 to 2020 (Home Office, 2016) highlighted several pieces of legislation introduced over the term of the prior government, legislating against: 'stalking, forced marriage, failure to protect from Female Genital Mutilation (FGM), and revenge pornography'.

Existing Good Practices to Support Victims of GBV

There is a plethora of charities and other NGOs in the UK operating with the goal of supporting victims of both gender-based violence and child abuse. Many of these organisations also work in partnership with each other as well as with governmental agencies in order to ensure that they are providing the most effective level of support. An example of this in regard to supporting women who have experienced GBV is End Violence Against Women, a coalition of many of the individual organisations in the UK who work towards this goal, such as Amnesty International UK, Women's Aid and Against Violence & Abuse.

Together, the coalition's main aims are to influence government policy and shape public attitudes in order to enable a better tackling of the issue[1]. Additionally, they also partake in specific campaigns, such as Step Up Migrant Women, which focuses on addressing the specific needs and barriers of migrant women who experience GBV, running joint campaigns working with other organisations primarily around the issue of migrant women having to 'risk being detained and deported if they report their abuser to the police.'. Rights of Women is an organisation which is part of both these coalitions and works to provide legal support to women in a variety of contexts. One of their focuses recently has been providing legal support to women who have experienced violence, with one of the target groups who they work with, in particular, being migrant women. The philosophy behind the project described on their website explains that regardless of the individual circumstances and factors of any situation where a woman is in need of aid, women want to know their legal rights and often need expert advice and guidance on how to legally navigate the situation. According to their website, Rights for Women employs a small team of legal staff who each specialise in various kinds of law useful for aiding women, as well as a supporting team for finance, administration and events, including volunteers. The director of the organisation has a background in campaigning for women's rights, having worked for organisations that specifically worked with human rights in conjunction with race and gender. Rights of Women is funded by a number of different funding bodies and organisations, which are listed on their website, are as follows: London Councils, Big Lottery Fund, Esmée Fairbairn Foundation, Trust for London, Garden Court Chambers, Lloyds Bank Foundation and The Henry Smith Charity. Rights of Women provide direct support to women across multiple different platforms, primarily online and over the phone. Their website offers extensive legal advice for women, including specifically on the subject of immigration rights in relation to domestic violence. Additionally, they also run multiple telephone advice lines for different specific branches of law, including one specifically for immigration and asylum law.

Another similar coalition, called the Tackling FGM Initiative, has published a specific best practice guide for working with FGM within communities in the UK (Khalifa and Brown, 2016). This guide is quite extensive and gives specific guidance for a variety of situations, including but not limited to working with: schools, religious leaders and newly arrived communities. For each category of guidance, the document explains the rationale, what's already been done and

---

[1] https://www.endviolenceagainstwomen.org.uk/about/our-goals/

lists best practices. As an example, some of the best practices it provides for working with newly arrived communities are: 'services should be holistic and provide a range of support' in order to adequately account for the complex needs and barriers newly arrived communities face; ensure information is communicated in an accessible format; developing 'robust arguments against FGM'; developing 'partnerships and a coordinated response' between local community organisations, migrant and refugee services and violence against women and girls services; and ensuring organisations are aware of any 'changes and updates in immigration legislation'.

Although there is undoubtedly a multitude of legislation and services in place aimed towards tackling GBV, and some specifically aimed at migrant women, there is also undeniably room for improvement in this respect, with certain gaps existing which decrease the effectiveness of support in the UK. One such gap, which has been criticised considerably, is the lack of effective legal protection for migrant women who experience domestic violence (Amnesty International UK, 2019). As briefly mentioned before, there is a recognised issue of migrant women being less inclined, and in some cases unable, to seek out support from the justice system and other institutions out of fear of being sent back to their country of origin due to their insecure immigration status. This has been a large part of the focus of the campaign Step Up Migrant Women and is well summarised by a press release from Amnesty International UK from this year, which is focused on highlighting how the proposed draft Domestic Violence Bill (Home Office & Ministry of Justice, 2019) fails to adequately address this issue. The main criticism is centred around the fact that although the bill addresses the issue, acknowledging that there is a need for considering additional barriers for migrant women when it comes to seeking help, the press release argues that no real new provisions have been devised and included in this draft bill (Amnesty International UK, 2019; Oppenheim, 2019). Step Up Migrant Women stresses that one of the causes for this is a lack of official guidance to police on how to act when the victim of a crime is a migrant, also quoting statistics suggesting that 60% of police 'shared victims' immigration details with the Home Office'. The campaign largely blames the 'hostile environment' policy for this, arguing that it puts human rights at risk, ultimately impeding the effect of aspects of the Human Rights Act 1998.

Highlighted in the joint Northern Rock Foundation and Trust for London report on the issue from 2012 (Towers and Walby, 2012), a potential cause for concern in the UK in terms of preventing GBV and supporting victims has been continuous cuts to both government and non-government services. Although this report is from 2012, the concerns that it highlights are arguably still of relevance today, with the government's austerity policy still not having officially ended. An example of one of the effects which the report highlights is reduced statutory provision, such as police and court services, having less funding, and therefore being less able to effectively operate specific services for things such as FGM and domestic violence. An article by Imkaan, an NGO which specifically focuses on addressing violence against women from BME backgrounds, published in 2017, confirmed that this issue, in particular, was still ongoing, concluding that in addition to cuts and in reference to Crown Prosecution Service statistics, existing legislation is not effective at enabling prosecutions, giving an example reflected by the statistics of there only being one offence of forced marriage brought at the time of writing (Imkaan, 2017).

Migrant women and girls disproportionately experience a more severe impact in the UK. This can be attributed to a number of factors which occur both: prior to the violence, enabling GBV to happen in the first place, and afterwards when the woman or girl requires support and, for many reasons, may not receive adequate enough support or in some instances, any at all.

Ultimately, a large part of the issue seems to be centred around various social and legal factors contributing to migrant women not reporting GBV or seeking support for it. One of the main factors is undoubtedly immigration status and fear of facing repercussions as a result of it, arguably leading to migrant women not wanting government authorities, including police, to be too involved in their lives. Some of the research gathered has suggested that this issue is being amplified by the government's 'hostile environment' policy towards illegal immigrants, inevitably causing a policy conflict where on the one hand, the government is trying to eliminate GBV, but on the other is disincentivising putting trust in government services for many migrant women with insecure immigration statuses. Furthermore, as some of the campaigns referenced in this report have outlined, there appears to be no clear official guidance for these services on how to approach this issue. In addition to this, there are many social factors which prevent reporting, particularly sexual violence, which research suggests is much less likely to be reported by migrant women, arguably due to a sense of shame surrounding the issue propagated within communities. It could be argued that both of these examples could be at least somewhat rectified by focusing policy on integration, both in government and non-government services.

Lifelong Learning and Migrant Women Empowerment

In 1996 the Council of the European Union adopted a Strategy for Lifelong Learning in which the promotion of democratic principles and human rights values, along with the elimination of social exclusion and the promotion of active participation, are core. Later, in 2001, the Communication *Making a European Area of Lifelong Learning a Reality* referred to a definition *'all purposeful learning activity, undertaken on an on-going basis with the aim of improving knowledge, skills and competence'*, framing the process as learning throughout life within a personal, civic, social and/or employment-related perspective, the four broad objectives of lifelong learning. In 2006, the Commission for European Communities considered adult learning as key to counteract social exclusion. In its communication on adult learning, it stressed the importance of engaging migrants in society and in the economy,

> (...) the challenge for adult learning is to support the integration of migrants in society and the economy, and to make the most of the competences and educational experiences acquired prior to migration. This should involve (...) – expanding adult learning opportunities in relation to linguistic, social and cultural integration; – developing appropriate and effective teaching and promoting more inter-cultural learning.

Competences as Engines of Change

Between 2019 and 2021, a multidisciplinary consortium of organisations in 8 EU countries (Austria, Bulgaria, Cyprus, Greece, Italy, Portugal, Slovenia and the United Kingdom) developed and implemented *BASE: Migrant and refugee child-friendly support services in cases of sexual and gender-based violence*, to promote child-friendly support to migrant girls survivors of GBV and to counteract the phenomenon in the community through capacity building of migrant women and of support service professionals on the provision, awareness raising and cooperation. *BASE* was funded by the Rights, Equality & Citizenship Programme of the European Commission.[2] BASE has at its core the building of competencies towards the participation of migrant/refugee women as cultural advisors promoting strategies that nurture inclusive communication and a culture of trust between support services, survivors, families and communities to counteract GBV, prevent victim re-traumatisation and to encourage reporting of GBV. BASE approaches the emerging needs by developing and implementing activities around 4 pillars that encompass the philosophy of the work programme – Empowerment, Inclusion, Expertise, and Cooperation.

---

[2] Ref. 809952-BASE-REC-RDAP-GBV-AG-2017

Table 9.1: The Four Pillars of the BASE Programme

Empowerment	Inclusion	Expertise	Cooperation
Improvement of migrant and refugee women and girls experience during support, disclosure, reporting, investigation procedures in cases of GBV facilitated by the role of the cultural advisors. Engagement of migrant and refugee women and girls, and communities, in the counteraction of GBV through an improved understanding of the phenomenon, and of mechanisms to raise-awareness and counteract it.	Promote migrant and refugee women and girls' voice in the center of procedures through the transfer of knowledge on the victim's cultural background. Inclusion of migrant communities in needs assessment to enrich existing practices with intercultural approaches. Enhancing communication between migrant communities, authorities, and service providers, increasing resilience.	Migrant and refugee women and girls capacitated as cultural advisors, better informed about GBV, judicial procedures, and better equipped to support communication between support service professionals and girls victims of GBV. Support service professionals and stakeholders better equipped to communicate with migrant and refugee women and girls victim of GBV, the training events will directly contribute to the enrichment of professional's knowledge and expertise in the field of addressing cultural diversity and understand the impact of cultural specificities in the prevention and the handling of cases of sexual and gender based violence.	Improved common inter-sector and multidisciplinary approaches and practices in relation to GBV against migrant and refugee women and girls through the focus groups, which will gather agencies, authorities and support services handling cases of sexual and GBV.

The model provides a framework towards the improvement of migrant/ refugee girls GBV survivors' experience of support services and procedures through: a) Building the capacity of migrant/refugee women as cultural advisors with knowledge about the procedures and services and communication skills that potentiate their role and collaborative work with other relevant professionals. The *BASE Cultural Advisor Curriculum* was piloted by training 162 women from diverse migrant communities in 8 countries as cultural advisors. b) Enhancing professionals' capacity to communicate with GBV survivors and families in migrant communities with a better understanding of sociocultural factors and contexts. The *BASE Capacity Building Programme* was piloted by training 232 professionals in 8 countries working in areas related to judicial procedures in cases of GBV and close to migrant girls and communities. c) Lobbying for the sustainability of capacity-building practices and their wide dissemination nationally and transnationally through cross-country cooperation that brought together migrant women, professionals and partner organisations from 8 European countries at 2 Transnational Cooperation Meetings; and through the signature of Protocols of Cooperation with organisations and entities with the capacity to promote the role of the cultural advisors. The BASE White Paper (Lenarčič, B. 2020), provides a contextual overview of needs in view of contributing to the improvement of the standards of support services with an emphasis on overcoming communication barriers. d) Raising public awareness on the vulnerability of migrant/refugee girls to GBV, contributing to its visibility and counteraction, and on the relevance of promoting gender equality in migrant communities towards a positive change of attitudes and behaviours. This was done informally through partners' networks throughout project implementation and formally through the implementation of 25 national small-scale dissemination events and 1 final transnational conference.[3]

The BASE cultural advisor's role is to provide information and raise awareness in the community on GBV-related topics, as well as to support professionals in understanding gender relations within the community, preparing the ground for disclosure and reporting of GBV.

> The cultural advisor in the context of BASE project is not equivalent to a mediator in judicial procedures, he/she is also much more than interpreter and translator, they are members of migrant and refugee communities, who mediate the dissonances produced by cultural differences, and are trained to intervene in cases of GBV, facilitate communication between support services and survivors, and promote awareness in families and communities (Ibid).

The BASE Cultural Advisor Curriculum is a learning tool aimed at developing the capacity of migrant and/or refugee women to operate as Cultural Advisors collaborating with professionals working in cases of GBV against refugee/migrant girls. The curriculum addresses the need to enhance child-friendly mechanisms by focusing on developing the participants' knowledge on key aspects of judicial procedures, communication strategies and cultural understanding. Specifically, the tool created to support lifelong learning and competence building of migrant women focuses on sensitising and raising awareness on GBV including violence against children; developing cultural understanding to facilitate communication with girls' survivors of GBV, and their families; developing competences to facilitate communication about the

---

[3] https://www.youtube.com/watch?v=vDSbC4WMcgU&t=492s

abuse between professionals and migrant girls' survivors of GBV; enhancing the capacity to provide guidance to professionals working in support services handling sexual violence and GBV against children; supporting communication at different moments, with an emphasis on disclosure and continuous support; basic understanding of the judicial procedures in cases of GBV against minors, including reporting and interviewing; enhancing the capacity to communicate and collaborate with stakeholders on awareness-raising on sexual abuse and GBV within migrant communities and applying such skills when working with any service in which professionals handle such cases.

BASE's model of sustainability was designed to place emphasis on the inclusion of migrant/refugee women and girls in the national systems of investigation of GBV, thus the development of the BASE curricula and the training of Cultural Advisors and Professionals whose added knowledge and skills can have a rippling effect in the communities and professional settings respectively. Inter-sector and multidisciplinary cooperation protocols were established in the framework of BASE to set a base for long-term and evolving cooperation, establishing common practices and approaches beyond the project duration. As illustrative examples, in the UK, Rinova Ltd engaged a different range of organisations, from grassroots organisations that work with migrant/refugee women in the community (The Light Project International and Kurdish and Middle Eastern Women's Organisation); local government councillors (Islington Council), hostel provisions which work with homeless people including migrant/refugee young people travelling alone (YMCA and Christian Action); Alternative Educational provider (WAC Arts school) and the Peer Outreach Team based at City Hall, 9 protocols for future cooperation were signed in February and March 2021.

Empowering UK Migrant Women and Communities to End FGM

Rinova Ltd, in collaboration with FGM campaigner Hibo Wardere, a Somali-born woman and a survivor of FGM, works as a mediator and regular FGM educator in the UK and whose support was crucial to reach young BAME girls, piloted the BASE tools with migrant women in London communities between March 2020 and July 2020. The women had Bangladeshi, Congolese, Algerian, Irish, Caribbean, British, Italian, Zambian, Moroccan, and Pakistani origins having a broad age range and different levels of experience. Hibo originally came to the UK as a refugee from Somalia and is herself an FGM survivor. Fleeing her much-loved home country at a young age, during her early years in the UK, there was little to indicate that Hibo would become such an influence in the fight against FGM in the UK and, indeed, across the world.

Despite the trauma of her childhood (Hibo was 6 when she was subjected to Type 3, Infibulation, one of the most severe forms of FGM). Hibo went on to become a mother and wife to a supportive husband. She continued to practice her strong Muslim faith, treasuring and valuing her strong ties to Somalian culture and working in the community with other refugee women.

Hibos' journey to becoming an activist and one of the strongest and most influential voices against FGM in the UK began when she was volunteering at an East London School and voiced her suspicion that young girls, who had often been born in the UK, were being taken away under the guise of visiting relatives abroad, to undergo FGM. Hibo made her concerns about a particular pupil known to the Senior Leadership at the School, and so began her mission to educate not only those girls directly affected by FGM but also to raise awareness in all those who were in a position to identify, support and protect those at risk. Initially, this began with talking to her own colleagues in the school, where she realised that there was really no understanding or comprehension of what FGM involved and that there were many preconceptions that would often prevent those in a position to support potential victims from acting. Concerns about appearing to not respect a culture or practice they did not understand, a misconception that FGM is a religious requirement, and not wanting to be perceived as ignorant, racially biased or intolerant of other cultures. Hibo set about dispelling the many myths that exist around the practice of FGM and also set herself the goal of informing and educating as many young people as possible. Hibo recognized that while there was still so much secrecy even within the community of women who had been victims of FGM, and little understanding even within this same community of the long-term effects of FGM on ALL aspects of a woman's life, physically and mentally, girls and mothers wouldn't be in a position to make their own informed decisions about the practice. A 2013 UNICEF report revealed that social acceptance is still the most frequently cited reason for supporting the practice of FGM.

Hibo also realised that it was not enough to try and stop the practice within the communities that had carried out FGM throughout generations and that educating potential victims and their families was only part of the issue. And so began Hibos' mission to work with the police, midwives, the legal system and the community to stop new instances of FGM and to support those who had already been victims in appropriate and informed ways, began.

The overarching objective of the BASE project to build migrant women's competencies as cultural advisors promoting strategies that nurture inclusive communication and a culture of trust to counteract GBV, prevent victim re-traumatisation and encourage reporting of GBV seemed to tie in perfectly with Hibos mission and during 2020 Rinova and Hibo began a collaboration. Initially, as part of BASE, Hibo delivered an inspiring programme of awareness raising to local community groups, where she detailed in a no-holds-barred and very personal account her own experience of FGM, including the long-term effects and the struggles it had caused. Working with women's groups, refugee associations and culturally diverse community groups, Hibo was able to provide a safe, judgement-free space for women to talk about their own experiences, how their own cultures viewed FGM and also what they saw happening in the UK community and diaspora at the current time. Through these sessions delivered as part of the BASE project, Hibo was able to help identify Community Advocates able to support her in her campaigning. During this phase of the project, Hibo also delivered sessions to groups of midwives, social workers and teachers.

At the same time as taking this message to the community, through BASE, we were able to work with Hibo to take the message into schools, where Hibo's lively and very direct sessions proved to be extremely popular with Teachers and pupils alike. Working with mixed groups of pupils from Year 8 upwards, through BASE, Hibo was able to address 800 young people over 4 months, delivering her message of awareness raising. Through her open and honest dialogue with young people, Hibo aimed to dispel myths, raise awareness and encourage young people to challenge ingrained acceptance of the practice in their communities. A practice that she was able to demonstrate to young people is still very much alive. According to the City University London/ Equality Now report published in 2014, 21 out of every 1000 are victims of FGM in London. Between September 2014 and January 2015, more than 2,600 cases of FGM were identified in the UK; 44 of those were children under 18, and more than 9,500 women were deinfibulated, and these are only the women who have sought medical treatment while others will be suffering in silence.

Feedback from these sessions was enlightening and inspiring. Young women, and notably also young men, armed with a better understanding of the practice and the traditions that have kept it going, felt empowered to identify and challenge the practice within their own communities and to support those at risk, along with protecting their own safety. While young boys who had previously not understood the practicalities and implications of the practice were able to make informed commitments not to continue to turn a blind eye to what many considered to be outside their control and the domain of the females in the community.

Feedback from pupils who participated in Hibo's BASE sessions illustrates the impact:

> ... your lesson was the best!! You helped me open my eyes to see the real world we live in and I have learnt so much from you.

> thank you for todays assembly, it was honestly amazing and great to hear that it happens to loads of families. My mum had it too but she

didn't many any of her daughers do it and she's told my family back home that we have done it, even though we haven't. So she's protecting up by also keeping the hour we have as a family. Thank you once again.

I thought it was very inspiring and you helped bring awareness to young girls who might be at risk. I also thought that it was very interesting and Hibo was stupendous.

I had heard a bit about it from other men in my family but I think boys don't realize how bad this is for the girls. I am glad that I understand now what really FGM and how it affects girls.

An important part of the programme of delivery was explaining current UK legislation against FGM, the rights of the child and the pathways those suspecting FGM is being practised, can take to report and stop the practice from happening. This legislation, including the FGM Protection Order, in place since 17th July 2015, in the UK, was still relatively unknown by teachers and community leaders. Teachers also reported feeling far more informed and empowered; they were now able to identify risks and understand what they could do to support a child they felt to be at risk or had already been subjected to FGM. with information and discussion focusing on how they could support that individual, personally, professionally and through the legal system.

Thank you so much. Quite simply, the most important, enlightening, moving training I have experienced in three decades of teaching.

Feedback from teachers participating in these sessions included:

What an absolutely phenomenal training session! FM is always a taboo subject that we try and address as adults in school, but today I feel empowered to deliver this. Thank you so much.

What an inspirational session this afternoon. Thank you, Hibo, for telling your story and sharing how we can be part of the solution.

Conclusion

While the impact on those individuals who attended the training delivered under BASE was profound, the longer-term impact of the work of BASE was perhaps even more relevant. The schools involved in the pilot requested that Hibo return annually to speak to students, and her presentations are now part of the calendar in over 30 schools across the capital. The presentation, which was developed as part of the BASE project, has now been shown to over 5000 young people across the London Boroughs. In addition, as a result of the message she was spreading, Hibo was approached by the Metropolitan Police and the Association of Midwives, with both organisations recognizing the need for their members and staff to be trained properly in all aspects of working with survivors and potential victims of FGM. Hibo now delivers regular training to new recruits of the London Metropolitan Police, and her sessions also now form an intrinsic part of the Association of Midwives programme of training.

Since her work with BASE, Hibos work has gone from strength to strength and has gained much-needed recognition and support. This has included features in national magazines and on national TV, awards for services to the community and an audience at the Old Bailey to speak directly to the UK's top judges on the matter of legislation and accountability for those still practising or allowing the practice of FGM. But while Hibo has gained the support of politicians and many well-known celebrities who have added weight to her message, she continues to prioritize her work developing awareness in local communities and identifying Advocates and Ambassadors within those communities. In this way, the initial message of the BASE project continues. It is with the support of these community Advocates and Ambassadors that Hibo has set up the charity Educate Not Mutilate, which will take the message to a wider audience whilst providing practical, on-the-ground help and support to those affected by FGM. ENM embodies everything that the BASE project was set up to achieve, and its impact project will far exceed our original expectations and continue to impact not just on communities and individuals but also on the legal, health and education systems.

References

Against Violence & Abuse. 2019, March 14. *What is Gender Based Violence.* Viewed 2.20.23 from https://avaproject.org.uk/about/gender-based-violence-and-abuse/

Amnesty International UK. 2019 *UK: Domestic Abuse Bill risks failing migrant women.* Viewed 2.20.23 from https://www.amnesty.org.uk/press-releases/uk-domestic-abuse-bill-risks-failing-migrant-women (14th March 2019)

Bates, L., *et al.*, 2018. *Policy Evidence Summary 1: Migrant Women.* Bristol: University of Bristol.

Brown, E. and Porter, C. 2016. *Evaluation of FGM Prevention among Communities Affected by FGM: A Participatory Ethnographic Evaluation Research (PEER) Study.* Viewed on 3.13.2022 from https://www.trustforlondon.org.uk/publications/tackling-female-genital-mutilation-uk-views-people-communities-affected-fgm/

Clinical Audit and Registries Management Service. 2017. *Female Genital Mutilation (FGM) Enhanced Dataset: England, April 2016 - March 2017, experimental statistics.* NHS Digital.

Department for Children Schools and Families. 2003. *Every Child Matters.* London: The Stationery Office.

Department for Education. 2018. *Working Together to Safeguard Children.* Viewed on 3.13.2022 from https://www.gov.uk/government/publications/working-together-to-safeguard-children--2

Department for Education, Department of Health and Social Care., and Home Office. 2016. *Multi-agency statutory guidance on female genital mutilation.* Viewed on 3.13.2022 from https://www.gov.uk/government/publications/multi-agency-statutory-guidance-on-female-genital-mutilation

Hester, M. *et al.*, 2015. *Victim/survivor voices – a participatory research project.* Report for HMIC honour-based violence inspection. Bristol: University of Bristol.

Home Office. 2005. *Guidance on offences against children.* Home Office Circular 16/2005. London: Home Office. Viewed on 3.13.2022 from http://www.home office.gov.uk/about-us/corporate-publications-strategy/home-office-circulars/circulars-2005/016-2005/

Home Office. 2012. *Cross-Government Definition of Domestic Violence – A Consultation Summary of Responses.* London: Home Office. Viewed on 3.13.2022 from https://assets.publishing.service.gov.uk/government/uploads/system/uploads/attachment_data/file/157800/domestic-violence-definition.pdf

Home Office. 2016. *Ending violence against women and girls strategy: 2016 to 2020.* London: Home Office.

Home Office. 2019a. *Ending violence against women and girls strategy refresh: 2016 to 2020.* London: Home Office.

Home Office. 2019b. *Ending violence against women and girls strategy action plan update.* London: Home Office.

Home Office and Ministry of Justice. 2019. *Transforming the response to domestic abuse: consultation response and draft bill.* London: Home Office.

Imkaan. 2017. *New reports: BME women and survivors of violence bear the brunt of public funding cuts.* Viewed on 3.13.2022 from https://www.imkaan.org.uk/new-reports-funding-cuts

Khalifa, S, Brown, E . 2016. 'Communities Tackling FGM in the UK: Best Practice Guide', the Tackling Female Genital Mutilation Initiative and Options Consultancy Services Limited, London. Viewed 2.12.22 from https://www.basw.co.uk/resources/communities-tackling-fgm-uk-best-practice-guide

Lenarčič, B *et al.*, 2020. *BASE White Paper.* BASE White Paper. Viewed on 27.03.23 from https://cesie.org/media/BASE_White-Paper_ENG.pdf

Krug, E. G., *et al.*, 2002. *World report on violence and health.* Geneva: World Health Organisation.

Laming, H., *et al.*, 2003. *The Victoria Climié Inquiry: Report of an Inquiry by Lord Laming.* London: The Stationery Office.

Logan, E. 2008. *Janusz Korczak Lecture: The child's best interest: a generally applicable principle.* Stockholm: Council of Europe.

Mayock, P. *et al.*, 2012. Migrant women and homelessness: the role of gender-based violence. *European Journal of Homelessness*, 6(1).

NHS Health and Social Care Information Centre 2015 Feb 27. *Female Genital Mutilation.* Viewed on 1.13.22 at https://digital.nhs.uk/data-and-information/publications/statistical/female-genital-mutilation/female-genital-mutilation-fgm-january-2015-experimental-statistics

NSPCC. 2012. *NSPCC factsheet: An introduction to child protection legislation in the UK.* Viewed on 3.13.2022 from http://www.erscb.org.uk/EasySiteWeb/GatewayLink.aspx%3FalId%3D167501

Oppenheim, M. 2019. *Domestic Abuse Bill fails migrant women whose perpetrators use immigration status as a 'weapon to abuse'.* Independent. Viewed on 3.13.2022 from https://www.independent.co.uk/news/uk/home-news/domestic-abuse-bill-migrant-women-immigration-status-amnesty-a8741206.html

Ott, M. 2017. *Series: What Does That Mean? Gender-based Violence.* Viewed on 3.13.2022 from https://www.womenforwomen.org/blogs/series-what-does-mean-gender-based-violence

Radford, L. *et al.*, 2011. *Child Abuse and Neglect in the UK Today.* NSPCC. Viewed on 3.13.2022 from https://www.researchgate.net/publication/23055 8737_Child_Abuse_and_Neglect_in_the_UK_Today

Rights of Women. 2015. *Annual Report 2015.* Viewed on 3.13.2022 from https://rightsofwomen.org.uk/about-us/what-do-we-do/our-annual-report/

Strickland, P., and Allen, G. 2018. *Domestic Violence in England and Wales.* (House of Commons Library No. 6337) London: House of Commons Library.

Towers, J. and Walby, S. 2012. *Measuring the impact of cuts in public expenditure on the provision of services to prevent violence against women and girls.* Viewed on 3.13.2022 from https://www.trustforlondon.org.uk/publications/measuring-impact-cuts-public-expenditure-provision-services-prevent-violence-against-women-and-girls/

UN. 1997. *Strategy for Lifelong Learning, Council of the European Union, 97/C 7/02, 20 December 1996.* Viewed on 3.13.2022 from https://www.ohchr.org/en/resources/educators/human-rights-education-training/5-council-conclusions-strategy-lifelong-learning-1996

UN General Assembly. 1989 *Declaration of the Rights of the Child.* A/RES/1386 (XIV). Viewed on 3.13.2022 from https://documents-ddsny.un.org/doc/RESOLUTION/GEN/NR0/142/09/IMG/NR014209.pdf?OpenElement

UN General Assembly. 1979. *Convention on the Elimination of All Forms of Discrimination Against Women.* Treaty Series, 1249. Viewed on 3.13.2022 from https://documents-dds-ny.un.org/doc/RESOLUTION/GEN/NR0/378/07/IMG/NR037807.pdf?OpenElement

UN General Assembly. 1989. *Convention on the Rights of the Child.* Treaty Series, 1577. Viewed on 3.13.2022 from https://daccess-ods.un.org/TMP/2859217.5245285.html

UN General Assembly. 1993. *Declaration on the Elimination of Violence against Women.* A/RES/48/104. Viewed on 3.13.2022 from http://www.un.org/documents/ga/res/48/a48r104.htm

UNICEF. 2013. *Female Genital mutilation/Cutting: A statistical overview and exploration of the dynamics of change.* Viewed 3.16.22 from https://data.unicef.org/resources/fgm-statistical-overview-and-dynamics-of-change/

Walby, S.and Allen, J. 2004. *Domestic violence, sexual assault and stalking: Findings from the British Crime Survey.* London: Home Office.

Walby, S. and Myhill, A. 2001. 'New Survey Methodologies in Researching Violence Against Women'. *The British Journal of Criminology,* 41(3), 502-522. doi:10.1093/bjc/41.3.502.

Wardere, H., 2016. *CUT – One Woman's Fight Against FGM in Britain Today.* NY: Simon and Schuster.

Chapter 10

Integration is the Process of Accumulating Micro Integrations Over Time

Richard Thickpenny

University of West of England; Aston University; The New Penny Ltd

Abstract

This chapter explores how refugee communities have given so much to their own children at great cost to themselves. Through a practitioner lens, it shows how systems coalescing out of immediate humanitarian need can lead to refugees being kept in silos. With policy influenced by abstract terms such as society, integration, and inclusion, it illustrates how unpicking the accepted norms of the abstract terms approach can lead to a greater understanding of, and commitment to individual refugee needs and their family's future well-being. Instead of trying to define what success can look like from the perspective of the policy controllers, the chapter explores what can be achieved if you look at what needs to be good enough to make the refugee service work well for each individual.

Keywords: Education, Supplementary school, social inclusion, policies and measures to support immigrants and refugees, UK

***

Introduction

During the 80's and 90's, the UK welcomed a steady flow of refugees fleeing the civil war in Somalia, which grew significantly during the period 2000 to 2005. Years of fighting had led to a diaspora adjusting to circumstances and cultures in countries across the globe. They were arriving in the UK at the same time as the concept of multiculturalism was working itself into local and national government agendas. The assumption behind multiculturalism – i.e., that society as a whole benefits from increased diversity through the harmonious coexistence of different cultures, whilst noble in its outlook, lacked in its practical application.

The 2001 census figure showed only 2,310 Black Africans in Bristol (Mills, 2014), and a further 936 identifying as Black Other. By the time of the 2011 census, the largely Somali population had grown to over 19,000 people, with 4,614 under the age of 15 and 1,948 between the ages of 16 and 24. For those refugees looking to settle in Bristol, conflict soon arose as the pressure of numbers meant the concept of 'harmonious coexistence' was difficult to establish. The type of coexistence being experienced by Somali refugees is described in the following news story: (Casciani, 2006)

> Bristol has a large Somali community in Lawrence Hill, an area among the most deprived in the UK. Rumours are rife of huge state handouts, queue jumping on housing lists, and even cash benefits for car purchases, and resentment is building among other black and white communities. It's time for Somalis and the local government to speed up integration and dispel these dangerous rumours before community relations reach a crisis point. (Simon Bartlett, Bristol)

The accession of Eastern European states to the European Union in 2004 added to the pressures in a small city like Bristol, as the booming regional economy turned it into a preferred location for both forced and economic migrants. The rhetoric of multiculturalism was not often represented in the daily lives of the children caught up in these migrations. They were distributed through the school system into classes based on their age. Those who arrived as part of the EU accession process found it difficult to adjust to their new school, but cultural familiarity, and the fact that their migration was voluntary, helped to mitigate the impact of their academic dislocation. Children of refugees experienced considerable damaging consequences due to a lack of supportive mechanisms to mitigate trauma, disrupted or insufficient prior schooling, the necessity for rapid language acquisition, adjusting to new cultural norms, and so on. According to empirical information, older children were pursuing criminal routes to establish a sense of stability in their lives.

Faced with such catastrophic consequences for their children, parents banded together to help their children and those in their communities. As parents attempted to augment the school-based curriculum in whatever manner they could, voluntary out-of-school programming began to emerge. The anxiety they felt for their children's futures was tangible.

The Accidental Integrationalist

The author had never set out to become an expert on refugee integration, having begun his working career as an apprentice with British Telecom in rural Norfolk. Working in the sector for 35 years, it was not until a combination of recession and having undertaken a degree in Manufacturing System Management that he had accumulated sufficient skills to secure - by accident - a project officer role with Bristol's Neighbourhood Renewal Fund. Entering the field of economic development for the first time in 2004, he was soon exposed to the needs of communities he knew little about and began meeting with some of the most influential people in his life. These ranged from community activists in white working-class areas of Bristol suffering intergenerational poverty and deprivation to community leaders within newly arrived inner-city communities.

It was in this project officer role that he began to see how so many lives were defined by negative stereotypes, entrenched attitudes, poor perceptions and 'othering'. He began to see the conflicts that arise between those wanting change in communities and those who control the purse strings of change. Tasked with discussing projects with an approval board, he became a part of this control process. As he progressed through community projects, it became clear that, often, the quality of writing and advocacy was more important for the project approval process than the level of needs within the communities themselves.

Whilst projects were beginning to be developed to meet the needs of the Somali refugee community, there was a reticence to use too much funding for a community which so few knew about. In the period leading up to the publication of the 2011 census results, this lack of population data impacted service design. The author recalls a conversation in 2006 with an NHS manager who couldn't understand why they were having 'more people coming to their health sessions than the population figures suggested.'

Soon, the reticence faded, and programmes financed by public funds, such as Community at Heart and Neighbourhood Renewal, as well as government money aimed at preventing gun violence, knife crime, and gang crime, were accessed to help the Somali and other 'newly arrived populations' with their resettlement needs. Many such projects focused on diversionary or health activities such as cycling, football, and gardening alongside research into vitamin D deficiency, mental health and FGM. However, funding for infrastructure groups developed by, and for, the Somali community was still in short supply.

It was around this time, in 2005, the author left his project officer role to concentrate on securing funds for refugee community infrastructure – initially with the Somali community, then subsequently, as word spread, working with the Libyan, Zimbabwean and more widely. For the next four years, this work was focused strongly on securing funding for supplementary schooling and adult community learning.

From Supplementary to Mainstream

Rapid inward migration from EU accession nations and Somalia created community friction in Bristol, especially in areas with a lot of social housing, resulting in a rash of racial incidents, including a pregnant Somali woman having stones thrown at her (Anon, 2007.) These attacks arose as a result of social housing programmes that were not designed to account for the social consequences of rapid demographic change (Hogget *et al.*, 2008.)

The fear of racist attacks led to constraints being placed on children's opportunities to play and interact with other children and adults. For many, living in isolated family groups across social housing estates or in small flats within tower blocks further limited the opportunities available. Within the estates, drug crime was becoming an issue, which meant green spaces were also off-limits for unsupervised play. In larger families, the lack of available space for siblings to study was severe and impacted children's ability to complete homework or catch up on their disrupted education. Those within the community with a background, or with an interest, in education, began to support parents to help their children study, providing tutoring and showing them techniques to use their living space in a way better suited for study.

This initial self-help provision could not keep pace with demand, soon leading to the development of a grassroots supplementary school movement providing after-school and weekend schooling to hundreds of children. Such schooling provided additional support for national curriculum subjects (particularly Mathematics, English, and Science), culturally specific teaching in family languages, religious studies, and enrichment activities, such as visits to the Degmo centre in Herefordshire and to the beach at Weymouth.

The benefits for the children were significant, including increased motivation, self-esteem and confidence, improved behaviour and social skills, and better school results alongside wellbeing improvements from having opportunities for leisure, fun and enjoyment. The evidence for this was evident in the ever-increasing numbers attending and monitoring of attainment within the supplementary school setting. The supplementary schools also lessened the isolation felt by the family groups as a result of living in mostly white regions and boosted their involvement in their children's education.

With support from the supplementary school forums (Ata-Amonoo, 2008), the supplementary schools were linked to the local implementation of the UK's 'Every Child Matters' policy agenda and benefited from professional support. At this stage, initial small grant funding became available (typically in the region of £10 to £20k), which enabled the supplementary schools to scale up and professionalise their provision. This included securing places on a teaching training course designed specifically for supplementary school organisers run by the University of the West of England, community development courses run by the City of Bristol College, places on the Common Purpose executive leaders' course and other continuous professional development (CPD) activities. In addition, the funding allowed volunteers to reclaim their expenses, as well as support volunteer student teachers from local universities with purchasing essential resources and improving the quality of service.

During 2006-08 a large-scale project, the Mainstreaming Supplementary School Support Project (MSSP) received over £150k to establish a partnership between four secondary schools and their local supplementary schools. This project had more resources to analyse the benefits of the supplementary school process. It demonstrated that within the target group of MSSP students, 75% attending the project achieved 5 or more A* to C achievement grades, compared to 33% of the control group who did not attend (Cousins, 2005).

At this point, the author was more focused on bid writing, helping to scale up three supplementary schools, a youth forum, migrant support hub and providing mentoring and coaching to nearly 20 community activists and organisers. Many of those who were supported went on to successful professions in the civil service, mainstream teaching, or establishing their own successful businesses and specialist organisations.

Grants became particularly vital to support the development of programmes, and one of the most successful was a Paul Hamlyn Foundation grant, which allowed the Amana Education Trust to create stability over three years, giving both child and adult-centred training. This helped provide intensive curriculum support in English, Maths and Science to Somali pupils in Key Stage (KS)2, KS3 and KS4. It also provided Statutory Assessment Tests (SATs) and revision classes organised through a supplementary weekend school run by specialist and mainstream teachers and was attended by over 100 pupils. SATs are the current process in Primary Schools to measure teaching success.

Adults associated with Amana have gone on to set up many organisations and businesses, including Autism Independence (autism-independence.org), which works to combat the stigma of autism and raise awareness of it among the British Somali community, and ACH (ach.org.uk), which works to build a better future for refugees and migrants in the UK.

For another group, SEDSOB (Somali Education Development Society of Bristol), the focus was on revision and study classes for children in preparation for SATs and General Certificate of Secondary Education (GCSEs), in Maths and English, alongside citizenship and cultural identity. GCSEs are the essential qualification for children at the age of 16 in the UK. Working with over 70 children, this organisation also raised donations to reconstruct hospital and medical infrastructure in Mogadishu, as well as supporting an orphanage for displaced children in Aliyale, Somalia. Those that volunteered have also gone on to have successful professional careers.

With stable funding in place, the training that became available for parents, accompanied by the opportunity to study while their children were in the supplementary school, had significant impacts. Subjects covered ranged from understanding the education system to setting up a business in the UK. Mostly taught in informal ways and in informal settings by their peers or mentors from the mainstream community, such training proved valuable in helping parents become school governors, volunteer teaching assistants and community champions for mainstream services. A local University even trained a cohort to become community researchers, producing a widely read report at the time into the mental health needs of the Somali community in Bristol.

However, the initial volunteers' commitment could not be easily compensated with money for wages, and over time, these volunteers went on to other careers or commitments, and both Amana and SEDSOB came to a natural end in 2010. New provisions began to emerge as a result of government-provided childcare funding, but the Author had moved on by that time. Throughout the process of writing funding proposals, funding for professional English was difficult to come by, resulting in a reliance on adult education-funded English for Speakers of Other Languages (ESOL), which limited many adults' hopes of attending university (White, 2021). This situation was exacerbated further by any such training ceasing to be funded once an individual progresses into work. As a result, many individuals with degree-level ambitions were stuck with little more than primary school English. With the pressures arising from families left behind or dispersed widely around the world, many adults had to abandon schooling and secure work with the levels of English they had managed to achieve. Whilst their ambitions may have been to take up professional careers, it meant that, for many, without their own family funds to secure additional support, they quickly filled vacancies for taxi drivers, cleaners and security guards. In the UK, the only refugees consistently provided with English training and access to regular conversational English language opportunities are refugee children.

Within the multiculturalism narrative, the state of employment is usually seen as the point when refugees are able to contribute to society. However, the reality is that for many securing entry-level employment, this represents the point when they are destined to live in poverty (within the EU, this is defined as 60% of the median salary or below). Indeed, it has been reported by leading organisations that 75% of refugees who start in entry-level jobs never progress from this level of employment throughout their work careers. Unfortunately, these individuals pay taxes and thus 'contribute' to society but never earn sufficient to establish themselves and thrive as vital parts of society. This stymieing of ambition has resulted in populations with limited social capital and non-co-ethnic networks. It also gives rise to the all too familiar anecdote that 'my taxi driver used to have a good job in his own country but can only get work as a taxi driver in the UK'.

For many of the parents of the supplementary school children, whilst they were able to commit to their children's futures, they themselves had to abandon their futures to ensure there was sufficient money available to cover bills and day-to-day costs of living. As a consequence, their social networks are quite limited outside their own social bond group and rarely include mainstream professionals. As a result, those children whose educational experience was boosted by supplemental schooling, who went on to earn degrees, and so on, are still at a disadvantage 20 years later since they cannot rely on their parents' networks to open doors.

Pivotal Conversations

The author closely worked with his Somali colleagues and had numerous opportunities to discuss their goals and learn more about their life. It is these conversations, and many subsequent ones, that inform his subsequent approach to refugee integration, centred around ensuring personal ambitions are not halted by arbitrary eligibility criteria. From these conversations, it became clear that refugee communities were being held back as much by barriers caused by policy as the maintaining of accepted practices.

One of the most important conversations held, which illustrated what was happening in practice, concerned self-esteem and confidence. Two of the Amana Somali volunteer teachers were not joining their degree seminars and workshops because they had no confidence in their English language. Observing them speaking Somali to Somali, it was clear they were confident, adept at using language and could talk with great rapport. Asked to estimate a value to how they felt when speaking Somali, they both said $100. However, when asked to similarly estimate how they felt speaking English, their reply was $1. Through further conversations over the next 2 to 3 weeks, their confidence grew to the point they valued their English at $40. They began to feel more confident when taking part in discussion groups.

Using this self-estimation approach highlighted how little self-esteem had been developed around their conversational English. Although the two volunteers had attended lessons, they had never been in a position to practice their spoken English in a professional setting or to compare it against others who were still learning. Informal conversations lasting less than one hour in total altered their degree outcomes from a possible dropout to successful completion. The fact that two individuals could have their academic careers turned around through a self-esteem-boosting conversation was not to be forgotten.

Another conversation concerned the Somali nomadic practice of Sahan. Given that a family's wealth is tied up in their livestock and with all their lives depending on safe grazing with plentiful water supplies, great care has to be taken moving from one area of grazing to another. To make this decision, pathfinder scouts, called Sahan, travel to potential grazing sites to determine their safety, pasture conditions etc. The scouts return with this information to the elders, and between them, they identify the best path and pasture. The knowledge and skills developed by this approach are still relevant and transferable to their new settlement situations informing how families identify where it is safe to travel in an urban context. It helped explain why the community activists had been able to secure such high attendance of children at the supplementary schools. They had been established in safe places and provided the community with vital resources.

Other conversations revealed how volunteers working to support education or social care needs were being ignored by the professionals who equated refugee volunteers with being unprofessional and unskilled. At the same time, such professionals were failing to deliver their services adequately because they themselves lacked key skills such as cultural competency and lived experience. This lack of recognition of the volunteer's competency resulted in professionals adopting a top-down approach with no true understanding of whether the services they commission were good enough, barely acceptable or even wholly inappropriate. This reliance by the professionals on their own knowledge and expertise led to dissatisfaction with many services, which is why the refugee volunteers had to provide additional support.

The workaround at the time was to find a professional whose status was higher than those designing the services. Using this method, it was possible to build professional advocacy for the volunteers and improve service design. There is increasing recognition of the need to consult those with lived experience when designing services.

A key part of the author's work at this stage also involved writing CVs and developing business ideas with the many volunteers he worked with. This exercise revealed not just the past experience and skills and experiences of refugees but also the sheer scale of their personal and community commitments. This included their own studies from basic level qualifications through to Master's degrees but revealed how much time each individual was committing to their community, the children and young people in their community diaspora across the globe, and their own families and communities in Somaliland and Somalia. This contribution to multiple communities included work to secure foster families in the UK, libraries in the Ogaden, fundraising for medical supplies for projects across the Horn of Africa, supporting orphanages for internally displaced children, and raising support standards for learning-disabled children and adults. When labelled as refugees, this capability and drive was rarely visible.

From Conversations to Innovations

Taking forward the experiences of the supplementary schools and the many conversations, the Author began working with Asylum Care and Housing (now ACH). This had been set up by one of his colleagues from Amana, Fuad Mahamed. This began the process of developing innovative approaches to refugee integration, which has led to ACH being recognised as a thought leader in the refugee sector, winning recognition through a Queen's Award for Enterprise for its work on social mobility.

The vision within ACH has always been to reduce the time taken to integrate and to ensure that the integration level achieved was as high as possible. ACH has pushed forward with ambitious growth plans, linking world-renowned academics, such as Professor Monder Ram, Centre Manager at CREME, with its own '#rethinkingrefugee' ethos. Aiming to drive forward a new narrative highlighting the refugee as an individual person with skills, ambitions, and unlimited potential. This has driven an ambition to challenge the systems currently in place and push an agenda designed to help refugees progress towards median salary roles.

With a vision for change, those initial dialogues, as well as ongoing 'we're living through it' conversations, proved critical to the social enterprise's growth. The knowledge of what was needed to create successful integration journeys rested within the communities. This had already been demonstrated through the supplementary school movement, and with ACH came the opportunity to truly explore refugee needs from a researcher-practitioner perspective. Now, with over 900 refugees going through its accommodation-based integration services and a further 1,500 going through its community-based integration provision, ACH sought to bring this accumulated knowledge to bear into the transformation of refugee-focused services in Bristol and beyond

In 2016, ACH visited the Paris November 2016 OECD conference just over a week after a major terrorist bombing incident. Despite concerns over safety and security responses, its CEO attended, and as a result, the organisation was invited to participate in its first Erasmus+ project. From this beginning, it developed relationships with Rick Parkes and his team at Rinova (rinova.co.uk), whose mentoring enabled ACH to build its research capability and to establish in prototype three ground-breaking services.

First, from the ARIVE Erasmus+ Project (Arrived, Respected, Integrated, Valued and Enabled) grew the Integrass toolkit. This was designed to measure an individual's ability to progress in their integration journey. Designed as a front-line tool, this created personal integration plans designed to provide support staff with guidance on what services and/or support was needed by an individual. Integrass provides vital insight into the impact of service by providing a before and after score for individuals as well as a comparison to the local society, indicating the difference between the individual and the existing societal midpoint. As a result, rather than remaining in a binary state, integration is seen more as how an individual transforms in relation to the majority community.

Second, we were able to generate other areas of study as a result of the data we gathered, which led to our 2018 SEESI (Strengthening Education and Employment Skills for Integration) project. SEESI looked at the 'de-integration phase' of refugees moving away from their past and how to improve the integration phase. It recognises that refugee knowledge is more valuable than professional service provider knowledge when considering refugee needs. By raising the status of the volunteer, it enables co-design of responsive and relevant services for refugees as opposed to the design of services which are predicated on evidencing service provider success in relation to funding criteria.

SEESI (ACH, 2021) created the concept of the *professionalised refugee volunteer*, able to provide other refugees with the knowledge required to be able to advocate confidently for themselves with early-stage English. Training is supported with booklets and other resources which enable the SEESI volunteer to discuss employment rights, climate action, citizenship and other key areas of their lives. ACH and its European partners have used this approach to great effect. With project partners reporting volunteers establishing themselves as trusted community voices and others moving into paid professional advisor roles.

ACH used this method to great effect to rapidly deploy advice into the community in response to taxi and Uber driver unemployment resulting from the pandemic. Ten volunteers were trained in key aspects of self-employment and social benefits to ensure those who were outside of the UK furlough schemes could access necessary support and finance. Over a two-month period, they were able to provide support to over 500 individuals through direct contacts and WhatsApp group information sharing.

The success of SEESI has led to the development of ACH's Livelihoods and Futures Methodology focused on career management and entrepreneurship to progress, the #Rethinkingrefugee ethos of supporting individuals' progression towards median salary and increasing family income. Important when you consider the difference between the National Minimum wage and the median salary is more than £10k per year, which over a working lifetime will amount to over £400k of non-achieved earnings. The recent innovation in media will see this methodology shift towards a social media-led response (using TikTok, FB reels and Discord) using 'community influencers' and drawing on the capabilities of young people from refugee backgrounds.

Third, taking forward the aim of bringing about change through increased availability of knowledge and understanding, the final project put forward is IEEDO (Integrated Education and Employment Digital Opportunities). Starting in 2020, this project is based on the premise that integration is a variable with a rate of change over time in relation to the local population. This rate of change can be broken down into the accumulation of a succession of 'Micro Integrations' that eventually lead to full integration. This method moves away from the use of traditional metrics like 'how many people in a community have ESOL at a given level' to focus on everyday skills which enable individual convergence with local norms. The IEEDO approach enables integration to be measured in terms of softer intangible behavioural adjustments that have arisen from learning and experience. For example, finding a friend who understands how to go to university, navigating bus services to reach destinations for pleasure and work, accumulating skills necessary to choose and follow a career path, using a volunteering opportunity to practice a skill and broaden personal networks.

With IEEDO, an app is being created that gamifies this accumulation of micro integrations with a multi-level play designed to develop the behaviours and increase necessary knowledge to support positive self-directed integration. By the end of the project in 2023, IEEDO will consist of:-

Coaching Curriculum Program – to support Digital Self-Learning with specified and detailed learning objectives and content development for tutors working with refugee and migrant communities – many whom are earlier generation refugees themselves.

The **IEEDO Digital Kit** – to build resilience and progression in Digital Self-Learning skills. The Digital Kit (VGWB, 2023) will be an interactive eLearning resource using a videogame-based approach. Designed to provide stimulation and take individuals beyond the poor digital inclusion offer.

The **Pedagogical Guide and Digital Resource Pack for Coaches** (Rinova, 2023) – to ensure adult/ community learning organisations and tutors are equipped with the skills and knowledge to accompany the IEEDO Digital Kit.

The author hopes through this work and forming communities of interest and partnerships across the UK, children of refugees from 20 years ago will be able to cash in and succeed in a country where there are severe labour shortages and that new groups of refugees will not face the same integration obstacles.

Conclusion

Coming into refugee integration from a background in telecommunications is far from typical in the sector, let alone study in manufacturing systems and lean management. But this background has been influential in developing an approach to refugee integration that reflects the realities of refugee life and focuses on developing solutions that are good enough to meet refugee individuals' needs but which are robust enough to create an evidence base for change.

As a lived experience ally and accomplice, hearing the voice of refugees is so important not just at the point of crisis but for many years afterward. As refugees live through their own experiences, their knowledge is a vital input into ensuring the sector creates the 'right solution for the right problem'. Without this input, any solution will risk entrenching poverty and denying opportunity. The narrative needs to move away from one of 'contributing to society' to one of being able to 'establish and thrive in society'. Refugee children benefit when their parents and guardians are able to establish and thrive as well.

Lean management has its roots in manufacturing and has many critics within the public sector, but its emphasis on meeting the needs of customers requires that you understand and listen to your customers. Too often, the funder of refugee projects is seen to be the customer. They're not. Their financial input helps to create refugee services, but ultimately the customer whose future depends on those services are refugees. Their voice needs to be heard to ensure relevant services are designed to be good enough to meet the needs of the refugees themselves. By listening, discussing, challenging and linking conversations, it is possible to bring about innovation and truly change refugee lives.

References

ACH. 2021. Celebrating the SEESI Project. Viewed on 24.03.23 from https://ach. org.uk/news-and-features/celebrating-seesi-project

Casciani, D. 2006. Somalis struggle in the UK. BBC. Viewed on 24.03.23 from http://news.bbc.co.uk/1/hi/magazine/5029390.stm

Cousins, L. 2005. Developing Effective Partnerships - Supplementary Schools in Bristol: their Contribution to Raising Attainment. Viewed on 24.03.23 from https://ec.europa.eu/migrant-integration/integration-practice/supplementary -schools-forum_en

Hogget, P. et al. 2008. Class, race, and community cohesion: A profile of Hillfields, Bristol.

University of West England. Viewed on 24.03.23 from https://www.researchgate. net/publication/254411750_Class_Race_And_CommunityCohesion_A_Profile _of_Hillfields_Bristol

Mills, J. 2014. Equalities Profile Black Africans in Bristol. Viewed on 24.03.23 from https://www.bristol.gov.uk/council-and-mayor/statistics-census-information/ census-2011

Rinova. 2023. Welcome to the IEEDO Pedagogical Guide and Digital resource Pack for Coaches. Viewed on 24.03.23 from https://ieedo.rinova.co.uk/

VGWB. 2023. IEEDO. Viewed on 24.03.23 from https://vgwb.org/projects/ieedo/

White, S. 2021. 'An investigation into the value of informal and experiential learning with Syrian refugees in the ESOL.' Viewed 24.03.23 from https://sure. sunderland.ac.uk/id/eprint/13601/

Conclusion

Yvonne Vissing

Salem State University

Sofia Leitão

Rinova Ltd

The chapters in this book have showcased how the structures and processes that communities use impact the well-being and future of refugees. The world is facing its biggest refugee crisis since the Second World War, with over 23 million people who have been forcibly displaced from their country by war, poverty, and persecution. It is important to put ourselves in the role of the other, as socialization expert and sociologist George Herbert Mead *et al.* (2015) reminded us.

The authors of the chapters in this book have imagined what it would be like to be a person who is living in distress and danger, someone who seeks safe refuge in another country where they may not know a soul, not know the language, not understand the culture, not have any money, indeed, they may have travelled to a new land alone with nothing except the clothes on their back. These are people who have endured violence, abuse, horrific situations, the loss of valued possessions, separation from loved ones, or the death of those whom they hold dear.

But the authors have not just imagined what the experiences of the refugees have been like. All of them have worked with refugees in various capacities. They have come to know their faces, their tears, their laughter, their bravery, and their fears. The authors have held their hands, helped them fill out paperwork, figured out what they need, and taken them to resources that may help them. They have watched communities wrestle with how they can help the refugees to have better lives. Community leaders and service providers have been challenged to figure out how to provide refugees with the help they need with the limited resources the community may have. The authors and the community providers that they discuss are people who have stayed awake at night, trying to figure out how best they can help the refugees. In welcoming the stranger, they have come to feel their hearts beating as one.

This book has offered a window into the complex work of how to create structures, buildings, housing, education, food, transportation, and services to people who come with nothing but who are willing to offer everything in exchange. Refugees have run away from situations and lifestyles that were not in their best interest. Will the places they have run be able to help them not just survive but also thrive? History has shown us the power, beauty, and economic benefits gained from the gifts that immigrants and refugees bring to communities, states, and nations. The way that communities choose to interact with them, and the interpersonal and systemic processes they put into place for refugee utilization are formative in creating a fork in the road for refugees. The authors in this book have shown how it is possible to build structures and processes that help refugees to build happy, successful, healthy, and productive lives for themselves, their families, and their communities. If communities turn their back and refuse to address the needs of this vulnerable group of human beings, we all suffer needlessly. From a public health approach, prevention is always more effective than after-the-fact efforts to fix personal or social problems. From a civic engagement model, finding opportunities for individuals to use their gifts, talents, and gratitude empower not just them but enriches the community as a whole. Failure to do so may result in alienated people who seek dysfunctional means to express themselves.

A truth that we have come to appreciate is that all of us want to know that we matter. Communities that welcome refugees and figure out solutions to help them show refugees that we know that they matter; that the refugees have important things to contribute. Communities step forward to help the refugees to get past the struggles that have been brought to their door. Government, faith, NGO, teachers, shelter providers, and others who give of themselves matter not just to the refugees but to the entire community. They send forth the message that every person who is in distress matters and that, as a caring community, we will be there for not just the refugees but for one another in times of crisis. This creates a climate of care that cannot be bought or sold. It has to be earned, and the providers who have stepped forth to invest their time, energy, and resources are to be honoured, for they could have made their contributions in countless other ways and to countless other peoples and issues.

This book, therefore, is a celebration of the brave people who have come to ask for help and for the heart-full people who have opened their lives and offered their resources to help them.

José Noronha Rodrigues and Dora Cabete remind us to look at the strength of transnational families since it is clear that around the world, families take different forms than a cisgender, heterosexual family that consists of a breadwinner father, a stay-at-home mother, and children who live with them. There are new family scenarios, de facto unions (no marriage contract), single-parent or LGBTQ+ families with children, recomposed families (arising after divorces or separations), extended families (including grandparents, uncles and cousins), large families (those with three or more children), and transnational families resulting from the migration process.

As a solicitor trainee in the United Kingdom, social worker, and international human rights expert with a business background, Tanya Herring, in her chapter, points to the importance of the General Comments and Recommendations on interpreting procedural requirements of treaties like the UN Convention on the Rights of the Child. Article 22 is a section of Child Law in an international context and sets out that State Parties shall take appropriate measures to ensure that a child seeking refugee status or considered a refugee receives appropriate protection and humanitarian assistance outlined in the Convention. Nations are obligated to provide special care to refugee children and protect them from persecution that may include subjection to genital mutilation, underage recruitment, sex trafficking for prostitution, forced organ transplant, and other assaults.

Isolde Quadranti addresses the tension of how communities choose to care for refugees who are already a part of the community versus the arrival of new illegal immigrants. Legal complexities are elucidated in her chapter. She brings forth the issue of humane treatment for children, especially those who have self-harmed, attempted suicide, been exposed to violence, separated from family members, denied essential needs, and received inadequate care for the mental suffering that even young children experience. In many communities, minor refugees and their suffering are treated as if they were invisible, which is a direct violation of their human rights.

In the chapter by Blaž Lenarčič and Zorana Medarić, information-communication technologies (ICTs) play an important role in the lives of migrant children at different stages of their migration process. These include the pre-departure stage, during the journey, and upon arrival at the destination. This technology holds huge potential for helping especially unaccompanied migrant children to prevail in the transition to their new community and to stay in touch with family and friends in their countries of origin and beyond, build new relationships, and orient themselves in the transition countries.

Dialechti Chatzoudi provides a rich discussion on the 'Homes for Hope' in Cyprus, which serves unaccompanied children. Built to incorporate the articles of provision, protection, and participation outlined in the UN Convention on the Rights of the Child, this program goes beyond providing the basic needs to more advanced care, especially in the area of psychological services.

Refugee children benefit significantly through education. Refugee children can learn new and different languages so they can better function in their communities; they can learn norms and cultural expectations, and they can build friendships and relationships with others. Integrating into the community and finding one's place in it, along with resources that can be accessed, is of utmost importance to their ability to thrive. Graça Santos and Sofia Bergano explore the right to education for both children and adult refugees in Portugal. In this chapter, they analyse how Portugal has developed the work of integrating refugee immigrants through the mobilisation of specific services and resources.

In the chapter by Regina Bernadin, Cristobal Pérez, and Raúl Fernández-Calienes, the authors explore three different types of federally funded programmes in Florida (USA) that offer support through education, social services, and social integration. They include Post Release Services for Unaccompanied Children, an Unaccompanied Refugee Minors Program and Services for Survivors of Human Trafficking. They explain why comprehensive services are necessary for assisting unaccompanied refugees, asylees, and trafficked youth, all of whom will have experienced trauma.

Greg Carroll, Allan Shwedel, George Weagba, Joe Buttner, and David Mercer discuss the importance of resilience for youth in Liberia. They found in their study that despite having suffered through two civil wars, two pandemics (Ebola and COVID-19), the loss of family members, dislocation, and high ACES scores, refugee children showed a level of optimism for the future. Their work points to the importance of resilience that can be found and cultivated in even people who have experienced significant trauma. Community structures and processes are wise to build upon the natural resilience that youth may hold.

Building safe and empowered individuals are a mission of caring, safe, and empowered communities, as shown in the chapter by Sami Atif, Amanda Francis, and Sofia Leitão. Their study of female genital mutilation and gender-based violence against refugee and migrant girls demonstrates the power of inclusivity, good communication, trust, and respect in helping traumatized people to recover. Utilizing a diverse, multifaceted team of social workers, health professionals, NGO support officers, psychologists, school staff, and law enforcement, the authors advocate for continuous educational programmes in order to change attitudes and behaviours from within the community.

Richard Thickpenny's chapter reminds us about the importance of social integration for refugees. Instead of trying to define what success can look like from the perspective of the policy controllers, his chapter explores what can be achieved when viewing not just community needs but identifying how to make the refugee service work well for each individual.

The authors in this book bring to our attention the similarities that face all communities and providers. Their works prompt us to see the similarities that bond all refugees together, no matter where they hail from or where they land. We are a global community which faces common challenges and obstacles. We are also a global community of caring communities who are wise to consider what is in 'the best interest of the child', as codified in the Convention on the Rights of the Child. It is clear that there are many dedicated professionals and communities around the world trying to help this vulnerable population of people. Learning from one another about how to identify common needs and challenges, to see what people are doing, and where the gaps are will help us to better implement best practices. We will all benefit when we do.

References

Mead, G. H., Huebner, D. R., and Joas, H. 2015. *Mind, self, and society* (C. W. Morris, Ed.). Chicago: University of Chicago Press.

Index

www.ingramcontent.com/pod-product-compliance
Lightning Source LLC
Chambersburg PA
CBHW072101020426

42334CB00017B/1594